PRINCIPLES, DIALOGUES,
AND
PHILOSOPHICAL
CORRESPONDENCE

The Library of Liberal Arts
OSKAR PIEST, FOUNDER

The Library of Liberal Arts

PRINCIPLES, DIALOGUES, AND PHILOSOPHICAL CORRESPONDENCE

GEORGE BERKELEY

Edited, with an Introduction, by
COLIN MURRAY TURBAYNE
Professor of Philosophy, University of Rochester

The Library of Liberal Arts
published by
THE BOBBS-MERRILL COMPANY, INC.
INDIANAPOLIS · NEW YORK

George Berkeley: 1685-1753

COPYRIGHT © 1965
THE BOBBS-MERRILL COMPANY, INC.
Printed in the United States of America
Library of Congress Catalog Card Number 64-66065
Fourth Printing

CONTENTS

EDITOR'S INTRODUCTION	vii
OUTLINE ANALYSIS	xxxv
CHRONOLOGY	xl
SELECTED BIBLIOGRAPHY	xlii
NOTE ON THE TEXTS	xlv

PRINCIPLES, DIALOGUES, AND PHILOSOPHICAL CORRESPONDENCE

A Treatise Concerning the Principles of Human Knowledge

Preface	3
Introduction	4
Of the Principles of Human Knowledge	22

Three Dialogues Between Hylas and Philonous

Preface	105
The First Dialogue	108
The Second Dialogue	149
The Third Dialogue	171

Philosophical Correspondence Between Berkeley and Samuel Johnson

I. Johnson to Berkeley	215
II. Berkeley to Johnson	224
III. Johnson to Berkeley	229
IV. Berkeley to Johnson	239
INDEX	243

INTRODUCTION

I. BERKELEY AND SKEPTICISM

George Berkeley's two major works, *A Treatise Concerning the Principles of Human Knowledge* and *Three Dialogues Between Hylas and Philonous,* are presented here, together with perhaps the most searching examination his ideas received during his lifetime, that of the American Samuel Johnson, who corresponded with Berkeley during his stay in this country.

Two and a half centuries after the publication of these masterpieces Berkeley's position in the front rank of the great philosophers is secure. His original contribution, commonly presented as the denial of matter and the assertion of *"esse* is *percipi* or *percipere,"* has been near the center of philosophical debate from his day to ours. In addition, his criticism of the fixed infinitesimal presented in his *Analyst* is now regarded as monumental in the history of mathematics. His *Essay Towards a New Theory of Vision*, the first argument in the classical debate between nativism and empiricism in optics, is also the first work in physiological optics, a discipline defined by Helmholtz a century and a half later. His revolutionary rejection of Newtonian absolute motion and his corresponding acceptance of the essential relativity of motion in his Latin tract *De Motu,* however ineffective it was at the time, anticipated in all its essentials the ideas of Ernst Mach, and foreshadowed those of Einstein. Since Berkeley's death, interest in his philosophy has continued; and there are now signs of a quickening of interest. Demand for editions of his two major works has increased enormously in the last three decades, especially in America.

After all this time, however, an aura of paradox pervades

his life and work. He is, as it were, a successful failure, for his fame rests largely upon his apparently inadvertent defense of skepticism, a philosophical position that he not only never held but sought most earnestly to refute. In the words of David Hume, "all his arguments, though otherwise intended, are in reality merely skeptical."[1] But if this is so, how is it that arguments that failed in their purpose could constitute Berkeley's subsequent success? Hume gives us a plausible answer: Most of these arguments "form the best lessons of skepticism."[2] If this is so, we have also a plausible explanation of Berkeley's importance in contemporary philosophy in which all the emphasis is placed upon argument. At any rate, the *Principles* and *Dialogues* are paradigms of argumentative discourse in philosophical literature. In addition, Berkeley's arguments, like those of Zeno, are often used as a pedagogical device. Both present paradoxes conjoined with uncannily consistent argument, and they offer a challenge to the student to detect the submerged fallacy assumed to be present.

Berkeley was classified as a skeptic as soon as the *Principles* was published, and he has been placed in the skeptical tradition ever since. In England during his lifetime his works were either barely reviewed or treated with hostility. By the time of his death, however, some of the seeds of his later eminence had been sown, especially in Scotland. Hume, perhaps through the influence of the members of the Rankenian Club, had already recognized and acknowledged his greatness. Moreover, on the Continent, Voltaire, Diderot, and Condillac had been influential in spreading the ideas presented in the *Essay on Vision*. In America, Samuel Johnson had already published his *Elementa Philosophica* and had dedicated it to Berkeley. It was in Scotland, however, that Berkeley's fame

---

[1] David Hume, *An Inquiry Concerning Human Understanding*, "Library of Liberal Arts," No. 49 (New York: The Liberal Arts Press, Inc., 1955), p. 163 n.

[2] *Ibid.*

and the traditional attitude to his work were made secure. A series of Scottish thinkers, Baxter, Hume, Beattie, and Reid, held in common the view that Berkeley was a skeptic, and all but one took issue with his skepticism. Of these thinkers, the influence of Hume and Reid was powerful and long-lasting, extending through Kant and subsequent Scottish and English philosophers to the present.

Is there another way of interpreting Berkeley's philosophy, a way that is more in keeping with his own intentions? After all, Berkeley tried to refute skepticism, not to embrace it. If, from Berkeley's point of view, a gross misinterpretation of his philosophy has become the traditional interpretation, it should be possible to account for the mistake or, at least, to show how it has arisen. To this end, one may consider how one of Berkeley's own discoveries may be applied to the interpretation of his life and his philosophy.

One of Berkeley's enduring contributions as a philosopher was his rejection of the doctrine of abstract ideas together with his corresponding acceptance of the view that the qualities of things always come in bundles or contexts—always, to use his words, "mixed," "blended," "complicated," or "concreted" together. This discovery, pronounced by David Hume "to be one of the greatest and most valuable discoveries that has been made of late years in the republic of letters," [3] illuminates Berkeley's life as well as his philosophy. The one is as interesting and unusual as the other. It is little wonder that Dr. Johnson, the famous lexicographer, sought permission to write Berkeley's life. (Unfortunately for posterity, permission was refused.)

Consider, first, Berkeley's typical assertions. More, perhaps, than those of any of the other great philosophers, Berkeley's assertions are liable to misinterpretation and the charge of absurdity. This is so because many of them, taken in themselves or abstracted from their contexts, are paradoxes—for example: "All those bodies which compose the mighty frame

[3] *A Treatise of Human Nature* (London, 1739), Bk. I, Pt. I, sec. 7.

of the world have not any subsistence without a mind"[4]; "When we do our utmost to conceive the existence of external bodies we are all the while only contemplating our own ideas"[5]; "We eat and drink ideas and are clothed with ideas"[6]; "The soul always thinks."[7] Such paradoxes, of the same order as "The child is father of the man," and "No man born of woman can harm Macbeth," constitute part of Berkeley's strength, but also part of his weakness, for they lay him wide open to attack and easy conquest. In uttering them, he commands attention, but he takes an enormous risk, for in the literal-minded reader they generate, first, that momentary sense of amazement and irresolution that prompts him to ask and exclaim, "How could this be? The words are wild!"; secondly, the denial of their literal truth; and, finally (at times), an attack upon the character of their author. Dr. Johnson refuted Berkeley's assertion that matter does not exist by kicking a stone, while Leibniz accused him of seeking notoriety by his paradoxes.

It is easy, however, to force the literal truth and hence the absurdity present in any paradox. It is correspondingly difficult, at times, to see the partially hidden truth, especially for the literal-minded reader and the advocate of robust common sense. Berkeley was aware of this. As a corollary to his denial that there are any abstract ideas and his assertion of concrete ones only, Berkeley rejected an "abstract" theory of meaning, according to which words have meaning separately or in themselves, and subscribed to a "context" theory of meaning. Consequently, he frequently implored his readers not to "stick in this or that phrase" but to collect his meaning from "the whole sum and tenor" of his discourse, because "there are some passages that, taken by themselves, are very liable to gross misinterpretation and to be charged with the

---

[4] *A Treatise Concerning the Principles of Human Knowledge*, sec. 6.
[5] *Ibid.*, sec. 23.
[6] *Ibid.*, sec. 38.
[7] *Ibid.*, sec. 98.

most absurd consequences."[8] Thus, in the context of the whole play we are able to collect the real meaning of the utterance that pleased the literal-minded Macbeth. In similar fashion, in the context of Berkeley's whole system we are able to discern the real meanings of assertions, such as "We eat and drink ideas," which so disturbed those other Scotsmen, Baxter and Beattie, that they thought Berkeley actually meant "we eat and drink our own mental states."

Similar considerations apply to the interpretation of Berkeley's method, except that it is more difficult to grasp and lends itself more readily to misunderstanding. Berkeley, it is true, makes use of skeptical arguments. Fully aware of this, he puts these words into the mouth of Hylas: "For a long time it looked as if you were advancing their philosophical skepticism." Perhaps he was not fully aware of the gamble he was taking. At any rate, he lost the gamble. What was for him a device, an appearance, was taken for the real thing. He was, in fact, making use of the indirect approach of the way of hypothesis, presenting essentially destructive arguments, and in the course of it temporarily adopting the assumptions of his opponents. His seeming to join the skeptics, in order to refute them, is a dialectical ploy of great power before a sophisticated audience; but, with a naïve audience, it is one that can recoil upon the user.

We can extend further the application of Berkeley's rejection of abstract ideas. Certain events in his life, when taken by themselves and abstracted from their context, are liable to gross misinterpretation and to the charge of absurdity. For example, he hit upon the visionary scheme of founding a university for Europeans and American savages in the Bermudas. As a bishop he experimented with tar-water, administered it to his flock, and tried to disseminate information on its medicinal value. In his will he left the strangest of instructions about the disposal of his body. It was to lie, before burial,

---

[8] *An Essay Towards a New Theory of Vision* (Dublin, 1709), sec. 120. See also the Prefaces to *Principles* and *Three Dialogues Between Hylas and Philonous*.

unwashed, undisturbed, and covered by the same bedclothes until it "grow offensive by the cadaverous smell." Such incidents in his life made conservatives shake their heads. Some said he was mad. Doubtless in any age and place he would be called eccentric, but many of the facts about his life lose much of their queer and sometimes macabre quality when seen within the context of his life and thought as a whole.

To ponder the evidence bearing upon Berkeley's character, including his portraits and what was said about him by his friends and enemies, is, I think, to drop the common judgment of him as an impractical dreamer and to replace it with a view of a man many-sided, vigorous, strong-minded, independent, and full of charm, and yet to understand both Pope's tribute, "to Berkeley every virtue under heaven," and Swift's, "an absolute philosopher with regard to money, titles and power."

II. REACTION TO THE SCIENTIFIC REVOLUTION

Born at the end of the "Century of Genius," Berkeley inherited a rich legacy. He followed Swift and Congreve, first to Kilkenny College, and then to Trinity College, Dublin, one of the most forward-looking universities in the British Isles. When he entered it in 1700, three men who were dominant influences upon the character of his thought were still alive: Locke, whose *Essay Concerning Human Understanding*, introduced to Trinity College by William Molyneux two years after its publication in 1690 and long before it was accepted at Locke's own Oxford, was being avidly read; Newton, whose *Philosophiae Naturalis Principia Mathematica* had been published in 1687, and whose *Opticks* was to appear in 1704; and Malebranche, whose *De la recherche de la vérité* (1674) had been translated by T. Taylor (Oxford, 1694). Berkeley studied their works with the greatest care. In addition he studied Bacon and Descartes and read Hobbes, More, Leibniz, and Cudworth. He studied Greek, Latin, and Hebrew. He became proficient in the mathematics, physics, and optics of Kepler, Descartes, and Newton. Another dominant influence in his formative years was Plato, "a philosopher whom," according to Stock, "he studied particularly," and who was "his favourite author from whom many of his notions were borrowed." [9]

Berkeley, however, reacted against his teachers as much as he learned from them. While he accepted the great scientific discoveries of his age, he quickly became and remained sharply antagonistic to the metaphysics and epistemology that accompanied them. Thus, in metaphysics he reacted against the Cartesian-Newtonian world-view, according to which the universe was nothing but a great machine, originally invented by a supreme mechanic. Berkeley saw that the machine, being automotive, no longer required the mechanic. Elbowed out of his traditional causal role, God became first "a distant deity" (deism), and then utterly redundant (atheism). In this view also, he saw that the human mind, shut up in the smaller clockwork of its body, lost its traditional freedom, being impelled and determined "as necessarily as [a ball in motion] is by the stroke of a racket." [10] In epistemology he saw that the view in which the common things of our daily life form merely an unreal screen of appearance between us and the unperceived real world of science must be mistaken. Moreover, if we cannot check the appearances against the realities, we cannot have knowledge of them (skepticism). Berkeley regarded these consequences of the scientific revolution as the main symptoms of a disease afflicting modern man.

III. ENDS AND MEANS

As a philosopher, religious apologist, and man of affairs Berkeley had many purposes, but in the hierarchy of these

[9] See Joseph Stock's "Life of the Author," added to *Works* (London, 1837; first published 1784), pp. vii and xi.
[10] *Principles*, sec. 144.

purposes it seems likely that a chief one was the betterment of human life. We can gather this from his other stated purposes. "The end of speculation," he held, "is practice or the improvement and regulation of our lives and actions." [11] In this he accepted the general opinion. Similarly, it appears that he held that the chief end of language is "the influencing our conduct and actions, which may be done either by forming rules for us to act by, or by raising certain passions, dispositions, and emotions in our minds." [12] The communication of ideas by words was subservient to this end. In this he corrected the general opinion. If this account is correct, then philosophical writing was only one (although the most important) of many instruments that Berkeley used to implement his ulterior philanthropic purposes.

As a philosopher, however, his procedure, like that of the Socratic dialectic, was characteristically indirect or oblique. This is manifested in four features:

First, and subservient to his main purpose, he chose not so much to build as to destroy. He used his instrument, language, as a surgeon uses a scalpel to remove diseased organs. He called his own philosophical position by the denying name "Immaterialism," and we associate his philosophy with the denial of the abstract, absolute, and infinite rather than with the assertion of the concrete, relative, and finite. At an early age he was already a dissenter and, by disposition, an iconoclast: "Mem. that I was ~~sceptical~~ distrustful at 8 years old and consequently by nature disposed for these new doctrines." [13] His wife, Anne, regarded him as a destroyer rather than a builder and understood the nature of his oblique attack upon the materialists and minute philosophers: "He has taken from them their ground they stand on, and had he

[11] *Dialogues*, Preface.
[12] *Alciphron*, Dialogue VII, sec. 5. The same view is presented in *Principles*, Introduction, sec. 20.
[13] *Philosophical Commentaries* (probably composed 1707–1708), ed. A. A. Luce (Edinburgh: Thomas Nelson, 1944), Entry 266.

built as he has pulled down he had been then a master builder indeed. But unto every man his work. Some must remove rubbish. . . ."[14]

Secondly, always the aetiologist, he wasted no effort in direct attacks on symptoms or effects, but tried to expose their causes or principles: "To behold the deformity of error, we need only undress it."[15] This procedure is discernible in his speculative and practical writings. He prescribed the task of his two major works as an inquiry into the "causes of error" and into the "grounds of skepticism, atheism, and irreligion," and he diagnosed the bursting of the South Sea Bubble in 1720 as merely a symptom of a deeper ailment: "The South-Sea Affair . . . is not the original evil or the great source of our misfortunes; it is but the natural effect of those principles which for many years have been propagated with great industry. . . . Other nations have been wicked, but we are the first who have been wicked upon principle."[16]

Thirdly, having exposed the false principles, he adduced his own rival principles which, he thought, would free us from the consequences of the false principles of his opponents.

Fourthly, he used an effective dialectical ploy: "He that would win another over to his opinion must seem to harmonize with him at first and humour him in his own way of talking," to which Berkeley added: "From my childhood I had an unaccountable turn of thought that way."[17]

---

[14] Letter from Mrs. Anne Berkeley to her son, in *The Works of George Berkeley, Bishop of Cloyne*, ed. A. A. Luce and T. E. Jessop (9 vols.; Edinburgh: Thomas Nelson, 1948–1957), VII (ed. Luce, 1955), 388.

[15] *Principles*, Introduction, First Draft, sec. 22.

[16] *An Essay Towards Preventing the Ruin of Great Britain* (London, 1721). The South Sea Bubble was named after the projects of the South Sea Company. Formed in 1711, the company conducted trade in the South Seas. At first successful, it produced many imitators and then extravagant speculation leading to its collapse and the ruin of many investors.

[17] *Commonplace Book*, in *Works*, ed. A. C. Fraser (4 vols; Oxford: Oxford University Press, 1901), I, 92.

IV. THE CREATIVE YEARS

The period from 1707 to 1713 was Berkeley's most creative. Within it he produced three philosophical masterpieces, the *Essay on Vision,* the *Principles,* and the *Dialogues.* Taken as a whole they present three steps in one argument unified by the theme of immaterialism, and they exemplify the oblique approach already indicated. Thus, in the first step he humored the materialists by allowing that matter existed even though he tried to undermine it; in the second, he exploded the whole materialist doctrine; and in the third, he tried to show that nothing material had been lost. During this period apparently he thought that the re-education of a few would help to alleviate the illness of Western man, the symptoms of which illness, skepticism and atheism, were caused by the false principles of the scientists and philosophers. Accordingly, with language as his instrument, the main purpose of which was to direct action and regulate conduct, he chose to "affect only a few speculative persons." [18] He realized that such re-education of the elite few could have at best only "a gradual influence." [19]

Having published his *Essay on Vision* in 1709, Berkeley wrote to Percival [20] on March 1, 1710: "I hope to make what is there laid down appear subservient to the ends of morality and religion in a treatise I have now in the press." This treatise was the *Principles,* published in Dublin in May 1710, when Berkeley was twenty-five years old. The book was an immediate failure. In London it was received with raillery and scorn but barely examined. "I did but name the subject matter of your book to some ingenious friends of mine," Percival wrote from London on August 26, "and they immediately treated it with ridicule, at the same time refusing to read it."

---

[18] *Dialogues,* Preface.
[19] *Ibid.*
[20] Sir John Percival (1683–1748), Berkeley's lifetime friend, was one of his two principal correspondents. See B. Rand, *Berkeley and Percival* (Cambridge: Cambridge University Press, 1914); and *Letters,* in *Works,* Vol. VIII (ed. Luce, 1956).

Berkeley knew that his theory was new and his theme paradoxical. On September 6 he replied to Percival: "I imagine whatever doctrine contradicts vulgar and settled opinion had need been introduced with great caution into the world. For this reason it was I omitted all mention of the nonexistence of matter in the title page, dedication, preface, and introduction, so that the notion might steal unawares on the reader, who possibly would never have meddled with a book that he had known contained such paradoxes." He then entreated Percival not to mention the paradox, namely, the denial of matter, in discourse with potential readers. But the book could not be rescued.

Several factors may have contributed to the failure of the *Principles*. The paradox that matter does not exist was a bold one. The whole book, but especially the Introduction, was extremely critical of contemporary English philosophy, including Locke's doctrine of abstract ideas. There were many sections devoted to criticism of contemporary physics and mathematics, especially of Newton's views. Finally, the book was written by an Irishman and published in Ireland.

Berkeley tried once more. Three years later he arrived in London carrying with him the manuscript of the *Three Dialogues*. His *Principles* had formed only the first part of a projected series of books which included a second part on psychology and ethics, a third on physics, and probably a fourth on mathematics. Probably because of the failure of the first part, Berkeley shelved the project and composed the *Dialogues*, in the Preface of which he wrote: "Before I proceed to publish the second part, I thought it requisite to treat more clearly and fully of certain principles laid down in the first and to place them in a new light." He wrote in "the most easy and familiar manner," weeding out philosophical jargon wherever possible. He excised the front part on abstract ideas and the sections on physics and mathematics. He tried to soften his paradox by admitting the word "matter" even into his own immaterialist vocabulary. He continued to exercise his first-rate logical ability, but this time, with a somewhat wider audience in mind, he hid his syllogisms. He used all his skill in an effort to show that immaterialism was the ally, not the opponent, of common sense against materialism and skepticism. The result was a unique combination of philosophical insight with high literary art. The *Three Dialogues* was published in London in May 1713, but, like his previous works, it received little attention.

In October Berkeley caught the boat for Calais and the Continent, where he spent five of the next seven years. During this time he resumed his ambitious project. Unfortunately, he lost the manuscript of the second part somewhere in Italy. Ideas from this section were incorporated, in part, into his later works.

V. THE AMERICAN DREAM

Returning to London in the fall of 1720 from his second Continental tour, Berkeley soon became deeply involved in one of the central projects of his life, the founding of a university in the New World. The idea was new, but once more it reflected his abiding ulterior purpose. The means this time were different, and the returns might have been quicker and surer. His three books had failed to produce enough response to suggest that they would have even the "gradual influence" for which he had hoped. As an educator in America, however, he envisaged his task as easier than that of a re-educator in England: "That ignorance is not so incurable as error; that you must pull down as well as build, erase as well as imprint, in order to make proselytes at home: whereas the savage Americans, if they are in a state purely natural and unimproved by education, they are also unencumbered with all that rubbish of superstition and prejudice, which is the effect of a wrong one." [21] With his classical, mathematical, and scientific background, he was intellectually well-equipped for the task of founding an academy of learning, and, like Plato prepara-

---

[21] *A Proposal for the Better Supplying of Churches in Our Foreign Plantations* . . . (London, 1725).

tory to the founding of *his* academy, he had widened his horizon by travel.

The idea may have come to him at the time of the South Sea Bubble in 1720. In his *Essay Towards Preventing the Ruin of Great Britain,* he conceived this affair along with the general degeneracy of the Old World as symptoms or effects traceable to false principles, doubtless the same ones that he sought to expose in his philosophy. "The truth is," he wrote, "our symptoms are so bad that, notwithstanding all the care and vigilance of the legislature, it is to be feared the final period of our State approaches." Accordingly, instead of persevering in his vain attempt to contribute to the repair of a broken-down society, he decided to withdraw from it and start afresh with a new one. He decided to found a college in Bermuda for the education of the colonists and natives of America. On March 4, 1723, he wrote to Percival: "It is now about ten months since I determined with myself to spend the residue of my days in the Island of Bermuda, where I trust in Providence I may be the mean instrument of doing good to mankind." His prophetic vision of the future of America was expressed in the poem *America, or the Muses Refuge: A Prophecy,* which he wrote in 1726 and published in his *Miscellany* (1752) as follows:

> The Muse, disgusted at an Age and Clime
>   Barren of every glorious Theme,
> In distant Lands now waits a better Time,
>   Producing Subjects worthy Fame:
> In happy Climes, where from the genial Sun
>   And virgin Earth such Scenes ensue,
> The Force of Art by Nature seems outdone,
>   And fancied Beauties by the true:
> In happy Climes the Seat of Innocence,
>   Where Nature guides and Virtue rules,
> Where Men shall not impose for Truth and Sense,
>   The Pedantry of Courts and Schools:
> There shall be sung another golden Age,
>   The rise of Empire and of Arts,
> The Good and Great inspiring epic Rage,
>   The wisest Heads and noblest Hearts.

> Not such as *Europe* breeds in her decay;
>   Such as she bred when fresh and young,
> When heav'nly Flame did animate her Clay,
>   By future Poets shall be sung.
> Westward the Course of Empire takes its Way;
>   The four first Acts already past,
> A fifth shall close the Drama with the Day;
>   Time's noblest Offspring is the last.

Using his powers of persuasion, which were considerable, Berkeley solicited and obtained public support. He secured a royal charter and the promise of a grant of £20,000 from the English Parliament. Private subscriptions, including £200 from the prime minister, Sir Robert Walpole, amounted to several thousand pounds. But Berkeley met all sorts of difficulties and delays. In September 1728, as he later recounted in a letter to Percival (June 27, 1729), he "was reduced to a difficult situation"; if he had lingered in England it would have been thought that he had dropped the design; on the other hand, if he had taken leave of his supporters, they would have condemned him for departing before the grant was received. Caught in this dilemma, Berkeley thought to escape by slipping between the horns. He decided to leave England but without taking leave of his supporters. With his newly wedded wife and a few companions, he slipped away in a "private manner." Having hired a ship, he set sail for America, where he settled in Newport, Rhode Island, and awaited the promised grant. It did not come. Walpole let him know indirectly that it would never come. By March 1731, expressing himself as "absolutely abandoned" by all his supporters, Berkeley had given up all hope of executing his design. He now wished only to return to Europe, where he would "endeavour to be useful in some other way."

Berkeley's hopes for the second great project of his life had been as high as those he entertained for the first. Moreover, the preparation for it had been equally arduous, the planning as careful. Why then did this one also fail? The idea of a university in America was a noble one; but, owing perhaps to an inadequate appreciation of the situation, Berkeley apparently made two mistakes that he could not correct. (In his first project he had been able to correct his mistakes of imprudence. Specifically, he had rewritten the *Principles* eliminating the direct attacks upon Newton and Locke.) His first mistake, it seems, was to locate his university in Bermuda, several hundred miles from the mainland. This made the original scheme impracticable. Rhode Island itself would have been suitable. The second mistake was to leave England before the parliamentary grant was received. In retrospect we see that Berkeley gravely miscalculated. Out of sight was out of mind, and Berkeley's main asset in this project, his personal charm, was rendered valueless. Instead of trying to slip between the horns of his dilemma, he should have grasped it by the horns and tried to scotch the rumor that he had dropped the scheme.

This project had used up a decade of Berkeley's prime and had ended in failure. Nevertheless, it had some good consequences for American education and for philosophy. The most serious and respectful, as well as the most penetrating, criticism of immaterialism was not published during Berkeley's life. This criticism was made by an American, Samuel Johnson (1696–1772), the father of American philosophy. Educated at Yale, Johnson, who was first a Congregational minister, joined the Anglican Church in 1722 and was made a Doctor of Divinity by Oxford in 1743. In 1754 he became the first president of King's College, New York (later Columbia University). His *Elementa Philosophica,* published in 1752 by Benjamin Franklin in Philadelphia, was dedicated to Berkeley. Johnson made several visits to Berkeley at Newport from Stratford, Connecticut.

Johnson made his criticism in two letters written to Berkeley during his stay in this country. These letters, with Berkeley's replies, are included in the present edition.[22] Although

[22] From *Samuel Johnson, President of King's College: His Career and Writings,* ed. Herbert and Carol Schneider (4 vols.; New York: Columbia University Press, 1929).

the two men continued to correspond throughout Berkeley's life, only these letters are of philosophical interest. Johnson's examination is a significant contribution for several reasons, among these being that it makes Newton, rather than Locke, the focal point of the debate on immaterialism and examines Berkeley on his vague or indefinite account of archetypes.

VI. LATER YEARS

After his return from America, Berkeley lived in London for nearly three years awaiting preferment. Although he was ill most of the time, the period ending with his appointment as Bishop of Cloyne in 1734 was his second most productive period of authorship. He wrote *Alciphron* in America and *The Theory of Vision, or Visual Language Vindicated and Explained* and the *Analyst* in London. All were published anonymously, perhaps because he thought that the overt disclosure of his authorship would damage their effectiveness. They are works in religious apologetics, optics, and mathematics, respectively, but once more they are primarily destructive in nature. At one level Berkeley attacks Deism, geometrical optics, and the method of fluxions; but fundamentally he attacks materialists, freethinkers, and atheists, by trying to destroy their principles. In the naïve view of his opponents, there are mysterious entities in religion (Grace, Trinity, and the like) and none in science and mathematics (force, gravity, fluxions, infinitesimals, and so forth). Berkeley says: "He who can digest a second or third fluxion . . . need not, methinks, be squeamish about any point in divinity." [23] What is the solution? One solution, dependent upon the false doctrine of abstract ideas, is that we must end in a forlorn skepticism: There are mysterious entities in both realms. Berkeley's solution is to treat the supposed entities of both realms as directive devices, calling them, respectively, "mathematical hypotheses" and "lively operative principles."

The response to *Alciphron,* with the *Essay on Vision* appended, was hostile and short-lived. Berkeley was prompted

[23] *Analyst*, sec. 7.

to publish revised (and final) editions of his *Principles* and *Dialogues* in one volume (1734). Thus, within three years he placed before the public the three great works of his early period, as well as three new ones. Once more the response to the early works was negligible. However, beginning in this decade, his *Essay* began to receive considerable attention on the Continent from such authors as Voltaire, Condillac, and Diderot. Published in Italy in 1732, it became his first work to be translated into a foreign language. That very great, very small book, *The Theory of Vision*, went into oblivion, where it stayed for more than a century. The response to the *Analyst* was immediate, bitterly hostile at first, and long-lived. Berkeley's criticism of the calculus was an able logician's direct exposure of the bad logic of its presentation: "I beg leave to repeat and insist that I consider the geometrical analyst as a logician." [24] He showed how the premises were false and the conclusion true, how to resolve this apparently "unaccountable paradox," and "how error may bring forth truth, though it cannot bring forth science." [25] The ensuing controversy, which engaged such eminent thinkers as Robins, Maclaurin, Carnot, and Lagrange, did not end until Cauchy's reformulation of the calculus nearly a century later.

As Bishop of Cloyne, where he lived in relative seclusion for the next eighteen years, Berkeley, in Stock's words, "turned his thoughts to subjects of more apparent utility." Deeply disturbed by the distressing economic conditions in Ireland, he tried to ameliorate both the national housekeeping and that of his own area. He started a spinning school and built a workhouse for vagrants. Anticipating censure for once again "meddling out of [his] profession," he published *The Querist* (1735–1737), notable for its enlightened advocacy of a people's bank and for its views on the nature of money and on the relations between work, wealth, money, production, and employment. The pamphlets were widely read but his advice was not taken.

[24] *Analyst*, sec. 20.
[25] *Ibid.*

In his last years he became caught up in yet another project, one that was more practical and promised quicker returns than any of his others. This was the dispensing, administering, and promoting of tar-water. How could a great creative genius allow himself to become so deeply involved in a project that laid him open to censure for quackery and, again, for meddling out of his profession? From his middle thirties Berkeley had suffered off and on from one ailment which he called his "habitual cholic" and from another (or the same) which Stock called "hypochondria." At Cloyne his illness became severe at a time when, in the wake of famine, an epidemic of dysentery ("the bloody flux") hit southern Ireland. No medical men were available, and Berkeley sought a remedy for himself and his flock. He thought he had found it in tar-water, a cheap, easily procurable balsam, "the resinous exudation of pines and firs," a medicine he had come across in America. He presented the idea to the world in the most remarkable of all his books, *Siris* (1744), "a chain of philosophical reflections" upon various subjects beginning with tar and ending with God. If the *Essay on Vision* was written in praise of *lux*, *Siris* is a panegyric upon *lumen*. If the *Principles* is characterized by clarity, crispness, and vigor, *Siris* is pervaded by serenity and mystery. But in this book one may find some of Berkeley's most careful and penetrating statements upon the nature of science. The book was an immediate success and went into six editions in the first year.

In the fall of 1752, Berkeley went with his family to Oxford in order to superintend the education of his second son, George. On January 14, 1753, Berkeley died suddenly. In accordance with an item in his will, based on the report that putrefaction is the only infallible sign of death, he was buried several days later.

VII. A SHORT HISTORY OF IMMATERIALISM

Berkeley's life was marked by increasing disillusionment. His aims and expectations were lowered from a lofty beginning in a solution to the problem of modern philosophy, to a low ending in a cure for all our bodily troubles. His concern declined from soul therapy to body therapy, from the theoretical to the pragmatic. All his missions were failures in his own lifetime, except the last and meanest. His first great project, his attempt to persuade the scientists of his day to accept his reallocation of the facts, failed miserably. In the words of Whitehead, "he failed to affect the main stream of scientific thought. It flowed on as if he had never written." [26] His two major works received hardly any reviews in English journals. To my knowledge, the *Principles* received only two short reviews in Continental journals, while the *Dialogues* received five reviews, all but one in Continental journals.[27]

Doubtless he began to modify his aims and hopes after the scornful rejection of his books by the English. Unfortunately for posterity, whose judgment is usually more reliable, he first shelved and then abandoned his great project. By middle age he had lost his great expectations: "I do not therefore pretend that my books can teach truth. All I hope for is that they may be an occasion to inquisitive men of discovering truth by consulting their own minds and looking into their own thoughts." [28]

Berkeley's hopes have since been partly realized, but his predictions of imputations that would be charged on him were quickly fulfilled. In his letter to Percival of September 6, 1710, he indicated that he had expected two imputations: (1) that he was insincere and, motivated by vanity, sought notoriety by his paradoxes; and (2) that he was a skeptic. Percival's London friends made both these charges in 1710, and the second, or at least the charge that he was a skeptic *malgré lui*, has been made persistently ever since.

Ephraim Chambers' *Cyclopaedia* (1728 and later editions)

---

[26] Alfred North Whitehead, *Science and the Modern World* (Cambridge: Cambridge University Press, 1926), p. 83.

[27] See H. M. Bracken, *The Early Reception of Berkeley's Immaterialism, 1710–1733* (The Hague: Martinus Nijhoff, 1959).

[28] Letter to Johnson, November 25, 1729. See below, p. 228.

contains several references to Berkeley. According to H. M. Bracken, Chambers' articles are "calculated to give the impression that the *Principles* was simply an attack, though an important and ingenious one, on abstract ideas and the material world, and thus in the sceptical tradition." [29]

During his lifetime Berkeley's philosophy was being discussed by at least one important group of "inquisitive men." This was the Rankenian Club,[30] a student society which met in Edinburgh in the 1720's. Its members included Colin Maclaurin, John Smibert, John Stevenson, and George Turnbull. Mossner claims that this club was "perhaps the strongest unofficial influence" upon David Hume's intellectual development during his student days at Edinburgh. It is likely, also, that its influence upon the subsequent reception of Berkeley's philosophy was profound and enduring. Berkeley was a central topic of discussion at the club, which carried on a philosophical correspondence with him. Smibert went with him to America as his prospective professor of fine arts. The other members first introduced Berkeley's works into the Scottish curriculum at Edinburgh and Aberdeen. Colin Maclaurin, who won the prize offered by the French Academy of Sciences for the year 1724 (Berkeley's *De Motu* had been entered for the prize in 1720), was appointed professor of mathematics at Edinburgh in 1725 on Newton's recommendation. His *Treatise on Fluxions* (1742) was the best defense in English of the Newtonian calculus against Berkeley's *Analyst*. John Stevenson, professor of logic and metaphysics at Edinburgh, lectured on Berkeley in the 1730's. George Turnbull lectured on him at the Univeristy of Aberdeen in the late 'twenties to an audience which

---

[29] Bracken, p. 60. See chap. 4 for a detailed discussion of Chambers' references.

[30] See E. C. Mossner, *The Life of David Hume* (Edinburgh: Thomas Nelson, 1954), pp. 48 f.; and George E. Davie, "Hume in his Contemporary Setting," in *David Hume*, 250th Anniversary of the Birth of David Hume, 1711-1961, *University Gazette*, Suppl. (Edinburgh: University Press, 1961), pp. 11-15.

included Thomas Reid, the founder of the Scottish school of philosophy, often called the Common Sense School.

What was the attitude of the members of the Rankenian Club to Berkeley and their evaluation of him? With the exception of Turnbull, who, in his *Principles of Moral Philosophy* (1728), accepted immaterialism, it seems likely that they did not charge him with insincerity but that they did think his position entailed skepticism; they "pushed his singular tenets all the amazing lengths to which they have been carried in later publications." [31] The phrase "amazing lengths" suggests skeptical conclusions utterly at variance with common sense. Since that time Berkeley has influenced two main groups of theorists: Those who have accepted some of his "singular tenets," while being aware that they violated common sense; and those who have been emphatic in their rejection of them because they violated common sense.

Members of the second group have been legion. One of its influential originals was Andrew Baxter. Educated at Aberdeen, but probably not a Rankenian, he published his *Enquiry into the Nature of the Human Soul* in London in 1733, a successful book which went into three editions. He asserts that Berkeley, who "seems serious," nevertheless tries to introduce "the wildest and most unbounded scepticism"; that, according to him, all material things and other people are "mere illusions, and have no existence but in the fancy"; and that Berkeley's principles "contradict common language as much as common sense." Poor Berkeley! Students who saw Berkeley through Baxter's eyes could hardly fail to confound his immaterialism with what Berkeley himself called "the deepest and most deplorable skepticism," wherein one is forced "positively to deny the real existence of any part of the universe." [32] Baxter apparently thought that Berkeley seriously entertained the deepest skepticism, not merely that his doctrine entailed it.

If the Rankenians "pushed" Berkeley's tenets to "amazing

[31] *The Scots Magazine*, XXXIII (Edinburgh, 1771), 341, quoted by Mossner, p. 48.
[32] *Dialogues*, III, sec. 1.

lengths," who then was responsible for "carrying" them to these lengths in "later publications"? The most likely author was "that bright and ingenious young spark," David Hume, who was at Edinburgh University in the 1720's when the club was flourishing, and who was converted to philosophy in 1730.[33] Hume composed his *Treatise of Human Nature* in the middle 'thirties and published it in London in 1739. Among the zealots it excited even fewer murmurs than had Berkeley's *Principles* thirty years earlier. Hume cast the first part of his work anew in the *Inquiry Concerning Human Understanding* (1748). This performance, also, was "entirely overlooked and neglected." In these two works, Hume showed how much he had learned from Berkeley, now called for the first time "a great philosopher," and for the second time "that ingenious author," but all he acknowledged were Berkeley's "discovery" regarding abstract ideas [34] and his supremely powerful arguments for skepticism. Of the latter he claimed:

> ... most of the writings of that ingenious author form the best lessons of skepticism which are to be found either among the ancient or modern philosophers, Bayle not excepted. He professes, however, in his title page (and undoubtedly with great truth) to have composed his book against the skeptics as well as against the atheists and freethinkers. But that all his arguments, though otherwise intended, are in reality merely skeptical appears from this, *that they admit of no answer and produce no conviction.* Their only effect is to cause that momentary amazement and irresolution and confusion which is the result of skepticism.[35]

Thus Hume, more perceptive than most, saw that Berkeley was a skeptic *malgré lui*. Apparently he thought also that

---

[33] "His conversion to philosophy certainly happened in his eighteenth year." Charles W. Hendel, *Studies in the Philosophy of David Hume*, "Library of Liberal Arts," No. 116 (Indianapolis and New York: The Bobbs-Merrill Company Inc., 1963), p. 16.

[34] See above, p. ix and note 1.

[35] *Inquiry Concerning Human Understanding*, p. 163 n.

his skeptical arguments, better than Bayle's, were unanswerable. In fact, he used similar arguments and pushed some of Berkeley's tenets to lengths that Berkeley had anticipated and had tried to avoid;[36] for example, he extended the application of Berkeley's argument against material substance to mental substance. Hume adopted Berkeley's account of physical causation, but he extended the account to cover mental causes as well. He also adopted Berkeley's principle of association, used so effectively in the latter's theory of vision, but extended its application "into most of his philosophy." Hume said of himself that if anything entitled him to "so glorious a name as that of an 'inventor,' it is the use he makes of this principle."[37] Finally, Hume adopted what he thought to be Berkeley's discovery regarding abstract ideas. Accordingly, Hume belongs to the first group of theorists influenced by Berkeley, that is, those who accepted some of his tenets although they are contrary to common sense. But at the same time he tried to subscribe to common-sense notions.

Thomas Reid, from Aberdeen, at first accepted Berkeley's philosophy and then, in his *Inquiry into the Human Mind on the Principles of Common Sense* (1764) and later *Essays*, reacted against Hume's skeptical conclusions. He tried to refute "the ideal theory" by rejecting its assumptions, specifically, that separate ideas or impressions are the primary data which we compound into things. Against Berkeley he distinguished between the sensation which is in the mind and the quality which is in the object and which is perceived. In his appeal to "principles of common sense" and his claim that "all men that have common understanding agree in such principles," he anticipated some of the views of twentieth-century realism.

Another Scotsman, also from Aberdeen, was influential in establishing the tradition of Berkeley as a skeptic and a naïve idealist. He was James Beattie, whose *Essay on the Nature and*

[36] *Dialogues*, III, sec. 9.
[37] "An Abstract of a Treatise of Human Nature" (1740), in *Inquiry*, p. 198.

Immutability of Truth, in Opposition to Sophistry and Scepticism (1770) went into five editions. It won wide acclaim, a painting of him by Sir Joshua Reynolds called "The Triumph of Truth," and a pension of £200 a year from George III. His refutation of Berkeley also deserves a prize for the best caricature of immaterialism: "A great philosopher has actually demonstrated—we are told—that matter does not exist. . . . Where is the harm of my believing that if I were to fall down yonder precipice and break my neck, I should be no more a man of this world? My neck, sir, may be an *idea* to you, but to me it is a *reality,* and an important one too. . . . Berkeley's system . . . leads to atheism and universal scepticism. . . . From beginning to end it is all a mystery of falsehood, arising from the use of ambiguous words. . . ."

Beattie's main target, however, was not Berkeley but Hume, and the German translation of Beattie's work probably introduced Kant to the writings of Hume. Perhaps it also introduced him to the views of Berkeley. Nevertheless, Berkeley's *Dialogues* was available to Kant in a German translation by Eschenbach (Rostock, 1756) long before he composed his *Critique of Pure Reason* (published in 1781). The subtitle of the translation refers to Berkeley and Collier (whose *Clavis Universalis* was included) as "the most eminent repudiaters of the reality of the entire corporeal world." Thus, the common interpretation of Berkeley as a willful skeptic reached Germany long before Beattie's account.

Kant's relation to Berkeley is puzzling. On the face of it, however, there is no puzzle. Kant clearly belongs to the second group of theorists who reacted against the skepticism of Berkeley. In this he was merely following the tradition now well established by the Scottish philosophers. This is the obvious and still generally accepted view.

There is, however, another interpretation. Did Kant learn from Berkeley, consciously adopting many of his insights, and yet hide his debt to an eccentric whom he regarded as a mystic and a visionary, perverting his account of Berkeley and holding him up to ridicule? Kant exhibited more animus toward

Berkeley than toward any other philosopher, calling his doctrine a "chimera of the brain." And yet Kant repeated, using different terms, Berkeley's arguments against materialism (transcendental realism), skepticism (empirical idealism), and the doctrine of abstract ideas (the transcendental illusion). He incorporated Berkeley's axiom, *esse* is *percipi*, into his own transcendental idealism and produced a proof of the external world (empirical realism) identical with that which had been, until Kant, uniquely Berkeley's. We cannot be certain whether these are merely similarities or also results of influence; but we *can* be sure that the ghost of "the good Berkeley" influenced Kant to this extent: Stung by critics who labeled him a Berkeleian, he suppressed, in his second edition of the *Critique of Pure Reason*, what Schopenhauer called "the principal idealistic passage," the Fourth Paralogism, and took pains to distinguish his system from Berkeley's. But he could not suppress his underlying central argument against transcendental realism, an argument identical in all of its six steps with Berkeley's main argument against materialism. Perhaps the most striking feature of this common argument is its use of the oblique approach, specifically, the simple but devastating turning against itself of the game played by skepticism, a move which originated with Berkeley,[38] and which, incidentally, was the most likely source of the traditional misinterpretations of his philosophy. This feature is absent in Hume's philosophy. All the evidence, both internal and external, indicates that Kant probably studied Berkeley carefully, understood him better than most of his modern critics, and adopted many of Berkeley's insights and made them his own.[39] If this is so—if, in the words of Ernst Mach, "Berkeley's

[38] See Richard H. Popkin, "Berkeley and Pyrrhonism," *Review of Metaphysics*, V, No. 2 (December 1951), 223–246, in which the author brings out this feature of Berkeley's dialectic with great clarity.

[39] For a fuller discussion, see my article, "Kant's Refutation of Dogmatic Idealism," *The Philosophical Quarterly*, V, No. 20 (July 1955), 225–244.

point of view was latently present in Kant" [40]—then Berkeley's indirect influence on modern philosophy has extended further than his direct influence.

After Kant, many theorists fall into the first group, the members of which accept some of his "singular tenets." These theorists have abstracted an element in his system that they found true and have built upon it. After Kant, on the Continent Schopenhauer, Bergson, and Mach have been strongly affected by Berkeley. According to Schopenhauer, Berkeley was the first to proclaim that the world is my idea. The principle he found in Berkeley, that there can be no object without a subject, "condemns materialism forever." Bergson, who remarked that every philosophy of recent years must take its start by reckoning with the contentions of Berkeley, recognized Berkeley as one of his principal teachers and inspirers. Mach, whose doctrine had a profound effect upon modern physics, developed a philosophy of science strikingly similar to Berkeley's; his criticism of absolute space, time, and motion was anticipated in all its central features by Berkeley. The extent to which Mach was influenced by Berkeley is not known, but it is known that Mach, in his youth, studied Berkeley and remained convinced of the importance of his contribution.

In Britain problems raised by Berkeley have been the subject of constant discussion in philosophical circles since the time of the Scottish school. Russell, for two of the most active decades of his career, was primarily concerned with a problem "which has been acute since the time of Berkeley," [41] the problem of the relation between sense data and the entities of physics. In his answers, he vacillated between several positions, one of them, phenomenalism, being similar to Berke-

---

[40] Ernst Mach, *Die Analyse der Empfindungen* (9th edn.; Jena: G. Fischer, 1922), p. 299. Mach added, however, that he was convinced that Kant's philosophy was markedly less consistent than the systems of Berkeley and Hume.

[41] Bertrand Russell, *Our Knowledge of the External World* (London: Allen & Unwin, 1914), p. 107.

ley's position; phenomenalism has been a prominent subject of contemporary debate. Whitehead, on the other hand, singled out Berkeley's protest against the bifurcation of nature. He named the widespread error the "Fallacy of Misplaced Concreteness," defined as "the accidental error of mistaking the abstract for the concrete," and he seems to have been aware that this was the central part of the error Berkeley noted as the doctrine of abstract ideas.

Berkeley's influence on American thought has been even more substantial. Early American idealists recognized him as their founder. Royce regarded his work as the best introduction to idealism. Peirce called Berkeley "the introducer of pragmatism." William James, although he did not accept Berkeley's conclusions, adopted his method. It appears that today Berkeley is read far more widely in America than in England.

Since the time of Berkeley's final editions, interest in his two major works has developed steadily. Between 1734 and 1933 there were at least twenty-four different editions (including those in collected works) of the *Principles* and twenty-three of the *Dialogues*.[42] Recently, however, the demand has increased enormously. During the last three decades there have been at least twenty-five different editions of the *Principles* and twenty of its companion.[43]

In general, Berkeley's writing has aggravated and provoked rather than persuaded. The tradition suggested by the Rankenian Club and established by the Scottish school of common sense is still strong: His paradoxical utterances are plainly wrong since, as Baxter noted, they contradict ordinary language as much as common sense. But some of them are hard to refute. Hence, Berkeley has commanded attention. This is

[42] See T. E. Jessop, *A Bibliography of George Berkeley* (Oxford: Oxford University Press, 1934).

[43] See Colin M. Turbayne and Robert Ware, "A Bibliography of George Berkeley, 1933–1962," reprinted (New York, 1963) by and from *The Journal of Philosophy*, LX, No. 4 (February 14, 1963), 93–112.

the tradition. Although it is a respectable one, it has tended to obscure rich areas in Berkeley's thought, such as his account of language, his theory of universals, his treatment of the nature of illusions and of error in general, and his account of scientific method. There are signs that suggest that these other areas are being increasingly explored.

COLIN MURRAY TURBAYNE

Rochester, New York
February 1965

OUTLINE ANALYSIS

BERKELEY'S PRINCIPLES, DIALOGUES, AND
PHILOSOPHICAL CORRESPONDENCE WITH JOHNSON

INTRODUCTION (to *Principles,* Part I and projected parts)

1–5 The plain man is in no danger of becoming a skeptic until he studies the writings of the philosophers. At once he is drawn into paradoxes and inconsistencies, and eventually he finishes either where he started or as a skeptic. The fault lies neither in the obscurity of things nor in his faculties but in the false principles of the philosophers.

6–9 A chief false principle is the supposition that there are abstract ideas:
 (a) We can abstract one from another, or apprehend separately, those qualities which cannot exist so separated, e.g., color or motion without extension (7).
 (b) We can frame a general idea of a quality by abstracting what is common to several instances of it, e.g., color-in-general that is not any determinate color (8).
 (c) We can frame a general idea of a compound of qualities by abstracting what is common to several particular instances of it, in which abstraction the latter partake, e.g., man-in-general, human nature, etc. (9).

10–17 Criticism: (1) Abstract ideas are not discovered by introspection; (2) Words are general or universal without signifying abstract ideas, a particular becoming general by being made a sign of other particulars; (3) Abstract ideas are not necessary for communication or for increasing knowledge.

18–20 The source of this doctrine is the received opinion that the chief and only end of language is communication and that every common or abstract noun functions as a proper noun. But language has other ends, e.g., rousing emotion and directing action. Moreover, we must distinguish between designation and definition, realizing that although a common or abstract noun designates nothing, it is necessary to keep it constantly to the same definition.

21–25 Although words are of excellent use, they are, for the most part, abused. Even though it is practically impossible, let us try to meditate without words in order to get clear of eristic or purely verbal disputes, to extricate ourselves from the subtle net of abstract ideas, and to reduce the risk of error.

	Principles	*Dialogues*
IMMATERIALISM: ITS MAIN FEATURES	1–33	III. 24
The physical world: concrete and relative existence v. abstract and absolute		
Physical objects are qualities or ideas concreted, combined, or blended together	1	I. 2, III. 16, 19
Physical objects exist only in relation to a percipient mind, human or divine	2–7	II. 3, III. 5
The perceived object concreted with the perception of it	5–6	I. 9
Representative or Copy Theory rejected	8–9	I. 13, III. 17
Relativity and concreteness of		
(a) Secondary qualities	9–15	I. 3–5
(b) Primary qualities		I. 6–8
"Material *substratum* or support": the metaphor exposed	16–17	I. 10
Matter unknowable or unnecessary	18–20	cf. I. 13
Relativity of (a) any quality, (b) any combination of qualities	22–24	I. 11
Causes and effects, and the laws of nature		
Physical, including neuro-physiological, explanation of the production of ideas incomprehensible	cf. 18–20	II. 1, 8
The physical world is a series of events (commonly called "causes and effects") exhibited by God's will according to rules (commonly called "laws of nature")	25–33	II. 2, 4, III. 10

OUTLINE ANALYSIS

	Principles	Dialogues	Correspondence
OBJECTIONS TO IMMATERIALISM	34–84		
1. Reduces nature to illusion and ends in skepticism:	34–40	III. 1, 2, 6, 15	
(a) Takes away corporeal substances	37	II. 10	
(b) Goes against ordinary language	38–39	III. 6	
(c) Rejects the testimony of sense	40	III. 16	
2. Confuses real and imaginary	41	III. 18	
3. Cannot explain the seen externality of physical objects	42–44	I. 12	
4. Cannot explain the continued existence of physical objects	45–48	III. 3	
5. Makes mind extended	49	III. 20	
6. Undermines physics	50	III. 13	I. 1, II. 1
7. Takes away physical causes and makes God the author of sin	51–53	III. 7, II. 5	I. 2–4, II. 4
8. Opposes common sense	54–57	III. 8, III. 14	
9. and cannot explain this universal deception	cf. 73–76		
10. Cannot accommodate illusions	58–59	III. 9	
11. Cannot explain the elaborate machinery of nature	60–66	II. 6, cf. II. 4	I. 5, II. 1–3
12. Cannot refute occasionalism	67–76	II. 7, cf. II. 4	cf. II. 2
13. We merely lack a sense for perceiving matter	77–78		
14. Cannot show the impossibility of the existence of matter	79	II. 11	
15. Cannot show that matter does not exist as an unknown *somewhat*	80–81	II. 9	

	Principles	Dialogues	Correspondence
16. Contradicts the Scriptural account of:			
(a) the real existence of bodies	82–83		
(b) miracles	84		
(c) the creation		III. 21	
(d) the resurrection	cf. 95		I. 6, II. 6
17. Inconsistently rejects matter because we have no idea of it and retains mind although we have no idea of it		III. 4, cf. III. 20	
18. Offers merely a new way of speaking about the same things		III. 10	
19. Makes God imperfect since he suffers pain		III. 11	
20. Does not consider that matter is proportional to gravity		III. 12	II. 1
21. Absurdly supposes that no two people can see the same thing		III. 18	
22. Gives a vague or indefinite account of archetypes	(cf. Objections 4, 12, 16, 21)		I. 2–10, III. 1, IV. 1
23. Typical fallacies in the preceding objections:		III. 23	
(a) That which makes equally against two contradictory opinions can be proof against neither			
(b) *petitio principii*			
(c) *ignoratio elenchi*			

	Principles	Dialogues	Correspondence
CONSEQUENCES OF IMMATERIALISM	85–156	III. 22	
Knowledge and Religion			
Undermines skepticism	85–91	I. 1, 14, III. 1, 2, 19	

	Principles	Dialogues	Correspondence
Undermines atheism	92–96	II. 3	
Physics			
Concrete v. abstract time, space, motion	97–100		cf. III. 2–3, IV. 2–3
Rules v. essences: attraction	101–109		
Signs v. causes			
Relative v. absolute time, space, motion	110–117		cf. III. 2, IV. 2
Mathematics			
Arithmetic: symbols v. abstractions	119–122		
Geometry: finite quantities v. infinitesimals	123–134		
Psychology			
Self-knowledge	135–144	cf. III. 4	
Other minds	145		
Theology			
Knowledge of God	146–156	III. 4–5	II. 2–4

CHRONOLOGY

Early Years: 1685–1707

1685	Born near Kilkenny, March 12
1696	Entered Kilkenny College
1700	Entered Trinity College, Dublin
1704	Graduated B.A.

Creative Years: 1707–1713

1707	*Arithmetica Absque Algebra* and *Miscellanea Mathematica;* graduated M.A.; elected Junior Fellow
1707–1708	Composed *Philosophical Commentaries*
1709	*An Essay Towards a New Theory of Vision*
1710	*A Treatise Concerning the Principles of Human Knowledge*
1712	Junior Greek Lecturer; *Passive Obedience*
1713	First visit to England; *Three Dialogues Between Hylas and Philonous*

Continental Tours: 1713–1720

1713–1714	First Continental tour
1716–1720	Second Continental tour as tutor to son of Bishop of Clogher, mainly in Italy; wrote *De Motu*

The American Dream: 1720–1731

1720	The bursting of the South Sea Bubble and the Mississippi Bubble
1721	Returned to Ireland; *An Essay Towards Preventing the Ruin of Great Britain*
1722	Bermuda project privately announced

1723	Executor and legatee of Swift's Vanessa (Hester Van Homrigh)
1724	Appointed Dean of Derry and resigned fellowship at Trinity College; returned to England; Bermuda project publicly launched
1725	*A Proposal for the Better Supplying of Churches in Our Foreign Plantations*
1726	Charter approved and grant of £20,000 agreed
1728	Married Anne, eldest daughter of Sir John Forster, and set sail for America
1729–1731	Lived at Newport, Rhode Island
1731	Bermuda project abandoned; returned to London

AWAITING PREFERMENT: 1731–1734

1732	*Alciphron* (composed in Rhode Island)
1733	*The Theory of Vision, or Visual Language Vindicated and Explained*
1734	*The Analyst*

THE BISHOP OF CLOYNE: 1734–1753

1734	Bishop of Cloyne
1735	*A Defence of Freethinking in Mathematics*
1735–1737	*The Querist*
1744	*Siris*
1752	At Oxford
1753	Died, January 14; interred in the Chapel of Christ Church

SELECTED BIBLIOGRAPHY

PRINCIPAL WORKS BY BERKELEY

Philosophical Commentaries. Notebooks written 1707–1708.
An Essay Towards a New Theory of Vision. Dublin, 1709.
A Treatise Concerning the Principles of Human Knowledge. Dublin, 1710.
Passive Obedience. Dublin and London, 1712.
Three Dialogues Between Hylas and Philonous. London, 1713.
De Motu. London, 1721.
Alciphron: or the Minute Philosopher. London and Dublin, 1732.
The Theory of Vision, or Visual Language Vindicated and Explained. London, 1733.
The Analyst: or a Discourse Addressed to an Infidel Mathematician. Dublin and London, 1734.
A Defence of Freethinking in Mathematics. Dublin and London, 1735.
The Querist. Dublin and London, 1735–1737.
Siris: A Chain of Philosophical Reflexions and Inquiries Concerning the Virtues of Tar-Water, and Divers Other Subjects. Dublin and London, 1744.

COLLECTED EDITIONS

1784	Dublin and London. 2 vols. Edited probably by JOSEPH STOCK (reprinted London, 1820, 3 vols.; and London, 1837, 1 vol.).
1843	London. 2 vols. Edited by G. N. WRIGHT.
1871	Oxford. 4 vols. Edited by A. C. FRASER.
1897–1898	London. 3 vols. Edited by G. SAMPSON. With a biographical introduction by A. J. BALFOUR.
1901	Oxford. 4 vols. Edited by A. C. FRASER.
1948–1957	Edinburgh. 9 vols. Edited by A. A. LUCE and T. E. JESSOP.

BIBLIOGRAPHIES

JESSOP, T. E. *A Bibliography of George Berkeley*. With an inventory of Berkeley's manuscript remains by A. A. LUCE. Oxford: Oxford University Press, 1934.

TURBAYNE, C. M., and WARE, ROBERT. "A Bibliography of George Berkeley, 1933–1962," reprinted by and from *The Journal of Philosophy*, LX, No. 4 (February 14, 1963), 93–112. New York, 1963.

BIOGRAPHIES

ADAMSON, R., and MITCHELL, J. M. "Berkeley," in *Encyclopedia Britannica*. Edinburgh, 9th edn., 1875; 11th ed., 1910.

BALFOUR, A. J. "Biographical Introduction" in *The Works of George Berkeley, Bishop of Cloyne*, edited by GEORGE SAMPSON. London, 1897.

FRASER, A. C. *Life and Letters of George Berkeley*. Oxford, 1871.

HONE, J. M., and ROSSI, M. M. *Bishop Berkeley: His Life, Writings and Philosophy*. With an introduction by W. B. YEATS. London: Faber and Faber, 1931.

LUCE, A. A. *The Life of George Berkeley, Bishop of Cloyne*. Edinburgh: Thomas Nelson, 1949.

RAND, BENJAMIN. *Berkeley and Percival*. Cambridge: Cambridge University Press, 1914.

WORKS WITH DIRECT REFERENCE TO BERKELEY'S PHILOSOPHY

ARDLEY, G. W. R. *Berkeley's Philosophy of Nature*. Auckland: University of Auckland, Bulletin No. 63, 1962.

ARMSTRONG, DAVID M. *Berkeley's Theory of Vision: A Critical Examination of Bishop Berkeley's Essay Towards a New Theory of Vision*. Melbourne: Melbourne University Press, 1961.

BRACKEN, HARRY M. *The Early Reception of Berkeley's Immaterialism, 1710–1733*. The Hague: Martinus Nijhoff, 1959.

FRASER, A. C. *Berkeley*. Edinburgh, 1881. Reprinted 1901.

GUEROULT, MARTIAL. *Berkeley, quatre études sur la perception et sur Dieu*. Paris: Aubier, 1956.

HEDENIUS, INGEMAR. *Sensationalism and Theology in Berkeley's Philosophy*. Oxford: Blackwell, 1936.

HICKS, G. DAWES. *Berkeley*. London: Oxford University Press, 1932.

JESSOP, T. E. *George Berkeley*. London: Longmans Green, 1959.

JOHNSTON, G. A. *The Development of Berkeley's Philosophy*. London: Methuen, 1923.

JOUSSAIN, ANDRÉ. *Exposé critique de la philosophie de Berkeley*. Paris: Boivin, 1921.

LEROY, ANDRÉ-LOUIS. *George Berkeley*. Paris: Presses Universitaires, 1959.

LEVI, A. *La filosofia di Giorgio Berkeley*. Turin: Bocca, 1922.

LUCE, A. A. *Berkeley and Malebranche*. Oxford: Oxford University Press, 1934.

———. *Berkeley's Immaterialism*. Edinburgh: Thomas Nelson, 1945.

———. *The Dialectic of Immaterialism*. London: Hodder and Stoughton, 1963.

METZ, R. *George Berkeley, Leben und Lehre*. Stuttgart: H. Kurtz, 1925.

PEPPER, STEPHEN C., ASCHENBRENNER, KARL, and MATES, BENSON (eds.). *George Berkeley: Lectures Delivered Before the Philosophical Union of the University of California*. Berkeley: University of California Press, 1957.

SILLEM, EDWARD A. *George Berkeley and the Proofs for the Existence of God*. London: Longmans Green, 1957.

TURBAYNE, COLIN M. "Commentary" in George Berkeley, *Works on Vision*. Indianapolis and New York: The Bobbs-Merrill Company, Inc., 1963.

———. *The Myth of Metaphor*. New Haven and London: Yale University Press, 1962.

WARNOCK, G. J. *Berkeley*. London: Penguin, 1953.

WILD, JOHN. *George Berkeley: A Study of His Life and Philosophy*. Cambridge: Harvard University Press, 1936.

WISDOM, J. O. *The Unconscious Origins of Berkeley's Philosophy*. London: Hogarth, 1953. New York: Hillary House, 1957.

NOTE ON THE TEXTS

The texts of *A Treatise Concerning the Principles of Human Knowledge* and *Three Dialogues Between Hylas and Philonous* are those of Berkeley's final editions published in one volume in London in 1734, except that the two Prefaces which Berkeley omitted have been restored. The *Principles* was first published in Dublin in 1710. The *Dialogues,* which first appeared in London in 1713, was reissued unchanged in 1725 and styled "Second Edition." Significant additions in the final versions have been bracketed in the text, while significant earlier variants have been given in footnotes.

The four letters comprising the philosophical correspondence between Berkeley and Johnson were first printed as a unit in *Samuel Johnson, President of King's College: His Career and Writings,* edited by Herbert and Carol Schneider (4 vols.; New York: Columbia University Press, 1929), II, 261–284. Johnson's two letters were published there in full, for the first time, from copies made by Johnson. I should like to thank Mr. Roland Baughman of Butler Library, Columbia University, for making available to me copies of the originals of Samuel Johnson's letters. I am indebted to Columbia University Press for permission to reprint them. Berkeley's two letters were first published in A. C. Fraser, *The Works of George Berkeley* (Oxford, 1871).

Berkeley chose to present nearly all of his philosophical and scientific writings in numbered sections. He and Johnson even used section numbers in their letters. The prominent exception is the *Three Dialogues Between Hylas and Philonous.* Because the practice is helpful to the student I have numbered the points in the *Dialogues,* enclosing the numbers in brackets.

Many of Berkeley's italics which appear to function as quotation marks have been eliminated. Furthermore, in the *Principles* and *Dialogues* spelling, punctuation, and capitalization have been revised to conform to present-day American usage, as they were in my earlier editions of these works published in The Library of Liberal Arts. In the correspondence, spelling and punctuation appear as written by Berkeley and Johnson, except for correction of a few obvious misspellings.

C. M. T.

A TREATISE CONCERNING THE PRINCIPLES OF HUMAN KNOWLEDGE

WHEREIN THE CHIEF CAUSES OF ERROR AND DIFFICULTY IN THE SCIENCES, WITH THE GROUNDS OF SKEPTICISM, ATHEISM, AND IRRELIGION, ARE INQUIRED INTO.

PREFACE[1]

What I here make public has, after a long and scrupulous inquiry, seemed to me evidently true and not unuseful to be known—particularly to those who are tainted with skepticism or want a demonstration of the existence and immateriality of God or the natural immortality of the soul. Whether it be so or no, I am content the reader should impartially examine, since I do not think myself any further concerned for the success of what I have written than as it is agreeable to truth. But to the end this may not suffer I make it my request that the reader suspend his judgment till he has once at least read the whole through with that degree of attention and thought which the subject matter shall seem to deserve. For as there are some passages that, taken by themselves, are very liable (nor could it be remedied) to gross misinterpretation, and to be charged with most absurd consequences which, nevertheless, upon an entire perusal will appear not to follow from them, so likewise, though the whole should be read over, yet, if this be done transiently, it is very probable my sense may be mistaken; but to a thinking reader, I flatter myself, it will be throughout clear and obvious. As for the characters of novelty and singularity which some of the following notions may seem to bear, it is, I hope, needless to make any apology on that account. He must surely be either very weak or very little acquainted with the sciences who shall reject a truth that is capable of demonstration for no other reason but because it is newly known and contrary to the prejudices of mankind. Thus much I thought fit to premise in order to prevent, if possible, the hasty censures of a sort of men who are too apt to condemn an opinion before they rightly comprehend it.

[1] [This Preface was not included in the second edition.]

INTRODUCTION

1. Philosophy being nothing else but the study of wisdom and truth, it may with reason be expected that those who have spent most time and pains in it should enjoy a greater calm and serenity of mind, a greater clearness and evidence of knowledge, and be less disturbed with doubts and difficulties than other men. Yet so it is, we see the illiterate bulk of mankind that walk the high road of plain common sense, and are governed by the dictates of nature, for the most part easy and undisturbed. To them nothing that is familiar appears unaccountable or difficult to comprehend. They complain not of any want of evidence in their senses, and are out of all danger of becoming skeptics. But no sooner do we depart from sense and instinct to follow the light of a superior principle, to reason, meditate, and reflect on the nature of things, but a thousand scruples spring up in our minds concerning those things which before we seemed fully to comprehend. Prejudices and errors of sense do from all parts discover themselves to our view; and, endeavoring to correct these by reason, we are insensibly drawn into uncouth paradoxes, difficulties, and inconsistencies, which multiply and grow upon us as we advance in speculation, till at length, having wandered through many intricate mazes, we find ourselves just where we were, or, which is worse, sit down in a forlorn skepticism.

2. The cause of this is thought to be the obscurity of things, or the natural weakness and imperfection of our understandings. It is said the faculties we have are few and those designed by nature for the support and comfort of life, and not to penetrate into the inward essence and constitution of things. Besides, the mind of man being finite, when it treats of things which partake of infinity it is not to be wondered at if it run into absurdities and contradictions, out of which

it is impossible it should ever extricate itself, it being of the nature of infinite not to be comprehended by that which is finite.

3. But, perhaps, we may be too partial to ourselves in placing the fault originally in our faculties and not rather in the wrong use we make of them. It is a hard thing to suppose that right deductions from true principles should ever end in consequences which cannot be maintained or made consistent. We should believe that God has dealt more bountifully with the sons of men than to give them a strong desire for that knowledge which he had placed quite out of their reach. This were not agreeable to the wonted, indulgent methods of Providence, which, whatever appetites it may have implanted in the creatures, does usually furnish them with such means as, if rightly made use of, will not fail to satisfy them. Upon the whole, I am inclined to think that the far greater part, if not all, of those difficulties which have hitherto amused philosophers and blocked up the way to knowledge, are entirely owing to ourselves—that we have first raised a dust and then complain we cannot see.

4. My purpose therefore is to try if I can discover what those principles are which have introduced all that doubtfulness and uncertainty, those absurdities and contradictions, into the several sects of philosophy—insomuch that the wisest men have thought our ignorance incurable, conceiving it to arise from the natural dullness and limitation of our faculties. And surely it is a work well deserving our pains to make a strict inquiry concerning the first principles of human knowledge, to sift and examine them on all sides, especially since there may be some grounds to suspect that those lets and difficulties which stay and embarrass the mind in its search after truth do not spring from any darkness and intricacy in the objects or natural defect in the understanding so much as from false principles which have been insisted on, and might have been avoided.

5. How difficult and discouraging soever this attempt may seem when I consider how many great and extraordinary men

have gone before me in the same designs, yet I am not without some hopes—upon the consideration that the largest views are not always the clearest, and that he who is shortsighted will be obliged to draw the object nearer, and may, perhaps, by a close and narrow survey discern that which had escaped far better eyes.

6. In order to prepare the mind of the reader for the easier conceiving what follows, it is proper to premise somewhat, by way of introduction, concerning the nature and abuse of language. But the unraveling this matter leads me in some measure to anticipate my design by taking notice of what seems to have had a chief part in rendering speculation intricate and perplexed and to have occasioned innumerable errors and difficulties in almost all parts of knowledge. And that is the opinion that the mind has a power of framing *abstract ideas* or notions of things. He who is not a perfect stranger to the writings and disputes of philosophers must needs acknowledge that no small part of them are spent about abstract ideas. These are in a more especial manner thought to be the object of those sciences which go by the name of logic and metaphysics, and of all that which passes under the notion of the most abstracted and sublime learning, in all which one shall scarce find any question handled in such a manner as does not suppose their existence in the mind, and that it is well acquainted with them.

7. It is agreed on all hands that the qualities or modes of things do never really exist each of them apart by itself and separated from all others, but are mixed, as it were, and blended together, several in the same object. But we are told the mind, being able to consider each quality singly, or abstracted from those other qualities with which it is united, does by that means frame to itself abstract ideas. For example, there is perceived by sight an object extended, colored, and moved: this mixed or compound idea the mind, resolving into its simple, constituent parts and viewing each by itself, exclusive of the rest, does frame the abstract ideas of extension, color, and motion. Not that it is possible for color or motion

to exist without extension, but only that the mind can frame to itself by *abstraction* the idea of color exclusive of extension, and of motion exclusive of both color and extension.

8. Again, the mind having observed that in the particular extensions perceived by sense there is something common and alike in all, and some other things peculiar, as this or that figure or magnitude, which distinguish them one from another, it considers apart or singles out by itself that which is common, making thereof a most abstract idea of extension, which is neither line, surface, nor solid, nor has any figure or magnitude, but is an idea entirely prescinded from all these. So likewise the mind, by leaving out of the particular colors perceived by sense that which distinguishes them one from another, and retaining that only which is common to all, makes an idea of color in abstract, which is neither red, nor blue, nor white, nor any other determinate color. And, in like manner, by considering motion abstractedly not only from the body moved, but likewise from the figure it describes, and all particular directions and velocities, the abstract idea of motion is framed, which equally corresponds to all particular motions whatsoever that may be perceived by sense.

9. And as the mind frames to itself abstract ideas of qualities or modes, so does it, by the same precision or mental separation, attain abstract ideas of the more compounded beings which include several coexistent qualities. For example, the mind, having observed that Peter, James, and John resemble each other in certain common agreements of shape and other qualities, leaves out of the complex or compounded idea it has of Peter, James, and any other particular man that which is peculiar to each, retaining only what is common to all, and so makes an abstract idea wherein all the particulars equally partake—abstracting entirely from and cutting off all those circumstances and differences which might determine it to any particular existence. And after this manner it is said we come by the abstract idea of *man* or, if you please, humanity, or human nature; wherein it is true there is included color, because there is no man but has some color, but then it

can be neither white, nor black, nor any particular color, because there is no one particular color wherein all men partake. So likewise there is included stature, but then it is neither tall stature, nor low stature, nor yet middle stature, but something abstracted from all these. And so of the rest. Moreover, there being a great variety of other creatures that partake in some parts, but not all, of the complex idea of man, the mind, leaving out those parts which are peculiar to men, and retaining those only which are common to all the living creatures, frames the idea of *animal,* which abstracts not only from all particular men, but also all birds, beasts, fishes, and insects. The constituent parts of the abstract idea of animal are body, life, sense, and spontaneous motion. By "body" is meant body without any particular shape or figure, there being no one shape or figure common to all animals, without covering, either of hair, or feathers, or scales, etc., nor yet naked: hair, feathers, scales, and nakedness being the distinguishing properties of particular animals, and for that reason left out of the *abstract idea.* Upon the same account the spontaneous motion must be neither walking, nor flying, nor creeping; it is nevertheless a motion, but what that motion is it is not easy to conceive.

10. Whether others have this wonderful faculty of abstracting their ideas, they best can tell; for myself I find indeed I have a faculty of imagining, or representing to myself, the ideas of those particular things I have perceived, and of variously compounding and dividing them. I can imagine a man with two heads, or the upper parts of a man joined to the body of a horse. I can consider the hand, the eye, the nose, each by itself abstracted or separated from the rest of the body. But then whatever hand or eye I imagine, it must have some particular shape and color. Likewise the idea of man that I frame to myself must be either of a white, or a black, or a tawny, a straight, or a crooked, a tall, or a low, or a middle-sized man. I cannot by any effort of thought conceive the abstract idea above described. And it is equally impossible for me to form the abstract idea of motion distinct from the body

moving, and which is neither swift nor slow, curvilinear nor rectilinear; and the like may be said of all other abstract general ideas whatsoever. To be plain, I own myself able to abstract in one sense, as when I consider some particular parts or qualities separated from others, with which, though they are united in some object, yet it is possible they may really exist without them. But I deny that I can abstract one from another, or conceive separately, those qualities which it is impossible should exist so separated; or that I can frame a general notion by abstracting from particulars in the manner aforesaid—which two last are the two proper acceptations of "abstraction." And there are grounds to think most men will acknowledge themselves to be in my case. The generality of men which are simple and illiterate never pretend to abstract notions. It is said they are difficult and not to be attained without pains and study; we may therefore reasonably conclude that, if such there be, they are confined only to the learned.

11. I proceed to examine what can be alleged in defense of the doctrine of abstraction, and try if I can discover what it is that inclines the men of speculation to embrace an opinion so remote from common sense as that seems to be. There has been a late, deservedly esteemed philosopher [2] who, no doubt, has given it very much countenance by seeming to think the having abstract general ideas is what puts the widest difference in point of understanding betwixt man and beast.—

> The having of general ideas (he says) is that which puts a perfect distinction betwixt man and brutes, and is an excellency which the faculties of brutes do by no means attain unto. For, it is evident we observe no footsteps in them of

---

[2] [John Locke (1632–1704). He published his revolutionary *Essay Concerning Human Understanding* in 1690. This work, which had a profound influence upon the development of Berkeley's philosophy, was available to him when he entered Trinity in 1700. "Locke's *Essay* was on the course there, within two years of its publication, years before it received general recognition in England . . . and was working like leaven." A. A. Luce, *Life of George Berkeley* (Edinburgh: Thomas Nelson, 1949), pp. 31, 39.]

> making use of general signs for universal ideas; from which we have reason to imagine that they have not the faculty of abstracting, or making general ideas, since they have no use of words or any other general signs.

And a little after:

> Therefore, I think, we may suppose that it is in this that the species of brutes are discriminated from men, and it is that proper difference wherein they are wholly separated, and which at last widens to so wide a distance. For, if they have any ideas at all, and are not bare machines (as some would have them), we cannot deny them to have some reason. It seems as evident to me that they do, some of them, in certain instances reason as that they have sense; but it is only in particular ideas, just as they receive them from their senses. They are the best of them tied up within those narrow bounds, and have not (as I think) the faculty to enlarge them by any kind of abstraction.—*Essay on Human Understanding,* Bk. II, chap. 11, secs. 10f.

I readily agree with this learned author that the faculties of brutes can by no means attain to abstraction. But then if this be made the distinguishing property of that sort of animals, I fear a great many of those that pass for men must be reckoned into their number. The reason that is here assigned why we have no grounds to think brutes have abstract general ideas is that we observe in them no use of words or any other general signs; which is built on this supposition—that the making use of words implies the having general ideas. From which it follows that men who use language are able to abstract or generalize their ideas. That this is the sense and arguing of the author will further appear by his answering the question he in another place puts: "Since all things that exist are only particulars, how come we by general terms?" His answer is: "Words become general by being made the signs of general ideas."—(*Essay on Human Understanding,* Bk. III, chap. 3, sec. 6.) But it seems that a word becomes general by being made the sign, not of an abstract general idea, but of several particular ideas, any one of which it indifferently suggests to the mind. For example, when it is said, "the change of motion is proportional to the impressed force," or that, "whatever has extension is divisible," these propositions are to be understood of motion and extension in general; and nevertheless it will not follow that they suggest to my thoughts an idea of motion without a body moved, or any determinate direction and velocity, or that I must conceive an abstract general idea of extension which is neither line, surface, nor solid, neither great nor small, black, white, nor red, nor of any other determinate color. It is only implied that whatever motion I consider, whether it be swift or slow, perpendicular, horizontal, or oblique, or in whatever object, the axiom concerning it holds equally true. As does the other of every particular extension, it matters not whether line, surface, or solid, whether of this or that magnitude or figure.

12. By observing how ideas become general we may the better judge how words are made so. And here it is to be noted that I do not deny absolutely there are general ideas, but only that there are any *abstract* general ideas; for, in the passages above quoted, wherein there is mention of general ideas, it is always supposed that they are formed by abstraction, after the manner set forth in sections 8 and 9. Now, if we will annex a meaning to our words and speak only of what we can conceive, I believe we shall acknowledge that an idea which, considered in itself, is particular, becomes general by being made to represent or stand for all other particular ideas of the same sort. To make this plain by an example, suppose a geometrician is demonstrating the method of cutting a line in two equal parts. He draws, for instance, a black line of an inch in length: this, which in itself is a particular line, is nevertheless with regard to its signification general, since, as it is there used, it represents all particular lines whatsoever; for that which is demonstrated of it is demonstrated of all lines or, in other words, of a line in general. And, as that *particular* line becomes general by being made a sign, so the *name* "line," which taken absolutely is particular, by being a sign is made general. And as the former owes its generality not to its being the sign of an abstract or general line, but of all

particular right lines that my possibly exist, so the latter must be thought to derive its generality from the same cause, namely, the various particular lines which it indifferently denotes.

13. To give the reader a yet clearer view of the nature of abstract ideas, and the uses they are thought necessary to, I shall add one more passage out of the *Essay on Human Understanding,* which is as follows:

> *Abstract ideas* are not so obvious or easy to children or the yet unexercised mind as particular ones. If they seem so to grown men it is only because by constant and familiar use they are made so. For, when we nicely reflect upon them, we shall find that general ideas are fictions and contrivances of the mind, that carry difficulty with them, and do not so easily offer themselves as we are apt to imagine. For example, does it not require some pains and skill to form the general idea of a triangle (which is yet none of the most abstract, comprehensive, and difficult); for it must be neither oblique nor rectangle, neither equilateral, equicrural, nor scalenon, but *all and none* of these at once? In effect, it is something imperfect that cannot exist, an idea wherein some parts of several different and *inconsistent* ideas are put together. It is true the mind in this imperfect state has need of such ideas and makes all the haste to them it can, for the convenience of communication and enlargement of knowledge to both which it is naturally very much inclined. But yet one has reason to suspect such ideas are marks of our imperfection. At least this is enough to show that the most abstract and general ideas are not those that the mind is first and most easily acquainted with, nor such as its earliest knowledge is conversant about.—Bk. IV, chap. 7, sec. 9.

If any man has the faculty of framing in his mind such an idea of a triangle as is here described, it is in vain to pretend to dispute him out of it, nor would I go about it. All I desire is that the reader would fully and certainly inform himself whether he has such an idea or no. And this, methinks, can be no hard task for anyone to perform. What more easy than for anyone to look a little into his own thoughts, and there try whether he has, or can attain to have, an idea that shall correspond with the description that is here given of the general idea of a triangle, which is "neither oblique nor rectangle, equilateral, equicrural nor scalenon, but all and none of these at once"?

14. Much is here said of the difficulty that abstract ideas carry with them, and the pains and skill requisite to the forming them. And it is on all hands agreed that there is need of great toil and labor of the mind to emancipate our thoughts from particular objects and raise them to those sublime speculations that are conversant about abstract ideas. From all which the natural consequence should seem to be, that so difficult a thing as the forming abstract ideas was not necessary for *communication*, which is so easy and familiar to all sorts of men. But, we are told, if they seem obvious and easy to grown men, "it is only because by constant and familiar use they are made so." Now, I would fain know at what time it is men are employed in surmounting that difficulty and furnishing themselves with those necessary helps for discourse. It cannot be when they are grown up, for then it seems they are not conscious of any such painstaking; it remains, therefore, to be the business of their childhood. And surely the great and multiplied labor of framing abstract notions will be found a hard task for that tender age. Is it not a hard thing to imagine that a couple of children cannot prate together of their sugar plums and rattles and the rest of their little trinkets till they have first tacked together numberless inconsistencies and so framed in their minds abstract general ideas and annexed them to every common name they make use of?

15. Nor do I think them a whit more needful for the *enlargement of knowledge* than for *communication*. It is, I know, a point much insisted on, that all knowledge and demonstration are about universal notions, to which I fully agree; but then it does not appear to me that those notions are formed by abstraction in the manner premised—*universality*, so far as I can comprehend, not consisting in the ab-

solute, positive nature or conception of any thing, but in the relation it bears to the particulars signified or represented by it; by virtue whereof it is that things, names, or notions, being in their own nature *particular,* are rendered *universal.* Thus, when I demonstrate any proposition concerning triangles, it is to be supposed that I have in view the universal idea of a triangle, which ought not to be understood as if I could frame an idea of a triangle which was neither equilateral, nor scalenon, nor equicrural, but only that the particular triangle I consider, whether of this or that sort it matters not, does equally stand for and represent all rectilinear triangles whatsoever, and is in that sense *universal.* All which seems very plain and not to include any difficulty in it.

16. But here it will be demanded how we can know any proposition to be true of all particular triangles, except we have first seen it demonstrated of the abstract idea of a triangle which equally agrees to all? For, because a property may be demonstrated to agree to some one particular triangle, it will not thence follow that it equally belongs to any other triangle which in all respects is not the same with it. For example, having demonstrated that the three angles of an isosceles rectangular triangle are equal to two right ones, I cannot therefore conclude this affection agrees to all other triangles which have neither a right angle nor two equal sides. It seems therefore that, to be certain this proposition is universally true, we must either make a particular demonstration for every particular triangle, which is impossible, or once for all demonstrate it of the abstract idea of a triangle in which all the particulars do indifferently partake and by which they are all equally represented. To which I answer that, though the idea I have in view whilst I make the demonstration be, for instance, that of an isosceles rectangular triangle whose sides are of a determinate length, I may nevertheless be certain it extends to all other rectilinear triangles, of what sort or bigness soever. And that because neither the right angle, nor the equality, nor determinate length of the sides are at all concerned in the demonstration. It is true the

diagram I have in view includes all these particulars, but then there is not the least mention made of them in the proof of the proposition. It is not said the three angles are equal to two right ones, because one of them is a right angle, or because the sides comprehending it are of the same length. Which sufficiently shows that the right angle might have been oblique, and the sides unequal, and for all that the demonstration have held good. And for this reason it is that I conclude that to be true of any obliquangular or scalenon which I had demonstrated of a particular right-angled equicrural triangle, and not because I demonstrated the proposition of the abstract idea of a triangle. [And here it must be acknowledged that a man may consider a figure merely as triangular, without attending to the particular qualities of the angles or relations of the sides. So far he may abstract, but this will never prove that he can frame an abstract, general, inconsistent idea of a triangle. In like manner we may consider Peter so far forth as man, or so far forth as animal, without framing the forementioned abstract idea either of man or of animal, inasmuch as all that is perceived is not considered.] [3]

17. It were an endless as well as a useless thing to trace the Schoolmen, those great masters of abstraction, through all the manifold, inextricable labyrinths of error and dispute which their doctrine of abstract natures and notions seems to have led them into. What bickerings and controversies, and what a learned dust have been raised about those matters, and what mighty advantage has been from thence derived to mankind, are things at this day too clearly known to need being insisted on. And it had been well if the ill effects of that doctrine were confined to those only who make the most avowed profession of it. When men consider the great pains, industry, and parts that have for so many ages been laid out on the cultivation and advancement of the sciences, and that notwithstanding all this the far greater part of them remains full of darkness and uncertainty, and disputes that are like

[3] [This addition in 1734 does not represent a change of doctrine. The same view was presented in the first edition of the *Dialogues*, I, sec. 8.]

never to have an end, and even those that are thought to be supported by the most clear and cogent demonstrations, contain in them paradoxes which are perfectly irreconcilable to the understandings of men, and that, taking all together, a small portion of them does supply any real benefit to mankind, otherwise than by being an innocent diversion and amusement—I say the consideration of all this is apt to throw them into a despondency and perfect contempt of all study. But this may, perhaps, cease upon a view of the false principles that have obtained in the world, amongst all which there is none, methinks, has a more wide influence over the thoughts of speculative men than this of *abstract* general ideas.

18. I come now to consider the *source* of this prevailing notion, and that seems to me to be language. And surely nothing of less extent than reason itself could have been the source of an opinion so universally received. The truth of this appears, as from other reasons, so also from the plain confession of the ablest patrons of abstract ideas, who acknowledge that they are made in order to naming; from which it is a clear consequence that if there had been no such thing as speech or universal signs there never had been any thought of abstraction. See Bk. III, chap. 6, sec. 39, and elsewhere of the *Essay on Human Understanding*. Let us examine the manner wherein words have contributed to the origin of that mistake: First then, it is thought that every name has, or ought to have, one only precise and settled signification, which inclines men to think there are certain abstract, determinate ideas which constitute the true and only immediate signification of each general name; and that it is by the mediation of these abstract ideas that a general name comes to signify any particular thing. Whereas, in truth, there is no such thing as one precise and definite signification annexed to any general name, they all signifying indifferently a great number of particular ideas. All which does evidently follow from what has been already said, and will clearly appear to anyone by a little reflection. To this it will be objected that every name that has a definition is thereby restrained to one

certain signification. For example, a "triangle" is defined to be "a plane surface comprehended by three right lines," by which that name is limited to denote one certain idea and no other. To which I answer that in the definition it is not said whether the surface be great or small, black or white, nor whether the sides are long or short, equal or unequal, nor with what angles they are inclined to each other; in all which there may be great variety, and consequently there is no one settled idea which limits the signification of the word "triangle." It is one thing for to keep a name constantly to the same definition, and another to make it stand everywhere for the same idea; the one is necessary, the other useless and impracticable.

19. But, to give a further account how words came to produce the doctrine of abstract ideas, it must be observed that it is a received opinion that language has no other end but the communicating ideas, and that every significant name stands for an idea. This being so, and it being withal certain that names which yet are not thought altogether insignificant do not always mark out particular conceivable ideas, it is straightway concluded that they stand for abstract notions. That there are many names in use amongst speculative men which do not always suggest to others determinate, particular ideas is what nobody will deny. And a little attention will discover that it is not necessary (even in the strictest reasonings) that significant names which stand for ideas should, every time they are used, excite in the understanding the ideas they are made to stand for—in reading and discoursing, names being for the most part used as letters are in algebra, in which, though a particular quantity be marked by each letter, yet to proceed right it is not requisite that in every step each letter suggest to your thoughts that particular quantity it was appointed to stand for.

20. Besides, the communicating of ideas marked by words is not the chief and only end of language, as is commonly supposed. There are other ends, as the raising of some passion, the exciting to or deterring from an action, the putting the

mind in some particular disposition—to which the former is in many cases barely subservient, and sometimes entirely omitted, when these can be obtained without it, as I think does not unfrequently happen in the familiar use of language. I entreat the reader to reflect with himself and see if it does not often happen, either in hearing or reading a discourse, that the passions of fear, love, hatred, admiration, disdain, and the like, arise immediately in his mind upon the perception of certain words, without any ideas coming between. At first, indeed, the words might have occasioned ideas that were fit to produce those emotions; but, if I mistake not, it will be found that, when language is once grown familiar, the hearing of the sounds or sight of the characters is oft immediately attended with those passions which at first were wont to be produced by the intervention of ideas that are now quite omitted. May we not, for example, be affected with the promise of a *good thing,* though we have not an idea of what it is? Or is not the being threatened with danger sufficient to excite a dread, though we think not of any particular evil likely to befall us, nor yet frame to ourselves an idea of danger in abstract? If anyone shall join ever so little reflection of his own to what has been said, I believe that it will evidently appear to him that general names are often used in the propriety of language without the speaker's designing them for marks of ideas in his own, which he would have them raise in the mind of the hearer. Even proper names themselves do not seem always spoken with a design to bring into our view the ideas of those individuals that are supposed to be marked by them. For example, when a Schoolman tells me, "Aristotle has said it," all I conceive he means by it is to dispose me to embrace his opinion with the deference and submission which custom has annexed to that name. And this effect may be so instantly produced in the minds of those who are accustomed to resign their judgment to the authority of that philosopher, as it is impossible any idea either of his person, writings, or reputation should go before. Innumerable examples of this kind may be given, but why should

I insist on those things which everyone's experience will, I doubt not, plentifully suggest unto him?

21. We have, I think, shown the impossibility of abstract ideas. We have considered what has been said for them by their ablest patrons, and endeavored to show they are of no use for those ends to which they are thought necessary. And lastly, we have traced them to the source from whence they flow, which appears to be language.—It cannot be denied that words are of excellent use, in that by their means all that stock of knowledge which has been purchased by the joint labors of inquisitive men in all ages and nations may be drawn into the view and made the possession of one single person. But at the same time it must be owned that most parts of knowledge have been strangely perplexed and darkened by the abuse of words, and general ways of speech wherein they are delivered. Since therefore words are so apt to impose on the understanding, whatever ideas I consider, I shall endeavor to take them bare and naked into my view, keeping out of my thoughts so far as I am able those names which long and constant use has so strictly united with them; from which I may expect to derive the following advantages:

22. *First,* I shall be sure to get clear of all controversies purely verbal—the springing up of which weeds in almost all the sciences has been a main hindrance to the growth of true and sound knowledge. *Secondly,* this seems to be a sure way to extricate myself out of that fine and subtle net of *abstract ideas* which has so miserably perplexed and entangled the minds of men; and that with this peculiar circumstance, that by how much the finer and more curious was the wit of any man, by so much the deeper was he likely to be ensnared and faster held therein. *Thirdly,* so long as I confine my thoughts to my own ideas divested of words, I do not see how I can easily be mistaken. The objects I consider I clearly and adequately know. I cannot be deceived in thinking I have an idea which I have not. It is not possible for me to imagine that any of my own ideas are alike or unlike that are not truly so. To discern the agreements or disagreements there

are between my ideas, to see what ideas are included in any compound idea and what not, there is nothing more requisite than an attentive perception of what passes in my own understanding.

23. But the attainment of all these advantages does presuppose an entire deliverance from the deception of words, which I dare hardly promise myself—so difficult a thing it is to dissolve a union so early begun and confirmed by so long a habit as that betwixt words and ideas. Which difficulty seems to have been very much increased by the doctrine of *abstraction*. For so long as men thought abstract ideas were annexed to their words, it does not seem strange that they should use words for ideas—it being found an impracticable thing to lay aside the word and retain the *abstract* idea in the mind, which in itself was perfectly inconceivable. This seems to me the principal cause why those men who have so emphatically recommended to others the laying aside all use of words in their meditations, and contemplating their bare ideas, have yet failed to perform it themselves. Of late many have been very sensible of the absurd opinions and insignificant disputes which grow out of the abuse of words. And, in order to remedy these evils, they advise well that we attend to the ideas signified and draw off our attention from the words which signify them. But, how good soever this advice may be they have given others, it is plain they could not have a due regard to it themselves so long as they thought the only immediate use of words was to signify ideas, and that the immediate signification of every general name was a determinate abstract idea.

24. But, these being known to be mistakes, a man may with greater ease prevent his being imposed on by words. He that knows he has no other than *particular* ideas will not puzzle himself in vain to find out and conceive the *abstract* idea annexed to any name. And he that knows names do not always stand for ideas will spare himself the labor of looking for ideas where there are none to be had. It were, therefore, to be wished that everyone would use his utmost endeavors

to obtain a clear view of the ideas he would consider, separating from them all that dress and encumbrance of words which so much contribute to blind the judgment and divide the attention. In vain do we extend our view into the heavens and pry into the entrails of the earth, in vain do we consult the writings of learned men and trace the dark footsteps of antiquity—we need only draw the curtain of words, to behold the fairest tree of knowledge, whose fruit is excellent and within the reach of our hand.

25. Unless we take care to clear the first principles of knowledge from the embarrassment and delusion of words, we may make infinite reasonings upon them to no purpose; we may draw consequences from consequences, and be never the wiser. The further we go, we shall only lose ourselves the more irrecoverably, and be the deeper entangled in difficulties and mistakes. Whoever, therefore, designs to read the following sheets, I entreat him to make my words the occasion of his own thinking and endeavor to attain the same train of thoughts in reading that I had in writing them. By this means it will be easy for him to discover the truth or falsity of what I say. He will be out of all danger of being deceived by my words, and I do not see how he can be led into an error by considering his own naked, undisguised ideas.

OF THE PRINCIPLES OF HUMAN KNOWLEDGE

PART I [4]

It is evident to anyone who takes a survey of the *objects* of human knowledge that they are either ideas actually imprinted on the senses, or else such as are perceived by attending to the passions and operations of the mind, or lastly, ideas formed by help of memory and imagination—either compounding, dividing, or barely representing those originally perceived in the aforesaid ways. By sight I have the ideas of light and colors, with their several degrees and variations. By touch I perceive, for example, hard and soft, heat and cold, motion and resistance, and of all these more and less either as to quantity or degree. Smelling furnishes me with odors, the palate with tastes, and hearing conveys sounds to the mind in all their variety of tone and composition. And as several of these are observed to accompany each other, they come to be marked by one name, and so to be reputed as one thing. Thus, for example, a certain color, taste, smell, figure, and consistence having been observed to go together, are accounted one distinct thing signified by the name "apple"; other collections of ideas constitute a stone, a tree, a book, and the like sensible things—which as they are pleasing or disagreeable excite the passions of love, hatred, joy, grief, and so forth.

2. But, besides all that endless variety of ideas or objects of knowledge, there is likewise something which knows or perceives them and exercises divers operations, as willing, imagin-

[4] ["Part I" was omitted from the title page of the second edition, apparently because Berkeley had given up the plan of publishing Part II. See Correspondence, Letter II, sec. 6, and *Dialogues*, Preface.]

ing, remembering, about them. This perceiving, active being is what I call "mind," "spirit," "soul," or "myself." By which words I do not denote any one of my ideas, but a thing entirely distinct from them, wherein they exist or, which is the same thing, whereby they are perceived—for the existence of an idea consists in being perceived.

3. That neither our thoughts, nor passions, nor ideas formed by the imagination exist without the mind is what everybody will allow. And it seems no less evident that the various sensations or ideas imprinted on the sense, however blended or combined together (that is, whatever objects they compose), cannot exist otherwise than in a mind perceiving them.—I think an intuitive knowledge may be obtained of this by anyone that shall attend to what is meant by the term "exist" when applied to sensible things. The table I write on I say exists, that is, I see and feel it; and if I were out of my study I should say it existed—meaning thereby that if I was in my study I might perceive it, or that some other spirit actually does perceive it. There was an odor, that is, it was smelled, there was a sound, that is to say, it was heard; a color or figure, and it was perceived by sight or touch. This is all that I can understand by these and the like expressions. For as to what is said of the absolute existence of unthinking things without any relation to their being perceived, that seems perfectly unintelligible. Their *esse* is *percipi*, nor is it possible they should have any existence out of the minds or thinking things which perceive them.

4. It is indeed an opinion strangely prevailing amongst men that houses, mountains, rivers, and, in a word, all sensible objects have an existence, natural or real, distinct from their being perceived by the understanding. But with how great an assurance and acquiescence soever this principle may be entertained in the world, yet whoever shall find in his heart to call it in question may, if I mistake not, perceive it to involve a manifest contradiction. For what are the forementioned objects but the things we perceive by sense? And what do we perceive besides our own ideas or sensations?

And is it not plainly repugnant that any one of these, or any combination of them, should exist unperceived?

5. If we thoroughly examine this tenet it will, perhaps, be found at bottom to depend on the doctrine of *abstract ideas*. For can there be a nicer strain of abstraction than to distinguish the existence of sensible objects from their being perceived, so as to conceive them existing unperceived? Light and colors, heat and cold, extension and figures—in a word, the things we see and feel—what are they but so many sensations, notions, ideas, or impressions on the sense? And is it possible to separate, even in thought, any of these from perception? For my part, I might as easily divide a thing from itself. I may, indeed, divide in my thoughts, or conceive apart from each other, those things which, perhaps, I never perceived by sense so divided. Thus I imagine the trunk of a human body without the limbs, or conceive the smell of a rose without thinking on the rose itself. So far, I will not deny, I can abstract—if that may properly be called "abstraction" which extends only to the conceiving separately such objects as it is possible may really exist or be actually perceived asunder. But my conceiving or imagining power does not extend beyond the possibility of real existence or perception. Hence, as it is impossible for me to see or feel anything without an actual sensation of that thing, so it is impossible for me to conceive in my thoughts any sensible thing or object distinct from the sensation or perception of it.

6. Some truths there are so near and obvious to the mind that a man need only open his eyes to see them. Such I take this important one to be, to wit, that all the choir of heaven and furniture of the earth, in a word, all those bodies which compose the mighty frame of the world, have not any subsistence without a mind—that their *being* is to be perceived or known, that, consequently, so long as they are not actually perceived by me or do not exist in my mind or that of any other created spirit, they must either have no existence at all or else subsist in the mind of some eternal spirit—it being perfectly unintelligible, and involving all the absurdity of

abstraction, to attribute to any single part of them an existence independent of a spirit. To be convinced of which, the reader need only reflect, and try to separate in his own thoughts, the *being* of a sensible thing from its *being perceived*.

7. From what has been said it follows there is not any other substance than *spirit*, or that which perceives. But, for the fuller proof of this point, let it be considered the sensible qualities are color, figure, motion, smell, taste, and such like —that is, the ideas perceived by sense. Now, for an idea to exist in an unperceiving thing is a manifest contradiction, for to have an idea is all one as to perceive; that, therefore, wherein color, figure, and the like qualities exist must perceive them; hence it is clear there can be no unthinking substance or *substratum* of those ideas.

8. But, say you, though the ideas themselves do not exist without the mind, yet there may be things like them, whereof they are copies or resemblances, which things exist without the mind in an unthinking substance. I answer, an idea can be like nothing but an idea; a color or figure can be like nothing but another color or figure. If we look but ever so little into our thoughts, we shall find it impossible for us to conceive a likeness except only between our ideas. Again, I ask whether those supposed originals or external things, of which our ideas are the pictures or representations, be themselves perceivable or no? If they are, then they are ideas and we have gained our point; but if you say they are not, I appeal to anyone whether it be sense to assert a color is like something which is invisible; hard or soft, like something which is intangible; and so of the rest.

9. Some there are who make a distinction betwixt *primary* and *secondary* qualities.[5] By the former they mean extension, figure, motion, rest, solidity or impenetrability, and number; by the latter they denote all other sensible qualities, as colors, sounds, tastes, and so forth. The ideas we have of these they acknowledge not to be the resemblances of anything existing

[5] [E.g., Locke, *Essay*, Bk. II, chap. 8.]

without the mind, or unperceived, but they will have our ideas of the primary qualities to be patterns or images of things which exist without the mind, in an unthinking substance which they call "matter." By "matter," therefore, we are to understand an inert, senseless substance, in which extension, figure, and motion do actually subsist. But it is evident from what we have already shown that extension, figure, and motion are only ideas existing in the mind, and that an idea can be like nothing but another idea, and that consequently neither they nor their archetypes can exist in an unperceiving substance. Hence it is plain that the very notion of what is called "matter" or "corporeal substance" involves a contradiction in it.

10. They who assert that figure, motion, and the rest of the primary or original qualities do exist without the mind in unthinking substances do at the same time acknowledge that colors, sounds, heat, cold, and suchlike secondary qualities do not—which they tell us are sensations existing in the mind alone, that depend on and are occasioned by the different size, texture, and motion of the minute particles of matter. This they take for an undoubted truth which they can demonstrate beyond all exception. Now, if it be certain that those original qualities are inseparably united with the other sensible qualities, and not, even in thought, capable of being abstracted from them, it plainly follows that they exist only in the mind. But I desire anyone to reflect and try whether he can, by any abstraction of thought, conceive the extension and motion of a body without all other sensible qualities. For my own part, I see evidently that it is not in my power to frame an idea of a body extended and moved, but I must withal give it some color or other sensible quality which is acknowledged to exist only in the mind. In short, extension, figure, and motion, abstracted from all other qualities, are inconceivable. Where therefore the other sensible qualities are, there must these be also, to wit, in the mind and nowhere else.

11. Again, *great* and *small, swift* and *slow* are allowed to

exist nowhere without the mind, being entirely relative, and changing as the frame or position of the organs of sense varies. The extension, therefore, which exists without the mind is neither great nor small, the motion neither swift nor slow; that is, they are nothing at all. But, say you, they are extension in general, and motion in general: thus we see how much the tenet of extended movable substances existing without the mind depends on that strange doctrine of *abstract ideas*. And here I cannot but remark how nearly the vague and indeterminate description of matter or corporeal substance, which the modern philosophers are run into by their own principles, resembles that antiquated and so much ridiculed notion of *materia prima,* to be met with in Aristotle and his followers. Without extension, solidity cannot be conceived; since, therefore, it has been shown that extension exists not in an unthinking substance, the same must also be true of solidity.

12. That number is entirely the creature of the mind, even though the other qualities be allowed to exist without, will be evident to whoever considers that the same thing bears a different denomination of number as the mind views it with different respects. Thus the same extension is one, or three, or thirty-six, according as the mind considers it with reference to a yard, a foot, or an inch. Number is so visibly relative and dependent on men's understanding that it is strange to think how anyone should give it an absolute existence without the mind. We say one book, one page, one line; all these are equally units, though some contain several of the others. And in each instance it is plain the unit relates to some particular combination of ideas arbitrarily put together by the mind.

13. Unity I know some will have to be a simple or uncompounded idea accompanying all other ideas into the mind.[6] That I have any such idea answering the word "unity" I do not find; and if I had, methinks I could not miss finding it; on the contrary, it should be the most familiar to my understand-

[6] [E.g., Locke, *Essay,* Bk. II, chap. 16, sec. 1: "Amongst all the ideas we have, there is none more simple than that of unity."]

ing, since it is said to accompany all other ideas and to be perceived by all the ways of sensation and reflection. To say no more, it is an *abstract idea*.

14. I shall further add that, after the same manner as modern philosophers prove certain sensible qualities to have no existence in matter, or without the mind, the same thing may be likewise proved of all other sensible qualities whatsoever. Thus, for instance, it is said that heat and cold are affections only of the mind, and not at all patterns of real beings existing in the corporeal substances which excite them. for that the same body which appears cold to one hand seems warm to another. Now, why may we not as well argue that figure and extension are not patterns or resemblances of qualities existing in matter, because to the same eye at different stations, or eyes of a different texture at the same station, they appear various and cannot, therefore, be the images of anything settled and determinate without the mind? Again, it is proved that sweetness is not really in the sapid thing, because, the thing remaining unaltered, the sweetness is changed into bitter, as in case of a fever or otherwise vitiated palate. Is it not as reasonable to say that motion is not without the mind, since if the succession of ideas in the mind become swifter, the motion, it is acknowledged, shall appear slower without any alteration in any external object?

15. In short, let anyone consider those arguments which are thought manifestly to prove that colors and tastes exist only in the mind, and he shall find they may with equal force be brought to prove the same thing of extension, figure, and motion. Though it must be confessed this method of arguing does not so much prove that there is no extension or color in an outward object as that we do not know by sense which is the true extension or color of the object. But the arguments foregoing plainly show it to be impossible that any color or extension at all, or other sensible quality whatsoever, should exist in an unthinking subject without the mind, or, in truth, that there should be any such thing as an outward object.

16. But let us examine a little the received opinion.—It is

said extension is a mode or accident of matter, and that matter is the *substratum* that supports it. Now I desire that you would explain what is meant by matter's "supporting" extension. Say you, I have no idea of matter and, therefore, cannot explain it. I answer, though you have no positive, yet, if you have any meaning at all, you must at least have a relative idea of matter; though you know not what it is, yet you must be supposed to know what relation it bears to accidents, and what is meant by its supporting them. It is evident "support" cannot here be taken in its usual or literal sense—as when we say that pillars support a building; in what sense therefore must it be taken?

17. If we inquire into what the most accurate philosophers [7] declare themselves to mean by "material substance," we shall find them acknowledge they have no other meaning annexed to those sounds but the idea of being in general together with the relative notion of its supporting accidents. The general idea of being appears to me the most abstract and incomprehensible of all other; and as for its supporting accidents, this, as we have just now observed, cannot be understood in the common sense of those words; it must, therefore, be taken in some other sense, but what that is they do not explain. So that when I consider the two parts or branches which make the signification of the words "material substance," I am convinced there is no distinct meaning annexed to them. But why should we trouble ourselves any further in discussing this material *substratum* or support of figure and motion and other sensible qualities? Does it not suppose they have an existence without the mind? And is not this a direct repugnancy and altogether inconceivable?

18. But, though it were possible that solid, figured, movable substances may exist without the mind, corresponding to

[7] [E.g., Locke, *Essay*, Bk. II, chap. 23, sec. 2: "If anyone will examine himself concerning his notion of pure substance in general, he will find he has no other idea of it all but only a supposition of he knows not what support of such qualities which are capable of producing simple ideas in us; which qualities are commonly called accidents."]

the ideas we have of bodies, yet how is it possible for us to know this? Either we must know it by sense or by reason. As for our senses, by them we have the knowledge only of our sensations, ideas, or those things that are immediately perceived by sense, call them what you will; but they do not inform us that things exist without the mind, or unperceived, like to those which are perceived. This the materialists themselves acknowledge. It remains therefore that if we have any knowledge at all of external things, it must be by reason, inferring their existence from what is immediately perceived by sense. But what reason can induce us to believe the existence of bodies without the mind, from what we perceive, since the very patrons of matter themselves do not pretend there is any necessary connection betwixt them and our ideas? I say it is granted on all hands (and what happens in dreams, frenzies, and the like, puts it beyond dispute) that it is possible we might be affected with all the ideas we have now, though no bodies existed without resembling them. Hence it is evident the supposition of external bodies is not necessary for the producing our ideas; since it is granted they are produced sometimes, and might possibly be produced always in the same order we see them in at present, without their concurrence.

19. But though we might possibly have all our sensations without them, yet perhaps it may be thought easier to conceive and explain the manner of their production by supposing external bodies in their likeness rather than otherwise; and so it might be at least probable there are such things as bodies that excite their ideas in our minds. But neither can this be said, for, though we give the materialists their external bodies, they by their own confession are never the nearer knowing how our ideas are produced, since they own themselves unable to comprehend in what manner body can act upon spirit, or how it is possible it should imprint any idea in the mind. Hence it is evident the production of ideas or sensations in our minds can be no reason why we should

suppose matter or corporeal substances, since that is acknowledged to remain equally inexplicable with or without this supposition. If therefore it were possible for bodies to exist without the mind, yet to hold they do so must needs be a very precarious opinion, since it is to suppose, without any reason at all, that God has created innumerable beings that are entirely useless and serve to no manner of purpose.

20. In short, if there were external bodies, it is impossible we should ever come to know it; and if there were not, we might have the very same reasons to think there were that we have now. Suppose—what no one can deny possible—an intelligence without the help of external bodies, to be affected with the same train of sensations or ideas that you are, imprinted in the same order and with like vividness in his mind. I ask whether that intelligence has not all the reason to believe the existence of corporeal substances, represented by his ideas and exciting them in his mind, that you can possibly have for believing the same thing? Of this there can be no question—which one consideration is enough to make any reasonable person suspect the strength of whatever arguments he may think himself to have for the existence of bodies without the mind.

21. Were it necessary to add any further proof against the existence of matter after what has been said, I could instance several of those errors and difficulties (not to mention impieties) which have sprung from that tenet. It has occasioned numberless controversies and disputes in philosophy, and not a few of far greater moment in religion. But I shall not enter into the detail of them in this place as well because I think arguments a posteriori are unneccessary for confirming what has been, if I mistake not, sufficiently demonstrated a priori, as because I shall hereafter find occasion to speak somewhat of them.

22. I am afraid I have given cause to think me needlessly prolix in handling this subject. For to what purpose is it to dilate on that which may be demonstrated with the utmost

evidence in a line or two to anyone that is capable of the least reflection? It is but looking into your own thoughts, and so trying whether you can conceive it possible for a sound, or figure, or motion, or color to exist without the mind or unperceived. This easy trial may make you see that what you contend for is a downright contradiction. Insomuch that I am content to put the whole upon this issue: if you can but conceive it possible for one extended movable substance, or, in general, for any one idea, or anything like an idea, to exist otherwise than in a mind perceiving it, I shall readily give up the cause. And, as for all that compages of external bodies which you contend for, I shall grant you its existence, though you cannot either give me any reason why you believe it exists, or assign any use to it when it is supposed to exist. I say the bare possibility of your opinion's being true shall pass for an argument that it is so.

23. But, say you, surely there is nothing easier than to imagine trees, for instance, in a park, or books existing in a closet, and nobody by to perceive them. I answer you may so, there is no difficulty in it; but what is all this, I beseech you, more than framing in your mind certain ideas which you call books and trees, and at the same time omitting to frame the idea of anyone that may perceive them? But do not you yourself perceive or think of them all the while? This therefore is nothing to the purpose; it only shows you have the power of imagining or forming ideas in your mind; but it does not show that you can conceive it possible the objects of your thought may exist without the mind. To make out this, it is necessary that you conceive them existing unconceived or unthought of, which is a manifest repugnancy. When we do our utmost to conceive the existence of external bodies, we are all the while only contemplating our own ideas. But the mind, taking no notice of itself, is deluded to think it can and does conceive bodies existing unthought of or without the mind, though at the same time they are apprehended by or exist in itself. A little attention will discover

to anyone the truth and evidence of what is here said, and make it unnecessary to insist on any other proofs against the existence of *material substance*.

24. It is very obvious, upon the least inquiry into our own thoughts, to know whether it be possible for us to understand what is meant by "the absolute existence of sensible objects in themselves, or without the mind." To me it is evident those words mark out either a direct contradiction or else nothing at all. And to convince others of this, I know no readier or fairer way than to entreat they would calmly attend to their own thoughts; and if by this attention the emptiness or repugnancy of those expressions does appear, surely nothing more is requisite for their conviction. It is on this, therefore, that I insist, to wit, that "the absolute existence of unthinking things" are words without a meaning, or which include a contradiction. This is what I repeat and inculcate, and earnestly recommend to the attentive thoughts of the reader.

25. All our ideas, sensations, or the things which we perceive, by whatsoever names they may be distinguished, are visibly inactive—there is nothing of power or agency included in them. So that one idea or object of thought cannot produce or make any alteration in another. To be satisfied of the truth of this, there is nothing else requisite but a bare observation of our ideas. For since they and every part of them exist only in the mind, it follows that there is nothing in them but what is perceived; but whoever shall attend to his ideas, whether of sense or reflection, will not perceive in them any power or activity; there is, therefore, no such thing contained in them. A little attention will discover to us that the very being of an idea implies passiveness and inertness in it, insomuch that it is impossible for an idea to do anything or, strictly speaking, to be the cause of anything; neither can it be the resemblance or pattern of any active being, as is evident from sec. 8. Whence it plainly follows that extension, figure, and motion cannot be the cause of our sensations. To

say, therefore, that these are the effects of powers resulting from the configuration, number, motion, and size of corpuscles must certainly be false.

26. We perceive a continual succession of ideas, some are anew excited, others are changed or totally disappear. There is, therefore, some cause of these ideas, whereon they depend and which produces and changes them. That this cause cannot be any quality or idea or combination of ideas is clear from the preceding section. It must therefore be a substance; but it has been shown that there is no corporeal or material substance: it remains, therefore, that the cause of ideas is an incorporeal, active substance or spirit.

27. A spirit is one simple, undivided, active being—as it perceives ideas it is called "the understanding," and as it produces or otherwise operates about them it is called "the will." Hence there can be no *idea* formed of a soul or spirit; for all ideas whatever, being passive and inert (*vide* sec. 25), they cannot represent unto us, by way of image or likeness, that which acts. A little attention will make it plain to anyone that to have an idea which shall be like that active principle of motion and change of ideas is absolutely impossible. Such is the nature of *spirit,* or that which acts, that it cannot be of itself perceived, but only by the effects which it produces. If any man shall doubt of the truth of what is here delivered, let him but reflect and try if he can frame the idea of any power or active being, and whether he has ideas of two principal powers marked by the names "will" and "understanding," distinct from each other as well as from a third idea of substance or being in general, with a relative notion of its supporting or being the subject of the aforesaid powers—which is signified by the name "soul" or "spirit." This is what some hold; but, so far as I can see, the words "will," "soul," "spirit" do not stand for different ideas or, in truth, for any idea at all, but for something which is very different from ideas, and which, being an agent, cannot be like unto, or represented by, any idea whatsoever. [Though it must be owned at the same time that we have some notion of soul, spirit, and

the operations of the mind, such as willing, loving, hating—in as much as we know or understand the meaning of those words.] [8]

28. I find I can excite ideas in my mind at pleasure, and vary and shift the scene as oft as I think fit. It is no more than willing, and straightway this or that idea arises in my fancy; and by the same power it is obliterated and makes way for another. This making and unmaking of ideas does very properly denominate the mind active. Thus much is certain and grounded on experience; but when we talk of unthinking agents or of exciting ideas exclusive of volition, we only amuse ourselves with words.

29. But, whatever power I may have over my own thoughts, I find the ideas actually perceived by sense have not a like dependence on my will. When in broad daylight I open my eyes, it is not in my power to choose whether I shall see or no, or to determine what particular objects shall present themselves to my view; and so likewise as to the hearing and other senses; the ideas imprinted on them are not creatures of my will. There is therefore some *other* will or spirit that produces them.

30. The ideas of sense are more strong, lively, and distinct than those of the imagination; they have likewise a steadiness, order, and coherence, and are not excited at random, as those which are the effects of human wills often are, but in a regular train or series, the admirable connection whereof sufficiently testifies the wisdom and benevolence of its Author. Now the set rules or established methods wherein the mind we depend on excites in us the ideas of sense are called "the laws of nature"; and these we learn by experience, which teaches us that such and such ideas are attended with such and such other ideas in the ordinary course of things.

31. This gives us a sort of foresight which enables us to

---

[8] [This sentence, added to the second edition of 1734, introduces the technical term "notion," but it is doubtful whether it marks a change of doctrine. Similar changes were made in *Principles,* secs. 89, 140, 142; and *Dialogues,* III, sec. 4.]

regulate our actions for the benefit of life. And without this we should be eternally at a loss; we could not know how to act anything that might procure us the least pleasure or remove the least pain of sense. That food nourishes, sleep refreshes, and fire warms us; that to sow in the seedtime is the way to reap in the harvest; and in general that to obtain such or such ends, such or such means are conducive—all this we know, not by discovering any necessary connection between our ideas, but only by the observation of the settled laws of nature, without which we should be all in uncertainty and confusion, and a grown man no more know how to manage himself in the affairs of life than an infant just born.

32. And yet this consistent, uniform working which so evidently displays the goodness and wisdom of that Governing Spirit whose Will constitutes the laws of nature, is so far from leading our thoughts to Him that it rather sends them awandering after second causes. For when we perceive certain ideas of sense constantly followed by other ideas, and we know this is not of our own doing, we forthwith attribute power and agency to the ideas themselves and make one the cause of another, than which nothing can be more absurd and unintelligible. Thus, for example, having observed that when we perceive by sight a certain round, luminous figure, we at the same time perceive by touch the idea or sensation called "heat," we do from thence conclude the sun to be the cause of heat. And in like manner perceiving the motion and collision of bodies to be attended with sound, we are inclined to think the latter an effect of the former.

33. The ideas imprinted on the senses by the Author of Nature are called "real things"; and those excited in the imagination, being less regular, vivid, and constant, are more properly termed "ideas" or "images of things" which they copy and represent. But then our sensations, be they never so vivid and distinct, are nevertheless ideas, that is, they exist in the mind, or are perceived by it, as truly as the ideas of its own framing. The ideas of sense are allowed to have more reality in them, that is, to be more strong, orderly, and coherent than

the creatures of the mind; but this is no argument that they exist without the mind. They are also less dependent on the spirit, or thinking substance which perceives them, in that they are excited by the will of another and more powerful spirit; yet still they are *ideas;* and certainly no idea, whether faint or strong, can exist otherwise than in a mind perceiving it.

34. Before we proceed any further it is necessary to spend some time in answering objections which may probably be made against the principles hitherto laid down. In doing of which, if I seem too prolix to those of quick apprehensions, I hope it may be pardoned, since all men do not equally apprehend things of this nature, and I am willing to be understood by everyone.

First, then, it will be objected that by the foregoing principles all that is real and substantial in nature is banished out of the world, and instead thereof a chimerical scheme of *ideas* takes place. All things that exist, exist only in the mind, that is, they are purely notional. What therefore becomes of the sun, moon, and stars? What must we think of houses, rivers, mountains, trees, stones, nay, even of our own bodies? Are all these but so many chimeras and illusions on the fancy? To all which, and whatever else of the same sort may be objected, I answer that by the principles premised we are not deprived of any one thing in nature. Whatever we see, feel, hear, or anywise conceive or understand remains as secure as ever, and is as real as ever. There is a *rerum natura,* and the distinction between realities and chimeras retains its full force. This is evident from secs. 29, 30, and 33, where we have shown what is meant by "real things" in opposition to "chimeras" or ideas of our own framing; but then they both equally exist in the mind, and in that sense they are alike *ideas.*

35. I do not argue against the existence of any one thing that we can apprehend either by sense or reflection. That the things I see with my eyes and touch with my hands do exist, really exist, I make not the least question. The only

thing whose existence we deny is that which philosophers call matter or corporeal substance. And in doing of this there is no damage done to the rest of mankind, who, I dare say, will never miss it. The atheist indeed will want the color of an empty name to support his impiety; and the philosophers may possibly find they have lost a great handle for trifling and disputation.

36. If any man thinks this detracts from the existence or reality of things, he is very far from understanding what has been premised in the plainest terms I could think of. Take here an abstract of what has been said: there are spiritual substances, minds, or human souls, which will or excite ideas in themselves at pleasure, but these are faint, weak, and unsteady in respect of others they perceive by sense—which, being impressed upon them according to certain rules or laws of nature, speak themselves the effects of a mind more powerful and wise than human spirits. These latter are said to have more *reality* in them than the former—by which is meant that they are more affecting, orderly, and distinct, and that they are not fictions of the mind perceiving them. And in this sense the sun that I see by day is the real sun, and that which I imagine by night is the idea of the former. In the sense here given of "reality" it is evident that every vegetable, star, mineral, and in general each part of the mundane system, is as much a *real being* by our principles as by any other. Whether others mean anything by the term "reality" different from what I do, I entreat them to look into their own thoughts and see.

37. It will be urged that thus much at least is true, to wit, that we take away all corporeal substances. To this my answer is that if the word "substance" be taken in the vulgar sense—for a combination of sensible qualities, such as extension, solidity, weight, and the like—this we cannot be accused of taking away; but if it be taken in a philosophic sense—for the support of accidents or qualities without the mind—then indeed I acknowledge that we take it away, if one may be said to take away that which never had any existence, not even in the imagination.

38. But, say you, it sounds very harsh to say we eat and drink ideas, and are clothed with ideas. I acknowledge it does so—the word "idea" not being used in common discourse to signify the several combinations of sensible qualities which are called "things"; and it is certain that any expression which varies from the familiar use of language will seem harsh and ridiculous. But this does not concern the truth of the proposition which, in other words, is no more than to say we are fed and clothed with those things which we perceive immediately by our senses. The hardness or softness, the color, taste, warmth, figure, and suchlike qualities, which combined together constitute the several sorts of victuals and apparel, have been shown to exist only in the mind that perceives them; and this is all that is meant by calling them "ideas," which word if it was as ordinarily used as "thing," would sound no harsher nor more ridiculous than it. I am not for disputing about the propriety, but the truth of the expression. If therefore you agree with me that we eat and drink and are clad with the immediate objects of sense, which cannot exist unperceived or without the mind, I shall readily grant it is more proper or conformable to custom that they should be called "things" rather than "ideas."

39. If it be demanded why I make use of the word "idea," and do not rather in compliance with custom call them "things," I answer I do it for two reasons; first, because the term "thing" in contradistinction to "idea" is generally supposed to denote somewhat existing without the mind; secondly, because "thing" has a more comprehensive signification than "idea," including spirits or thinking things as well as ideas. Since therefore the objects of sense exist only in the mind and are withal thoughtless and inactive, I chose to mark them by the word "idea," which implies those properties.

40. But, say what we can, someone perhaps may be apt to reply he will still believe his senses, and never suffer any arguments, how plausible soever, to prevail over the certainty of them. Be it so; assert the evidence of sense as high as you please, we are willing to do the same. That what I see, hear,

and feel does exist—that is to say, is perceived by me—I no more doubt than I do of my own being. But I do not see how the testimony of sense can be alleged as a proof for the existence of anything which is not perceived by sense. We are not for having any man turn skeptic and disbelieve his senses; on the contrary, we give them all the stress and assurance imaginable; nor are there any principles more opposite to skepticism than those we have laid down, as shall be hereafter clearly shown.

41. *Secondly,* it will be objected that there is a great difference betwixt real fire, for instance, and the idea of fire, betwixt dreaming or imagining oneself burned, and actually being so. This and the like may be urged in opposition to our tenets. To all which the answer is evident from what has been already said; and I shall only add in this place that if real fire be very different from the idea of fire, so also is the real pain that it occasions very different from the idea of the same pain, and yet nobody will pretend that real pain either is, or can possibly be, in an unperceiving thing, or without the mind, any more than its idea.

42. *Thirdly,* it will be objected that we see things actually without or at a distance from us, and which, consequently, do not exist in the mind, it being absurd that those things which are seen at the distance of several miles should be as near to us as our own thoughts. In answer to this I desire it may be considered that in a dream we do oft perceive things as existing at a great distance off, and yet for all that those things are acknowledged to have their existence only in the mind.

43. But for the fuller clearing of this point it may be worth while to consider how it is that we perceive distance and things placed at a distance by sight. For that we should in truth see external space, and bodies actually existing in it, some nearer, others farther off, seems to carry with it some opposition to what has been said of their existing nowhere without the mind. The consideration of this difficulty it was that gave birth to my *Essay Towards a New Theory of*

Vision,[9] which was published not long since, wherein it is shown that distance or outness is neither immediately of itself perceived by sight, nor yet apprehended or judged of by lines and angles, or anything that has a necessary connection with it; but that it is only suggested to our thoughts by certain visible ideas and sensations attending vision, which in their own nature have no manner of similitude or relation either with distance or things placed at a distance; but by a connection taught us by experience they come to signify and suggest them to us after the same manner that words of any language suggest the ideas they are made to stand for; insomuch that a man born blind and afterwards made to see would not, at first sight, think the things he saw to be without his mind or at any distance from him. See sec. 41 of the forementioned treatise.

44. The ideas of sight and touch make two species entirely distinct and heterogeneous. The former are marks and prognostics of the latter. That the proper objects of sight neither exist without mind, nor are the images of external things, was shown even in that treatise. Though throughout the same the contrary be supposed true of tangible objects—not that to suppose that vulgar error was necessary for establishing the notion therein laid down, but because it was beside my purpose to examine and refute it in a discourse concerning *vision*. So that in strict truth the ideas of sight, when we apprehend by them distance and things placed at a distance, do not suggest or mark out to us things actually existing at a distance, but only admonish us what ideas of touch will be imprinted in our minds at such and such distances of time, and in consequence of such and such actions. It is, I say, evident from what has been said in the foregoing parts of

---

[9] [See the *Essay* (1709), *The Theory of Vision, or Visual Language Vindicated and Explained* (1733), and *Alciphron* (1732), excerpts from Dialogue IV, in Berkeley, *Works on Vision*, "Library of Liberal Arts," No. 83 (Indianapolis and New York: The Bobbs-Merrill Company, Inc., 1963).]

this treatise, and in sec. 147 and elsewhere of the *Essay Concerning Vision,* that visible ideas are the language whereby the Governing Spirit on whom we depend informs us what tangible ideas he is about to imprint upon us in case we excite this or that motion in our own bodies. But for a fuller information in this point I refer to the *Essay* itself.

45. *Fourthly,* it will be objected that from the foregoing principles it follows things are every moment annihilated and created anew. The objects of sense exist only when they are perceived; the trees, therefore, are in the garden, or the chairs in the parlor, no longer than while there is somebody by to perceive them. Upon shutting my eyes all the furniture in the room is reduced to nothing, and barely upon opening them it is again created. In answer to all which I refer the reader to what has been said in secs. 3, 4, etc., and desire he will consider whether he means anything by the actual existence of an idea distinct from its being perceived. For my part, after the nicest inquiry I could make, I am not able to discover that anything else is meant by those words; and I once more entreat the reader to sound his own thoughts and not suffer himself to be imposed on by words. If he can conceive it possible either for his ideas or their archetypes to exist without being perceived, then I give up the cause; but if he cannot, he will acknowledge it is unreasonable for him to stand up in defense of he knows not what and pretend to charge on me as an absurdity the not assenting to those propositions which at bottom have no meaning in them.

46. It will not be amiss to observe how far the received principles of philosophy are themselves chargeable with those pretended absurdities. It is thought strangely absurd that upon closing my eyelids all the visible objects around me should be reduced to nothing; and yet is not this what philosophers commonly acknowledge when they agree on all hands that light and colors, which alone are the proper and immediate objects of sight, are mere sensations that exist no longer than they are perceived? Again, it may to some, perhaps, seem very incredible that things should be every

moment creating, yet this very notion is commonly taught in the Schools. For the Schoolmen, though they acknowledge the existence of matter, and that the whole mundane fabric is framed out of it, are nevertheless of opinion that it cannot subsist without the divine conservation, which by them is expounded to be a continual creation.

47. Further, a little thought will discover to us that though we allow the existence of matter or corporeal substance, yet it will unavoidably follow, from the principles which are now generally admitted, that the particular bodies of what kind soever do none of them exist whilst they are not perceived. For it is evident from sec. 11 and the following sections that the matter philosophers contend for is an incomprehensible somewhat, which has none of those particular qualities whereby the bodies falling under our senses are distinguished one from another. But, to make this more plain, it must be remarked that the infinite divisibility of matter is now universally allowed, at least by the most approved and considerable philosophers, who on the received principles demonstrate it beyond all exception. Hence it follows that there is an infinite number of parts in each particle of matter which are not perceived by sense. The reason, therefore, that any particular body seems to be of a finite magnitude, or exhibits only a finite number of parts to sense, is not because it contains no more, since in itself it contains an infinite number of parts, but because the sense is not acute enough to discern them. In proportion, therefore, as the sense is rendered more acute, it perceives a greater number of parts in the object; that is, the object appears greater, and its figure varies, those parts in its extremities which were before unperceivable appearing now to bound it in very different lines and angles from those perceived by an obtuser sense. And at length, after various changes of size and shape, when the sense becomes infinitely acute, the body shall seem infinite. During all which there is no alteration in the body, but only in the sense. Each body, therefore, considered in itself, is infinitely extended, and consequently void of all shape or figure. From which it

follows that, though we should grant the existence of matter to be ever so certain, yet it is withal as certain—the materialists themselves are by their own principles forced to acknowledge—that neither the particular bodies perceived by sense, nor anything like them, exists without the mind. Matter, I say, and each particle thereof, is according to them infinite and shapeless, and it is the mind that frames all that variety of bodies which compose the visible world, any one whereof does not exist longer than it is perceived.

48. If we consider it, the objection proposed in sec. 45 will not be found reasonably charged on the principles we have premised, so as in truth to make any objection at all against our notions. For though we hold indeed the objects of sense to be nothing else but ideas which cannot exist unperceived, yet we may not hence conclude they have no existence except only while they are perceived by us, since there may be some other spirit that perceives them, though we do not. Wherever bodies are said to have no existence without the mind, I would not be understood to mean this or that particular mind, but all minds whatsoever. It does not therefore follow from the foregoing principles that bodies are annihilated and created every moment or exist not at all during the intervals between our perception of them.

49. *Fifthly*, it may perhaps be objected that if extension and figure exist only in the mind, it follows that the mind is extended and figured, since extension is a mode or attribute which (to speak with the Schools) is predicated of the subject in which it exists. I answer, those qualities are in the mind only as they are perceived by it—that is, not by way of *mode* or *attribute*, but only by way of *idea;* and it no more follows that the soul or mind is extended, because extension exists in it alone, than it does that it is red or blue, because those colors are on all hands acknowledged to exist in it, and nowhere else. As to what philosophers say of subject and mode, that seems very groundless and unintelligible. For instance, in this proposition "a die is hard, extended, and square," they

will have it that the word "die" denotes a subject or substance distinct from the hardness, extension, and figure which are predicated of it, and in which they exist. This I cannot comprehend; to me a die seems to be nothing distinct from those things which are termed its modes or accidents. And to say a die is hard, extended, and square is not to attribute those qualities to a subject distinct from and supporting them, but only an explication of the meaning of the word "die."

50. *Sixthly,* you will say there have been a great many things explained by matter and motion; take away these and you destroy the whole corpuscular philosophy and undermine those mechanical principles which have been applied with so much success to account for the phenomena. In short, whatever advances have been made, either by ancient or modern philosophers, in the study of nature do all proceed on the supposition that corporeal substance or matter does really exist. To this I answer that there is not any one phenomenon explained on that supposition which may not as well be explained without it, as might easily be made appear by an induction of particulars. To explain the phenomena is all one as to show why, upon such and such occasions, we are affected with such and such ideas. But how matter should operate on a spirit, or produce any idea in it, is what no philosopher will pretend to explain; it is therefore evident there can be no use of matter in natural philosophy. Besides, they who attempt to account for things do it not by corporeal substance, but by figure, motion, and other qualities, which are in truth no more than mere ideas and, therefore, cannot be the cause of anything, as has been already shown. See sec. 25.

51. *Seventhly,* it will upon this be demanded whether it does not seem absurd to take away natural causes and ascribe everything to the immediate operation of spirits? We must no longer say, upon these principles, that fire heats, or water cools, but that a spirit heats, and so forth. Would not a man be deservedly laughed at who should talk after this manner? I answer, he would so; in such things we ought to "think with

the learned and speak with the vulgar." [10] They who by demonstration are convinced of the truth of the Copernican system do nevertheless say, "the sun rises," "the sun sets," or "comes to the meridian"; and if they affected a contrary style in common talk it would without doubt appear very ridiculous. A little reflection on what is here said will make it manifest that the common use of language would receive no manner of alteration or disturbance from the admission of our tenets.

52. In the ordinary affairs of life, any phrases may be retained so long as they excite in us proper sentiments or dispositions to act in such a manner as is necessary for our well-being, how false soever they may be if taken in a strict and speculative sense. Nay, this is unavoidable, since, propriety being regulated by custom, language is suited to the received opinions, which are not always the truest. Hence it is impossible, even in the most rigid, philosophic reasonings, so far to alter the bent and genius of the tongue we speak, as never to give a handle for cavilers to pretend difficulties and inconsistencies. But a fair and ingenuous reader will collect the sense from the scope and tenor and connection of a discourse, making allowances for those inaccurate modes of speech which use has made inevitable.

53. As to the opinion that there are no corporeal causes, this has been heretofore maintained by some of the Schoolmen, as it is of late by others among the modern philosophers [11] who, though they allow matter to exist, yet will have God alone to be the immediate efficient cause of all things. These men saw that amongst all the objects of sense there was none which had any power or activity included in it, and that by consequence this was likewise true of whatever bodies they

[10] [Perhaps Berkeley found this epigram in Francis Bacon, *De Augmentis Scientiarium* (London, 1623), Bk. V, chap. 4: "Loquendum esse ut vulgus, sentiendum ut sapientes." A similar version was given in the sixteenth century by Augustine Niphus in his *Comm. in Aristotelem de Gen. et Corr.*, Bk. I, folio 29. G: "Loquendum enim est ut plures, sentiendum ut pauci." See *The Works of Francis Bacon*, ed. James Spedding (Boston: Brown and Taggard, 1861), II, 403.]

[11] [E.g., by the Occasionalists. See below, note 13, p. 55.]

supposed to exist without the mind, like unto the immediate objects of sense. But then, that they should suppose an innumerable multitude of created beings which they acknowledge are not capable of producing any one effect in nature, and which therefore are made to no manner of purpose, since God might have done everything as well without them—this I say, though we should allow it possible, must yet be a very unaccountable and extravagant supposition.

54. In the *eighth* place, the universal concurrent assent of mankind may be thought by some an invincible argument in behalf of matter, or the existence of external things. Must we suppose the whole world to be mistaken? And if so, what cause can be assigned of so widespread and predominant an error? I answer, first, that, upon a narrow inquiry, it will not perhaps be found so many as is imagined do really believe the existence of matter or things without the mind. Strictly speaking, to believe that which involves a contradiction, or has no meaning in it, is impossible; and whether the foregoing expressions are not of that sort, I refer it to the impartial examination of the reader. In one sense, indeed, men may be said to believe that matter exists, that is, they act as if the immediate cause of their sensations, which affects them every moment and is so nearly present to them, were some senseless unthinking being. But that they should clearly apprehend any meaning marked by those words, and form thereof a settled speculative opinion, is what I am not able to conceive. This is not the only instance wherein men impose upon themselves, by imagining they believe those propositions they have often heard, though at bottom they have no meaning in them.

55. But secondly, though we should grant a notion to be ever so universally and steadfastly adhered to, yet this is but a weak argument of its truth to whoever considers what a vast number of prejudices and false opinions are everywhere embraced with the utmost tenaciousness by the unreflecting (which are the far greater) part of mankind. There was a time when the antipodes and motion of the earth were looked upon as

monstrous absurdities even by men of learning; and if it be considered what a small proportion they bear to the rest of mankind, we shall find that at this day those notions have gained but a very inconsiderable footing in the world.

56. But it is demanded that we assign a cause of this prejudice and account for its obtaining in the world. To this I answer that men, knowing they perceived several ideas whereof they themselves were not the authors—as not being excited from within nor depending on the operation of their wills—this made them maintain those ideas, or objects of perception, had an existence independent of and without the mind, without ever dreaming that a contradiction was involved in those words. But philosophers having plainly seen that the immediate objects of perception do not exist without the mind, they in some degree corrected the mistake of the vulgar, but at the same time run into another which seems no less absurd, to wit, that there are certain objects really existing without the mind or having a subsistence distinct from being perceived, of which our ideas are only images or resemblances, imprinted by those objects on the mind. And this notion of the philosophers owes its origin to the same cause with the former, namely, their being conscious that they were not the authors of their own sensations, which they evidently knew were imprinted from without, and which therefore must have some cause distinct from the minds on which they are imprinted.

57. But why they should suppose the ideas of sense to be excited in us by things in their likeness, and not rather have recourse to *spirit* which alone can act, may be accounted for, first because they were not aware of the repugnancy there is, as well in supposing things like unto our ideas existing without, as in attributing to them power or activity. Secondly, because the supreme spirit which excites those ideas in our minds is not marked out and limited to our view by any particular finite collection of sensible ideas, as human agents are by their size, complexion, limbs, and motions. And thirdly, because His operations are regular and uniform.

Whenever the course of nature is interrupted by a miracle, men are ready to own the presence of a superior agent. But when we see things go on in the ordinary course, they do not excite in us any reflection; their order and concatenation, though it be an argument of the greatest wisdom, power, and goodness in their Creator, is yet so constant and familiar to us that we do not think them the immediate effects of a *free spirit,* especially since inconstancy and mutability in acting, though it be an imperfection, is looked on as a mark of *freedom.*

58. *Tenthly,* it will be objected that the notions we advance are inconsistent with several sound truths in philosophy and mathematics. For example, the motion of the earth is now universally admitted by astronomers as a truth grounded on the clearest and most convincing reasons. But on the foregoing principles there can be no such thing. For, motion being only an idea, it follows that if it be not perceived it exists not; but the motion of the earth is not perceived by sense. I answer, that tenet, if rightly understood, will be found to agree with the principles we have premised, for the question whether the earth moves or no amounts in reality to no more than this, to wit, whether we have reason to conclude, from what has been observed by astronomers, that if we were placed in such and such circumstances, and such or such a position and distance both from the earth and sun, we should perceive the former to move among the choir of the planets, and appearing in all respects like one of them; and this, by the established rules of nature which we have no reason to mistrust, is reasonably collected from the phenomena.

59. We may, from the experience we have had of the train and succession of ideas in our minds, often make, I will not say uncertain conjectures, but sure and well-grounded predictions concerning the ideas we shall be affected with pursuant to a great train of actions, and be enabled to pass a right judgment of what would have appeared to us in case we were placed in circumstances very different from those we

are in at present. Herein consists the knowledge of nature, which may preserve its use and certainty very consistently with what has been said. It will be easy to apply this to whatever objections of the like sort may be drawn from the magnitude of the stars or any other discoveries in astronomy or nature.

60. In the *eleventh* place, it will be demanded to what purpose serves that curious organization of plants and the admirable mechanism in the parts of animals; might not vegetables grow and shoot forth leaves and blossoms, and animals perform all their motions as well without as with all that variety of internal parts so elegantly contrived and put together; which, being ideas, have nothing powerful or operative in them, nor have any necessary connection with the effects ascribed to them? If it be a spirit that immediately produces every effect by a fiat or act of his will, we must think all that is fine and artificial in the works, whether of man or nature, to be made in vain. By this doctrine, though an artist has made the spring and wheels, and every movement of a watch, and adjusted them in such a manner as he knew would produce the motions he designed, yet he must think all this done to no purpose, and that it is an Intelligence which directs the index and points to the hour of the day. If so, why may not the Intelligence do it, without his being at the pains of making the movements and putting them together? Why does not an empty case serve as well as another? And how comes it to pass that whenever there is any fault in the going of a watch, there is some corresponding disorder to be found in the movements, which being mended by a skillful hand all is right again? The like may be said of all the clockwork of nature, great part whereof is so wonderfully fine and subtle as scarce to be discerned by the best microscope. In short, it will be asked how, upon our principles, any tolerable account can be given, or any final cause assigned, of an innumerable multitude of bodies and machines, framed with the most exquisite art, which in the common philosophy have very apposite uses assigned them and serve to explain abundance of phenomena?

61. To all which I answer, first, that though there were some difficulties relating to the administration of Providence, and the uses by it assigned to the several parts of nature which I could not solve by the foregoing principles, yet this objection could be of small weight against the truth and certainty of those things which may be proved a priori with the utmost evidence. Secondly, but neither are the received principles free from the like difficulties, for it may still be demanded to what end God should take those roundabout methods of effecting things by instruments and machines which no one can deny might have been effected by the mere command of His will without all that apparatus; nay, if we narrowly consider it, we shall find the objection may be retorted with greater force on those who hold the existence of those machines without the mind, for it has been made evident that solidity, bulk, figure, motion, and the like have no *activity* or *efficacy* in them so as to be capable of producing any one effect in nature. See sec. 25. Whoever, therefore, supposes them to exist (allowing the supposition possible) when they are not perceived does it manifestly to no purpose, since the only use that is assigned to them, as they exist unperceived, is that they produce those perceivable effects which in truth cannot be ascribed to anything but spirit.

62. But, to come nearer the difficulty, it must be observed that though the fabrication of all those parts and organs be not absolutely necessary to the producing any effect, yet it is necessary to the producing of things in a constant regular way according to the laws of nature. There are certain general laws that run through the whole chain of natural effects; these are learned by the observation and study of nature and are by men applied as well to the framing artificial things for the use and ornament of life as to the explaining the various phenomena—which explication consists only in showing the conformity any particular phenomenon has to the general laws of nature or, which is the same thing, in discovering the *uniformity* there is in the production of natural effects, as will be evident to whoever shall attend to the several instances

wherein philosophers pretend to account for appearances. That there is a great and conspicuous use in these regular, constant methods of working observed by the Supreme Agent has been shown in sec. 31. And it is no less visible that a particular size, figure, motion, and disposition of parts are necessary, though not absolutely, to the producing any effect, yet to the producing it according to the standing mechanical laws of nature. Thus, for instance, it cannot be denied that God, or the Intelligence which sustains and rules the ordinary course of things, might, if He were minded to produce a miracle, cause all the motions on the dial-plate of a watch, though nobody had ever made the movements and put them in it; but yet, if He will act agreeably to the rules of mechanism by Him for wise ends established and maintained in the Creation, it is necessary that those actions of the watchmaker, whereby he makes the movements and rightly adjusts them, precede the production of the aforesaid motions, as also that any disorder in them be attended with the perception of some corresponding disorder in the movements, which, being once corrected, all is right again.

63. It may indeed on some occasions be necessary that the Author of Nature display His overruling power in producing some appearance out of the ordinary series of things. Such exceptions from the general rules of nature are proper to surprise and awe men into an acknowledgment of the Divine Being; but then they are to be used but seldom, otherwise there is a plain reason why they should fail of that effect. Besides, God seems to choose the convincing our reason of His attributes by the works of nature, which discover so much harmony and contrivance in their make and are such plain indications of wisdom and beneficence in their Author rather than to astonish us into a belief of His being by anomalous and surprising events.

64. To set this matter in a yet clearer light, I shall observe that what has been objected in sec. 60 amounts in reality to no more than this: ideas are not anyhow and at random produced, there being a certain order and connection between

them, like to that of cause and effect; there are also several combinations of them made in a very regular and artificial manner, which seem like so many instruments in the hand of nature that, being hidden, as it were, behind the scenes, have a secret operation in producing those appearances which are seen on the theater of the world, being themselves discernible only to the curious eye of the philosopher. But, since one idea cannot be the cause of another, to what purpose is that connection? And, since those instruments, being barely *inefficacious perceptions* in the mind, are not subservient to the production of natural effects, it is demanded why they are made, or, in other words, what reason can be assigned why God should make us, upon a close inspection into His works, behold so great variety of ideas so artfully laid together, and so much according to rule, it not being credible that He would be at the expense (if one may so speak) of all that art and regularity to no purpose.

65. To all which my answer is, first, that the connection of ideas does not imply the relation of *cause* and *effect,* but only of a mark or *sign* with the thing *signified.* The fire which I see is not the cause of the pain I suffer upon my approaching it, but the mark that forewarns me of it. In like manner, the noise that I hear is not the effect of this or that motion or collision of the ambient bodies, but the sign thereof. Secondly, the reason why ideas are formed into machines, that is, artificial and regular combinations, is the same with that for combining letters into words. That a few original ideas may be made to signify a great number of effects and actions, it is necessary they be variously combined together. And, to the end their use be permanent and universal, these combinations must be made by *rule* and with *wise contrivance.* By this means abundance of information is conveyed unto us concerning what we are to expect from such and such actions and what methods are proper to be taken for the exciting such and such ideas, which in effect is all that I conceive to be distinctly meant when it is said that, by discerning the figure, texture, and mechanism of the inward parts of bodies,

whether natural or artificial, we may attain to know the several uses and properties depending thereon, or the nature of the thing.

66. Hence it is evident that those things which, under the notion of a cause cooperating or concurring to the production of effects, are altogether inexplicable and run us into great absurdities may be very naturally explained and have a proper and obvious use assigned to them when they are considered only as marks or signs for our information. And it is the searching after and endeavoring to understand [those signs instituted by] [12] the Author of Nature that ought to be the employment of the natural philosopher, and not the pretending to explain things by corporeal causes, which doctrine seems to have too much estranged the minds of men from that active principle, that supreme and wise Spirit "in whom we live, move, and have our being."

67. In the *twelfth* place, it may perhaps be objected that—though it be clear from what has been said that there can be no such thing as an inert, senseless, extended, solid, figured, movable substance existing without the mind, such as philosophers describe matter—yet, if any man shall leave out of his idea of *matter* the positive ideas of extension, figure, solidity, and motion and say that he means only by that word an inert, senseless substance that exists without the mind or unperceived, which is the occasion of our ideas, or at the presence whereof God is pleased to excite ideas in us—it does not appear but that matter taken in this sense may possibly exist. In answer to which I say, first, that it seems no less absurd to suppose a substance without accidents than it is to suppose accidents without a substance. But secondly, though we should grant this unknown substance may possibly exist, yet where can it be supposed to be? That it exists not in the mind is agreed; and that it exists not in place is no less certain—since all extension exists only in the mind, as has been already proved. It remains therefore that it exists nowhere at all.

[12] [The first edition reads: "this language (if I may so call it) of."]

68. Let us examine a little the description that is here given us of *matter*. It neither acts, nor perceives, nor is perceived, for this is all that is meant by saying it is an inert, senseless, unknown substance; which is a definition entirely made up of negatives, excepting only the relative notion of its standing under or supporting. But then it must be observed that it supports nothing at all, and how nearly this comes to the description of a *nonentity* I desire may be considered. But, say you, it is the *unknown occasion* [13] at the presence of which

[13] [Occasionalism was a development from Cartesian dualism. If mind and body are separate substances that cannot act upon one another, how do physical and mental events occur? A modified occasionalism was developed by Arnold Geulincx of Antwerp (1625–1669), author of *Metaphysica vera* (1691), while a more extreme view was elaborated by Nicolas Malebranche (1638–1715), author of *De la recherche de la vérité* (Paris, 1674). According to both views an event in one realm is merely an occasion on which God causes an event in that realm or the other. On the former view, we cause our own volitions; on the latter, these too are the effects of divine volition. Berkeley was partly occasionalist, "allowing occasional causes (which are in truth but signs)" (Correspondence, Letter II, sec. 2), partly not: "We move our legs our selves, 'tis we that will their movement. Herein I differ from Malbranch" (*Philosophical Commentaries*, Entry 548). In some points the similarity between the two philosophers is close, although Berkeley strongly denied any coincidence. Berkeley's friend and patron, Sir John Percival (1683–1748), reported to Berkeley on October 30, 1710, that Dr. Samuel Clarke (1675–1729), author of *On the Being and Attributes of God* (1705), having read the recently published *Principles*, had ranked Berkeley with Malebranche and John Norris (1657–1711), author of *An Essay Towards the Theory of an Ideal and Intelligible World* (1701–1704). Berkeley replied to Percival from Ireland on November 27, 1710: "I think the notions I embrace are not in the least coincident with, or agreeing with theirs, but indeed plainly inconsistent with them in the main points." See also *Dialogues*, II, secs. 4 and 7. It is probable that Berkeley and Malebranche met during Berkeley's first visit to Paris. In a letter to Percival from Paris dated November 24, 1713, Berkeley wrote: "Today he [l'abbé d'Aubigne] is to introduce me to Father Malebranche," and next day he wrote to Thomas Prior (1679–1751), Berkeley's closest friend: "Tomorrow I intend to visit Father Malebranche and discourse him on certain points." Joseph Stock, in his "Life of the Author," added to *Works* (London, 1837; first published 1784), p. iii, reported a meeting during Berkeley's second visit to Paris: "But the issue of this debate proved tragical to poor Male-

ideas are excited in us by the will of God. Now I would fain know how anything can be present to us which is neither perceivable by sense nor reflection, nor capable of producing any idea in our minds, nor is at all extended, nor has any form, nor exists in any place. The words "to be present," when thus applied, must needs be taken in some abstract and strange meaning, and which I am not able to comprehend.

69. Again, let us examine what is meant by "occasion." So far as I can gather from the common use of language, that word signifies either the agent which produces any effect or else something that is observed to accompany or go before it in the ordinary course of things. But when it is applied to matter as above described, it can be taken in neither of those senses, for matter is said to be passive and inert, and so cannot be an agent or efficient cause. It is also unperceivable, as being devoid of all sensible qualities, and so cannot be the occasion of our perceptions in the latter sense, as when the burning my finger is said to be the occasion of the pain that attends it. What therefore can be meant by calling matter an "occasion"? This term is either used in no sense at all or else in some sense very distant from its received signification.

70. You will perhaps say that matter, though it be not perceived by us, is nevertheless perceived by God, to whom it is the occasion of exciting ideas in our minds. For, say you, since we observe our sensations to be imprinted in an orderly and constant manner, it is but reasonable to suppose there are certain constant and regular occasions of their being produced. That is to say, that there are certain permanent and

---

branche. In the heat of disputation he raised his voice so high, and gave way so freely to the natural impetuosity of a man of parts and a Frenchman, that he brought on himself a violent increase of his disorder, which carried him off a few days after." Malebranche died on October 13, 1715, when, it seems, Berkeley was in England. The story that arose that Berkeley was the *occasional* cause of the death of Malebranche was developed further by Thomas de Quincey (1785–1859) in his "On Murder as One of the Fine Arts," *Blackwood's Magazine* (Edinburgh, 1827). See *Letters*, in *Works*, Vol. VIII (ed. Luce, 1956).]

distinct parcels of matter, corresponding to our ideas, which, though they do not excite them in our minds or anyways immediately affect us, as being altogether passive and unperceivable to us, they are nevertheless to God, by whom they are perceived, as it were, so many occasions to remind Him when and what ideas to imprint on our minds that so things may go on in a constant uniform manner.

71. In answer to this I observe that, as the notion of matter is here stated, the question is no longer concerning the existence of a thing distinct from *spirit* and *idea,* from perceiving and being perceived, but whether there are not certain ideas of I know not what sort in the mind of God which are so many marks or notes that direct Him how to produce sensations in our minds in a constant and regular method—much after the same manner as a musician is directed by the notes of music to produce that harmonious train and composition of sound which is called a "tune," though they who hear the music do not perceive the notes and may be entirely ignorant of them. But this notion of matter seems too extravagant to deserve a confutation. Besides, it is in effect no objection against what we have advanced, to wit, that there is no senseless, unperceived substance.

72. If we follow the light of reason we shall, from the constant uniform method of our sensations, collect the goodness and wisdom of the spirit who excites them in our minds; but this is all that I can see reasonably concluded from thence. To me, I say, it is evident that the being of a spirit infinitely wise, good, and powerful is abundantly sufficient to explain all the appearances of nature. But, as for *inert, senseless matter,* nothing that I perceive has any the least connection with it or leads to the thoughts of it. And I would fain see anyone explain any the meanest phenomenon in nature by it or show any manner of reason, though in the lowest rank of probability, that he can have for its existence, or even make any tolerable sense or meaning of that supposition. For as to its being an occasion we have, I think, evidently shown

that with regard to us it is no occasion. It remains therefore that it must be, if at all, the occasion to God of exciting ideas in us, and what this amounts to we have just now seen.

73. It is worth while to reflect a little on the motives which induced men to suppose the existence of *material substance;* that so having observed the gradual ceasing and expiration of those motives or reasons, we may proportionably withdraw the assent that was grounded on them. First, therefore, it was thought that color, figure, motion, and the rest of the sensible qualities or accidents did really exist without the mind; and for this reason it seemed needful to suppose some unthinking *substratum* or substance wherein they did exist, since they could not be conceived to exist by themselves. Afterwards, in process of time, men being convinced that colors, sounds, and the rest of the sensible, secondary qualities had no existence without the mind, they stripped this *substratum* or material substance of those qualities, leaving only the primary ones, figure, motion, and suchlike, which they still conceived to exist without the mind, and consequently to stand in need of a material support. But it having been shown that none even of these can possibly exist otherwise than in a spirit or mind which perceives them, it follows that we have no longer any reason to suppose the being of matter; nay, that it is utterly impossible there should be any such thing so long as that word is taken to denote an *unthinking substratum* of qualities or accidents wherein they exist without the mind.

74. But though it be allowed by the materialists themselves that matter was thought of only for the sake of supporting accidents, and, the reason entirely ceasing, one might expect the mind should naturally, and without any reluctance at all, quit the belief of what was solely grounded thereon, yet the prejudice is riveted so deeply in our thoughts that we can scarce tell how to part with it, and are therefore inclined, since the *thing* itself is indefensible, at least to retain the *name,* which we apply to I know not what abstracted and indefinite notions of being, or occasion, though without any show of reason, at least so far as I can see. For what is there

on our part, or what do we perceive among all the ideas, sensations, notions which are imprinted on our minds, either by sense or reflection, from whence may be inferred the existence of an inert, thoughtless, unperceived occasion? And, on the other hand, on the part of an all-sufficient Spirit, what can there be that should make us believe or even suspect He is directed by an inert occasion to excite ideas in our minds?

75. It is a very extraordinary instance of the force of prejudice, and much to be lamented, that the mind of man retains so great a fondness, against all the evidence of reason, for a stupid, thoughtless *somewhat*, by the interposition whereof it would as it were screen itself from the Providence of God and remove him farther off from the affairs of the world. But though we do the utmost we can to secure the belief of matter, though, when reason forsakes us, we endeavor to support our opinion on the bare possibility of the thing, and though we indulge ourselves in the full scope of an imagination not regulated by reason to make out that poor possibility, yet the upshot of all is that there are certain *unknown ideas* in the mind of God; for this, if anything, is all that I conceive to be meant by "occasion" with regard to God. And this at the bottom is no longer contending for the thing, but for the name.

76. Whether, therefore, there are such ideas in the mind of God, and whether they may be called by the name "matter," I shall not dispute. But if you stick to the notion of an unthinking substance or support of extension, motion, and other sensible qualities, then to me it is most evidently impossible there should be any such thing, since it is a plain repugnancy that those qualities should exist in or be supported by an unperceiving substance.

77. But, say you, though it be granted that there is no thoughtless support of extension and the other qualities or accidents which we perceive, yet there may, perhaps, be some inert, unperceiving substance or *substratum* of some other qualities, as incomprehensible to us as colors are to a man born blind, because we have not a sense adapted to them. But

if we had a new sense, we should possibly no more doubt of their existence than a blind man made to see does of the existence of light and colors. I answer, first, if what you mean by the word "matter" be only the unknown support of unknown qualities, it is no matter whether there is such a thing or no, since it no way concerns us; and I do not see the advantage there is in disputing about we know not *what,* and we know not *why.*

78. But, secondly, if we had a new sense, it could only furnish us with new ideas or sensations; and then we should have the same reason against their existing in an unperceiving substance that has been already offered with relation to figure, motion, color, and the like. Qualities, as has been shown, are nothing else but *sensations* or *ideas,* which exist only in a *mind* perceiving them; and this is true not only of the ideas we are acquainted with at present, but likewise of all possible ideas whatsoever.

79. But, you will insist, what if I have no reason to believe the existence of matter? What if I cannot assign any use to it or explain anything by it, or even conceive what is meant by that word? Yet still it is no contradiction to say that matter exists, and that this matter is in general a *substance,* or *occasion of ideas,* though, indeed, to go about to unfold the meaning or adhere to any particular explication of those words may be attended with great difficulties. I answer, when words are used without a meaning, you may put them together as you please without danger of running into a contradiction. You may say, for example, that twice two is equal to seven, so long as you declare you do not take the words of that proposition in their usual acceptation but for marks of you know not what. And, by the same reason, you may say there is an inert, thoughtless substance without accidents which is the occasion of our ideas. And we shall understand just as much by one proposition as the other.

80. In the *last* place, you will say, What if we give up the cause of material substance and assert that matter is an un-

known *somewhat*—neither substance nor accident, spirit nor idea, inert, thoughtless, indivisible, immovable, unextended, existing in no place? For, say you, whatever may be urged against *substance* or *occasion,* or any other positive or relative notion of matter, has no place at all so long as this *negative* definition of matter is adhered to. I answer, You may, if so it shall seem good, use the word "matter" in the same sense as other men use "nothing," and so make those terms convertible in your style. For, after all, this is what appears to me to be the result of that definition, the parts whereof, when I consider with attention, either collectively or separate from each other, I do not find that there is any kind of effect or impression made on my mind different from what is excited by the term "nothing."

81. You will reply, perhaps, that in the foresaid definition is included what does sufficiently distinguish it from nothing —the positive, abstract idea of *quiddity, entity,* or *existence.* I own, indeed, that those who pretend to the faculty of framing abstract general ideas do talk as if they had such an idea, which is, say they, the most abstract and general notion of all; that is, to me, the most incomprehensible of all others. That there are a great variety of spirits of different orders and capacities whose faculties both in number and extent are far exceeding those the Author of my being has bestowed on me, I see no reason to deny. And for me to pretend to determine by my own few, stinted, narrow inlets of perception what ideas the inexhaustible power of the Supreme Spirit may imprint upon them were certainly the utmost folly and presumption—since there may be, for aught that I know, innumerable sorts of ideas or sensations, as different from one another, and from all that I have perceived, as colors are from sounds. But how ready soever I may be to acknowledge the scantiness of my comprehension with regard to the endless variety of spirits and ideas that might possibly exist, yet for anyone to pretend to a notion of entity or existence, *abstracted* from *spirit* and *idea,* from perceiving and being per-

ceived is, I suspect, a downright repugnancy and trifling with words.—It remains that we consider the objections which may possibly be made on the part of religion.

82. Some there are who think that, though the arguments for the real existence of bodies which are drawn from reason be allowed not to amount to demonstration, yet the Holy Scriptures are so clear in the point as will sufficiently convince every good Christian that bodies do really exist, and are something more than mere ideas, there being in Holy Writ innumerable facts related which evidently suppose the reality of timber and stone, mountains and rivers, and cities, and human bodies. To which I answer that no sort of writings whatever, sacred or profane, which use those and the like words in the vulgar acceptation, or so as to have a meaning in them, are in danger of having their truth called in question by our doctrine. That all those things do really exist, that there are bodies, even corporeal substances, when taken in the vulgar sense, has been shown to be agreeable to our principles; and the difference betwixt *things* and *ideas, realities* and *chimeras* has been distinctly explained. See secs. 29, 30, 33, 36, etc. And I do not think that either what philosophers call "matter," or the existence of objects without the mind, is anywhere mentioned in Scripture.

83. Again, whether there be or be not external things, it is agreed on all hands that the proper use of words is the marking out conceptions, or things only as they are known and perceived by us; whence it plainly follows that in the tenets we have laid down there is nothing inconsistent with the right use and significance of *language,* and that discourse, of what kind soever, so far as it is intelligible, remains undisturbed. But all this seems so very manifest, from what has been set forth in the premises, that it is needless to insist any further on it.

84. But it will be urged that miracles do, at least, lose much of their stress and import by our principles. What must we think of Moses' rod? Was it not *really* turned into a serpent, or was there only a change of *ideas* in the minds of the

spectators? And can it be supposed that our Saviour did no more at the marriage-feast in Cana than impose on the sight and smell and taste of the guests, so as to create in them the appearance or idea only of wine? The same may be said of all other miracles, which, in consequence of the foregoing principles, must be looked upon only as so many cheats or illusions of fancy. To this I reply that the rod was changed into a real serpent, and the water into real wine. That this does not in the least contradict what I have elsewhere said will be evident from secs. 34 and 35. But this business of *real* and *imaginary* has been already so plainly and fully explained, and so often referred to, and the difficulties about it are so easily answered from what has gone before, that it were an affront to the reader's understanding to resume the explication of it in this place. I shall only observe that if at table all who were present should see, and smell, and taste, and drink wine, and find the effects of it, with me there could be no doubt of its reality, so that at bottom the scruple concerning real miracles has no place at all on ours, but only on the received principles, and consequently makes rather for than against what has been said.

85. Having done with the objections, which I endeavored to propose in the clearest light, and gave them all the force and weight I could, we proceed in the next place to take a view of our tenets in their consequences. Some of these appear at first sight—as that several difficult and obscure questions, on which abundance of speculation has been thrown away, are entirely banished from philosophy: whether corporeal substance can think; whether matter be infinitely divisible; and how it operates on spirit—these and the like inquiries have given infinite amusement to philosophers in all ages, but, depending on the existence of matter, they have no longer any place on our principles. Many other advantages there are, as well with regard to religion as the sciences, which it is easy for anyone to deduce from what has been premised; but this will appear more plainly in the sequel.

86. From the principles we have laid down it follows

human knowledge may naturally be reduced to two heads—that of *ideas* and that of *spirits*. Of each of these I shall treat in order.

And, *first,* as to ideas or unthinking things. Our knowledge of these has been very much obscured and confounded, and we have been led into very dangerous errors, by supposing a twofold existence of the objects of sense—the one *intelligible* or in the mind, the other *real* and without the mind, whereby unthinking things are thought to have a natural subsistence of their own distinct from being perceived by spirits. This, which, if I mistake not, has been shown to be a most groundless and absurd notion, is the very root of skepticism, for so long as men thought that real things subsisted without the mind, and that their knowledge was only so far forth *real* as it was conformable to *real things,* it follows they could not be certain they had any real knowledge at all. For how can it be known that the things which are perceived are conformable to those which are not perceived or exist without the mind?

87. Color, figure, motion, extension, and the like, considered only as so many *sensations* in the mind, are perfectly known, there being nothing in them which is not perceived. But if they are looked on as notes or images, referred to *things* or *archetypes* existing without the mind, then are we involved all in skepticism. We see only the appearances, and not the real qualities of things. What may be the extension, figure, or motion of anything really and absolutely, or in itself, it is impossible for us to know, but only the proportion or the relation they bear to our senses. Things remaining the same, our ideas vary, and which of them, or even whether any of them at all, represent the true quality really existing in the thing, it is out of our reach to determine. So that, for aught we know, all we see, hear, and feel may be only phantom and vain chimera, and not at all agree with the real things existing in *rerum natura.* All this skepticism follows from our supposing a difference between *things* and *ideas,* and that the former have a subsistence without the mind or unperceived. It were easy to dilate on this subject and show how

the arguments urged by skeptics in all ages depend on the supposition of external objects.

88. So long as we attribute a real existence to unthinking things, distinct from their being perceived, it is not only impossible for us to know with evidence the nature of any real unthinking being, but even that it exists. Hence it is that we see philosophers distrust their senses and doubt of the existence of heaven and earth, of everything they see or feel, even of their own bodies. And after all their labor and struggle of thought, they are forced to own we cannot attain to any self-evident or demonstrative knowledge of the existence of sensible things. But all this doubtfulness which so bewilders and confounds the mind and makes philosophy ridiculous in the eyes of the world vanishes if we annex a meaning to our words and do not amuse ourselves with the terms "absolute," "external," "exist," and suchlike, signifying we know not what. I can as well doubt of my own being as of the being of those things which I actually perceive by sense; it being a manifest contradiction that any sensible object should be immediately perceived by sight or touch and at the same time have no existence in nature, since the very *existence* of an unthinking being consists in *being perceived*.

89. Nothing seems of more importance toward erecting a firm system of sound and real knowledge, which may be proof against the assaults of skepticism, than to lay the beginning in a distinct explication of what is meant by "thing," "reality," "existence"; for in vain shall we dispute concerning the real existence of things or pretend to any knowledge thereof, so long as we have not fixed the meaning of those words. "Thing" or "being" is the most general name of all; it comprehends under it two kinds entirely distinct and heterogeneous, and which have nothing common but the name, to wit, *spirits* and *ideas*. The former are active, indivisible substances; the latter are inert, fleeting, dependent beings which subsist not by themselves, but are supported by or exist in minds or spiritual substances. [We comprehend our own existence by inward feeling or reflection, and that of other spirits by

reason. We may be said to have some knowledge or notion of our own minds, of spirits and active beings, whereof in a strict sense we have not ideas. In like manner, we know and have a notion of relations between things or ideas—which relations are distinct from the ideas or things related, in as much as the latter may be perceived by us without our perceiving the former. To me it seems that *ideas, spirits,* and *relations* are all in their respective kinds the object of human knowledge and subject of discourse, and that the term "idea" would be improperly extended to signify everything we know or have any notion of.]

90. Ideas imprinted on the senses are real things, or do really exist—this we do not deny, but we deny they can subsist without the minds which perceive them, or that they are resemblances of any archetypes existing without the mind, since the very being of a sensation or idea consists in being perceived, and an idea can be like nothing but an idea. Again, the things perceived by sense may be termed "external" with regard to their origin—in that they are not generated from within by the mind itself, but imprinted by a spirit distinct from that which perceives them. Sensible objects may likewise be said to be "without the mind" in another sense, namely, when they exist in some other mind; thus, when I shut my eyes, the things I saw may still exist, but it must be in another mind.

91. It were a mistake to think that what is here said derogates in the least from the reality of things. It is acknowledged, on the received principles, that extension, motion, and, in a word, all sensible qualities have need of a support, as not being able to subsist by themselves. But the objects perceived by sense are allowed to be nothing but combinations of those qualities, and consequently cannot subsist by themselves. Thus far it is agreed on all hands. So that in denying the things perceived by sense an existence independent of a substance or support wherein they may exist, we detract nothing from the received opinion of their *reality,* and are guilty of no innovation in that respect. All the difference is that, according to us,

the unthinking beings perceived by sense have no existence distinct from being perceived, and cannot therefore exist in any other substances than those unextended indivisible substances or *spirits* which act and think and perceive them; whereas philosophers vulgarly hold that the sensible qualities exist in an inert, extended, unperceiving substance which they call "matter," to which they attribute a natural subsistence, exterior to all thinking beings, or distinct from being perceived by any mind whatsoever, even the eternal mind of the Creator, wherein they suppose only ideas of the corporeal substances created by him, if indeed they allow them to be at all created.

92. For as we have shown the doctrine of matter or corporeal substance to have been the main pillar and support of skepticism, so likewise, upon the same foundation, have been raised all the impious schemes of atheism and irreligion. Nay, so great a difficulty has it been thought to conceive matter produced out of nothing that the most celebrated among the ancient philosophers, even of these who maintained the being of a God, have thought matter to be uncreated and coeternal with Him. How great a friend *material substance* has been to atheists in all ages were needless to relate. All their monstrous systems have so visible and necessary a dependence on it that, when this cornerstone is once removed, the whole fabric cannot choose but fall to the ground, insomuch that it is no longer worth while to bestow a particular consideration on the absurdities of every wretched sect of atheists.

93. That impious and profane persons should readily fall in with those systems which favor their inclinations by deriding immaterial substance and supposing the soul to be divisible and subject to corruption as the body, which exclude all freedom, intelligence, and design from the formation of things, and instead thereof make a self-existent, stupid, unthinking substance the root and origin of all beings; that they should hearken to those who deny a Providence, or inspection of a Superior Mind over the affairs of the world, attributing the whole series of events either to blind chance or fatal neces-

sity arising from the impulse of one body or another—all this is very natural. And, on the other hand, when men of better principles observe the enemies of religion lay so great a stress on *unthinking matter,* and all of them use so much industry and artifice to reduce everything to it, methinks they should rejoice to see them deprived of their grand support and driven from that only fortress without which your Epicureans, Hobbists, and the like, have not even the shadow of a pretense, but become the most cheap and easy triumph in the world.

94. The existence of matter, or bodies unperceived, has not only been the main support of atheists and fatalists, but on the same principle does idolatry likewise in all its various forms depend. Did men but consider that the sun, moon, and stars, and every other object of the senses are only so many sensations in their minds, which have no other existence but barely being perceived, doubtless they would never fall down and worship their own *ideas,* but rather address their homage to that Eternal Invisible Mind which produces and sustains all things.

95. The same absurd principle, by mingling itself with the articles of our faith, has occasioned no small difficulties to Christians. For example, about the resurrection, how many scruples and objections have been raised by Socinians [14] and others? But do not the most plausible of them depend on the supposition that a body is denominated "the same," with regard not to the form or that which is perceived by sense, but the material substance, which remains the same under several forms? Take away this *material substance,* about the identity whereof all the dispute is, and mean by "body" what every plain, ordinary person means by that word, to wit, that which is immediately seen and felt, which is only a combination of

[14] [Followers of Sozinus, i.e., Lelio Francesco Maria Sozini (1525–1562), or Socinus, i.e., Fausto Paolo Sozzini (1539–1604), both of Siena, Italy. Sozinus raised difficulties in regard to the resurrection, salvation, etc., in *De sacramentis dissertatio* and *De resurrectione,* first printed in *F. et L. Socini, item E. Soneri tractatus* (Amsterdam, 1654).]

sensible qualities or ideas, and then their most unanswerable objections come to nothing.

96. Matter being once expelled out of nature drags with it so many skeptical and impious notions, such an incredible number of disputes and puzzling questions, which have been thorns in the sides of divines as well as philosophers and made so much fruitless work for mankind, that if the arguments we have produced against it are not found equal to demonstration (as to me they evidently seem), yet I am sure all friends to knowledge, peace, and religion have reason to wish they were.

97. Beside the external existence of the objects of perception, another great source of errors and difficulties with regard to ideal knowledge is the doctrine of *abstract ideas,* such as it has been set forth in the Introduction. The plainest things in the world, those we are most intimately acquainted with and perfectly know, when they are considered in an abstract way, appear strangely difficult and incomprehensible. Time, place, and motion, taken in particular or concrete, are what everybody knows, but, having passed through the hands of a metaphysician, they become too abstract and fine to be apprehended by men of ordinary sense. Bid your servant meet you at such a *time* in such a *place,* and he shall never stay to deliberate on the meaning of those words; in conceiving that particular time and place, or the motion by which he is to get thither, he finds not the least difficulty. But if *time* be taken exclusive of all those particular actions and ideas that diversify the day, merely for the continuation of existence or duration in abstract, then it will perhaps gravel even a philosopher to comprehend it.

98. Whenever I attempt to frame a simple idea of *time,* abstracted from the succession of ideas in my mind, which flows uniformly and is participated by all beings, I am lost and embrangled in inextricable difficulties. I have no notion of it at all, only I hear others say it is infinitely divisible, and speak of it in such a manner as leads me to entertain odd thoughts of my existence; since that doctrine lays one under

an absolute necessity of thinking, either that he passes away innumerable ages without a thought or else that he is annihilated every moment of his life, both which seem equally absurd. Time therefore being nothing, abstracted from the succession of ideas in our minds, it follows that the duration of any finite spirit must be estimated by the number of ideas or actions succeeding each other in that same spirit or mind. Hence, it is a plain consequence that the soul always thinks; and in truth whoever shall go about to divide in his thoughts or abstract the *existence* of a spirit from its *cogitation* will, I believe, find it no easy task.[15]

99. So likewise when we attempt to abstract extension and motion from all other qualities, and consider them by themselves, we presently lose sight of them, and run into great extravagances. All which depend on a twofold abstraction; first, it is supposed that extension, for example, may be abstracted from all other sensible qualities; and secondly, that the entity of extension may be abstracted from its being perceived. But whoever shall reflect, and take care to understand what he says, will, if I mistake not, acknowledge that all **sensible qualities are alike** *sensations* **and alike** *real;* that where the extension is, there is the color, too, to wit, in his mind, and that their archetypes can exist only in some other *mind;* and that the objects of sense are nothing but those sensations combined, blended, or (if one may so speak) con-

[15] [The manuscript continued the section as follows: "Sure I am that should any one tell me there is a time wherein a spirit actually exists without perceiving, or an idea without being perceived, or that there is a third sort of being which exists though it neither wills nor perceives nor is perceived, his words would have no other effect on my mind than if he talked in an unknown language. It is indeed an easy matter for a man to say, 'the mind exists without thinking,' but to conceive a meaning that may correspond to those sounds, or to frame a notion of a spirit's existence abstracted from thinking, this seems to me impossible, and I suspect that even they who are the stiffest abettors of that tenet might abate somewhat of their firmness would they but lay aside the words and, calmly attending to their own thoughts, examine what they meant by them." This passage is from a manuscript of part of the *Principles*, now in the British Museum. Cf. *Works*, II (ed. Jessop, 1949), 84.]

creted together; none of all which can be supposed to exist unperceived.

100. What it is for a man to be happy, or an object good, everyone may think he knows. But to frame an abstract idea of happiness, prescinded from all particular pleasure, or of goodness from everything that is good, this is what few can pretend to. So likewise a man may be just and virtuous without having precise ideas of justice and virtue. The opinion that those and the like words stand for general notions, abstracted from all particular persons and actions, seems to have rendered morality difficult, and the study thereof of less use to mankind. And in effect the doctrine of *abstraction* has not a little contributed toward spoiling the most useful parts of knowledge.

101. The two great provinces of speculative science conversant about ideas received from sense and their relations are natural philosophy and mathematics; with regard to each of these I shall make some observations. And first I shall say somewhat of natural philosophy.[16] On this subject it is that the skeptics triumph. All that stock of arguments they produce to depreciate our faculties and make mankind appear ignorant and low are drawn principally from this head, to wit, that we are under an invincible blindness as to the *true* and *real* nature of things. This they exaggerate, and love to enlarge on. We are miserably bantered, say they, by our senses, and amused only with the outside and show of things. The real essence, the internal qualities and constitution of every the meanest object, is hidden from our view; something there is in every drop of water, every grain of sand, which it is beyond the power of human understanding to fathom or comprehend. But it is evident from what has been shown that all this complaint is groundless, and that we are influenced by false principles to that degree as to mistrust our senses and think we know nothing of those things which we perfectly comprehend.

[16] [See also *De Motu* (1721); *Alciphron*, Dialogue VII; *Siris* (1744), secs. 220–254.]

102. One great inducement to our pronouncing ourselves ignorant of the nature of things is the current opinion that everything includes within itself the cause of its properties; or that there is in each object an inward essence which is the source whence its discernible qualities flow, and whereon they depend. Some have pretended to account for appearances by occult qualities, but of late they are mostly resolved into mechanical causes, to wit, the figure, motion, weight, and suchlike qualities of insensible particles; whereas, in truth, there is no other agent or efficient cause than *spirit,* it being evident that motion, as well as all other *ideas,* is perfectly inert. See sec. 25. Hence, to endeavor to explain the production of colors or sounds by figure, motion, magnitude, and the like, must needs be labor in vain. And accordingly we see the attempts of that kind are not at all satisfactory. Which may be said in general of those instances wherein one idea or quality is assigned for the cause of another. I need not say how many hypotheses and speculations are left out, and how much the study of nature is abridged by this doctrine.

103. The great mechanical principle now in vogue is *attraction*. That a stone falls to the earth, or the sea swells toward the moon, may to some appear sufficiently explained thereby. But how are we enlightened by being told this is done by attraction? Is it that that word signifies the manner of the tendency, and that it is by the mutual drawing of bodies instead of their being impelled or protruded toward each other? But nothing is determined of the manner or action, and it may as truly (for aught we know) be termed "impulse," or "protrusion," as "attraction." Again, the parts of steel we see cohere firmly together, and this also is accounted for by attraction; but, in this as in the other instances, I do not perceive that anything is signified besides the effect itself; for as to the manner of the action whereby it is produced, or the cause which produces it, these are not so much as aimed at.

104. Indeed, if we take a view of the several phenomena and compare them together, we may observe some likeness

and conformity between them. For example, in the falling of a stone to the ground, in the rising of the sea toward the moon, in cohesion and crystallization, there is something alike, namely, a union or mutual approach of bodies. So that any one of these or the like phenomena may not seem strange or surprising to a man who has nicely observed and compared the effects of nature. For that only is thought so which is uncommon, or a thing by itself, and out of the ordinary course of our observation. That bodies should tend toward the center of the earth is not thought strange, because it is what we perceive every moment of our lives. But, that they should have a like gravitation toward the center of the moon may seem odd and unaccountable to most men, because it is discerned only in the tides. But a philosopher, whose thoughts take in a larger compass of nature, having observed a certain similitude of appearances, as well in the heavens as the earth, that argue innumerable bodies to have a mutual tendency toward each other, which he denotes by the general name "attraction," whatever can be reduced to that he thinks justly accounted for. Thus he explains the tides by the attraction of the terraqueous globe toward the moon, which to him does not appear odd or anomalous, but only a particular example of a general rule or law of nature.

105. If therefore we consider the difference there is betwixt natural philosophers and other men with regard to their knowledge of the phenomena, we shall find it consists not in an exacter knowledge of the efficient cause that produces them—for that can be no other than the *will of a spirit*—but only in a greater largeness of comprehension, whereby analogies, harmonies, and agreements are discovered in the works of nature, and the particular effects explained, that is, reduced to general rules, see sec. 62, which rules, grounded on the analogy and uniformness observed in the production of natural effects, are most agreeable and sought after by the mind; for that they extend our prospect beyond what is present and near to us, and enable us to make very probable conjectures touching things that may have happened at very

great distances of time and place, as well as to predict things to come; which sort of endeavor toward omniscience is much affected by the mind.

106. But we should proceed warily in such things, for we are apt to lay too great a stress on analogies, and, to the prejudice of truth, humor that eagerness of the mind whereby it is carried to extend its knowledge into general theorems. For example, gravitation or mutual attraction, because it appears in many instances, some are straightway for pronouncing "universal"; and that to attract and be attracted by every other body is an essential quality inherent in all bodies whatsoever. Whereas it appears the fixed stars have no such tendency toward each other; and so far is that gravitation from being *essential* to bodies that in some instances a quite contrary principle seems to show itself; as in the perpendicular growth of plants, and the elasticity of the air. There is nothing necessary or essential in the case, but it depends entirely on the will of the governing spirit, who causes certain bodies to cleave together or tend toward each other according to various laws, whilst he keeps others at a fixed distance; and to some he gives a quite contrary tendency to fly asunder just as he sees convenient.

107. After what has been premised, I think we may lay down the following conclusions. First, it is plain philosophers amuse themselves in vain when they inquire for any natural efficient cause distinct from a *mind* or *spirit*. Secondly, considering the whole creation is the workmanship of a *wise and good agent,* it should seem to become philosophers to employ their thoughts (contrary to what some hold) about the final causes of things; and I must confess I see no reason why pointing out the various ends to which natural things are adapted, and for which they were originally with unspeakable wisdom contrived, should not be thought one good way of accounting for them, and altogether worthy a philosopher. Thirdly, from what has been premised no reason can be drawn why the history of nature should not still be studied, and observations and experiments made; which, that they are of use

to mankind, and enable us to draw any general conclusions, is not the result of any immutable habits or relations between things themselves, but only of God's goodness and kindness to men in the administration of the world. See secs. 30 and 31. Fourthly, by a diligent observation of the phenomena within our view, we may discover the general laws of nature, and from them deduce the other phenomena; I do not say "demonstrate," for all deductions of that kind depend on a supposition that the Author of Nature always operates uniformly and in a constant observance of those rules we take for principles, which we cannot evidently know.

108. [Those men who frame general rules from the phenomena and afterwards derive the phenomena from those rules seem to consider signs rather than causes. A man may well understand natural signs without knowing their analogy,][17] or being able to say by what rule a thing is so or so. And, as it is very possible to write improperly, through too strict an observance of general grammar rules; so, in arguing from general rules of nature, it is not impossible we may extend the analogy too far, and by that means run into mistakes.

109. As, in reading other books, a wise man will choose to fix his thoughts on the sense and apply it to use, rather than lay them out in grammatical remarks on the language, so, in perusing the volume of nature, it seems beneath the dignity of the mind to affect an exactness in reducing each particular phenomenon to general rules, or showing how it follows from them. We should propose to ourselves nobler views, such as to recreate and exalt the mind with a prospect

---

[17] [Section 108 in the first edition began as follows: "It appears from secs. 66. etc., that the steady consistent methods of nature may not unfitly be styled the 'language' of its 'Author,' whereby He discovers His attributes to our view and directs us how to act for the convenience and felicity of life. And to me, those men who frame general rules from the phenomena, and afterwards derive the phenomena from those rules seem to be grammarians, and their art the grammar of nature. Two ways there are of learning a language, either by rule or by practice: a man may be well read in the language of nature without understanding the grammar of it, ..."]

of the beauty, order, extent, and variety of natural things: hence, by proper inferences, to enlarge our notions of the grandeur, wisdom, and beneficence of the Creator; and lastly, to make the several parts of the Creation, so far as in us lies, subservient to the ends they were designed for—God's glory and the sustentation and comfort of ourselves and fellow creatures.

110. [The best key for the aforesaid analogy or natural science will be easily acknowledged to be a certain celebrated treatise of *mechanics*.][18] In the entrance of which justly admired treatise, time, space, and motion are distinguished into *absolute* and *relative, true* and *apparent, mathematical* and *vulgar;* which distinction, as it is at large explained by the author, does suppose these quantities to have an existence without the mind; and that they are ordinarily conceived with relation to sensible things, to which nevertheless in their own nature they bear no relation at all.

111. As for "time," as it is there taken in an absolute or abstracted sense, for the duration or perseverance of the existence of things, I have nothing more to add concerning it after what has been already said on that subject. Secs. 97 and 98. For the rest, this celebrated author holds there is an *absolute space,* which, being unperceivable to sense, remains in itself similar and immovable; and relative space to be the measure thereof, which, being movable and defined by its situation in respect of sensible bodies, is vulgarly taken for

---

18 [Section 110 in the first edition began as follows: "The best grammar of the kind we are speaking of will be easily acknowledged to be a treatise of mechanics, demonstrated and applied to nature by a philosopher of a neighboring nation whom all the world admire. I shall not take upon me to make remarks on the performance of that extraordinary person: only some things he has advanced so directly opposite to the doctrine we have hitherto laid down, that we should be wanting in the regard due to the authority of so great a man did we not take some notice of them." The first edition appeared in Ireland; hence, Newton is spoken of as belonging to a "neighboring nation." The treatise referred to is Sir Isaac Newton's *Philosophiae Naturalis Principia Mathematica* (London, 1687).]

immovable space. "Place" he defines to be that part of space which is occupied by any body; and according as the space is absolute or relative, so also is the place. "Absolute motion" is said to be the translation of a body from absolute place to absolute place, as relative motion is from one relative place to another. And, because the parts of absolute space do not fall under our senses, instead of them we are obliged to use their sensible measures, and so define both place and motion with respect to bodies which we regard as immovable. But it is said in philosophical matters we must abstract from our senses, since it may be that none of those bodies which seem to be quiescent are truly so, and the same thing which is moved relatively may be really at rest; as likewise one and the same body may be in relative rest and motion, or even moved with contrary relative motions at the same time, according as its place is variously defined. All which ambiguity is to be found in the apparent motions, but not at all in the true or absolute, which should therefore be alone regarded in philosophy. And the true we are told are distinguished from apparent or relative motions by the following properties. —First, in true or absolute motion all parts which preserve the same position with respect to the whole partake of the motions of the whole. Secondly, the place being moved, that which is placed therein is also moved; so that a body moving in a place which is in motion does participate in the motion of its place. Thirdly, true motion is never generated or changed otherwise than by force impressed on the body itself. Fourthly, true motion is always changed by force impressed on the body moved. Fifthly, in circular motion, barely relative, there is no centrifugal force which, nevertheless, in that which is true or absolute, is proportional to the quantity of motion.

112. But, notwithstanding what has been said, it does not appear to me that there can be any motion other than *relative;* so that to conceive motion there must be at least conceived two bodies, whereof the distance or position in regard to each other is varied. Hence, if there was one only body in being it could not possibly be moved. This seems evident, in

that the idea I have of motion does necessarily include relation.

113. But, though in every motion it be necessary to conceive more bodies than one, yet it may be that one only is moved, namely, that on which the force causing the change of distance is impressed, or, in other words, that to which the action is applied. For, however some may define relative motion, so as to term that body "moved" which changes its distance from some other body, whether the force or action causing that change were applied to it or no, yet as relative motion is that which is perceived by sense, and regarded in the ordinary affairs of life, it should seem that every man of common sense knows what it is as well as the best philosopher. Now I ask anyone whether, in his sense of motion as he walks along the streets, the stones he passes over may be said to *move*, because they change distance with his feet? To me it seems that though motion includes a relation of one thing to another, yet it is not necessary that each term of the relation be denominated from it. As a man may think of somewhat which does not think, so a body may be moved to or from another body which is not therefore itself in motion.

114. As the place happens to be variously defined, the motion which is related to it varies. A man in a ship may be said to be quiescent with relation to the sides of the vessel, and yet move with relation to the land. Or he may move eastward in respect of the one, and westward in respect of the other. In the common affairs of life, men never go beyond the earth to define the place of any body; and what is quiescent in respect of that is accounted *absolutely* to be so. But philosophers, who have a greater extent of thought, and juster notions of the system of things, discover even the earth itself to be moved. In order therefore to fix their notions, they seem to conceive the corporeal world as finite, and the utmost unmoved walls or shell thereof to be the place whereby they estimate true motions. If we sound our own conceptions, I believe we may find all the absolute motion we can frame an idea of to be at bottom no other than relative motion thus

defined. For, as has been already observed, absolute motion, exclusive of all external relation, is incomprehensible; and to this kind of relative motion all the above-mentioned properties, causes, and effects ascribed to absolute motion will, if I mistake not, be found to agree. As to what is said of the centrifugal force, that it does not at all belong to circular relative motion, I do not see how this follows from the experiment which is brought to prove it. See *Philosophiae Naturalis Principia Mathematica, in Schol. Def. VIII.* For the water in the vessel at that time wherein it is said to have the greatest relative circular motion, has, I think, no motion at all; as is plain from the foregoing section.

115. For, to denominate a body "moved" it is requisite, first, that it change its distance or situation with regard to some other body; and secondly, that the force or action occasioning that change be applied to it. If either of these be wanting, I do not think that, agreeably to the sense of mankind, or the propriety of language, a body can be said to be in motion. I grant indeed that it is possible for us to think a body which we see change its distance from some other to be moved, though it have no force applied to it (in which sense there may be apparent motion), but then it is because the force causing the change of distance is imagined by us to be applied or impressed on that body thought to move; which indeed shows we are capable of mistaking a thing to be in motion which is not, and that is all.

116. From what has been said, it follows that the philosophic consideration of motion does not imply the being of an *absolute space,* distinct from that which is perceived by sense and related to bodies; which that it cannot exist without the mind is clear upon the same principles that demonstrate the like of all other objects of sense. And perhaps, if we inquire narrowly, we shall find we cannot even frame an idea of *pure space* exclusive of all body. This I must confess seems impossible, as being a most abstract idea. When I excite a motion in some part of my body, if it be free or without resistance, I say there is *space;* but if I find a resist-

ance, then I say there is *body;* and in proportion as the resistance to motion is lesser or greater, I say the space is more or less *pure*. So that when I speak of pure or empty space, it is not to be supposed that the word "space" stands for an idea distinct from or conceivable without body and motion—though indeed we are apt to think every noun substantive stands for a distinct idea that may be separated from all others; which has occasioned infinite mistakes. When, therefore, supposing all the world to be annihilated besides my own body, I say there still remains *pure space,* thereby nothing else is meant but only that I conceive it possible for the limbs of my body to be moved on all sides without the least resistance; but if that, too, were annihilated, then there could be no motion, and consequently no space. Some, perhaps, may think the sense of seeing does furnish them with the idea of pure space; but it is plain from what we have elsewhere shown, that the ideas of space and distance are not obtained by that sense. See the *Essay Concerning Vision*.

117. What is here laid down seems to put an end to all those disputes and difficulties that have sprung up amongst the learned concerning the nature of *pure space*. But the chief advantage arising from it is that we are freed from that dangerous dilemma to which several who have employed their thoughts on this subject imagine themselves reduced, to wit, of thinking either that real space is God, or else that there is something besides God which is eternal, uncreated, infinite, indivisible, immutable. Both which may justly be thought pernicious and absurd notions. It is certain that not a few divines, as well as philosophers of great note, have, from the difficulty they found in conceiving either limits or annihilation of space, concluded it must be divine. And some of late have set themselves particularly to show that the incommunicable attributes of God agree to it. Which doctrine, how unworthy soever it may seem of the Divine Nature, yet I do not see how we can get clear of it so long as we adhere to the received opinions.

118. Hitherto of natural philosophy: we come now to make

some inquiry concerning the other great branch of speculative knowledge, to wit, mathematics.[19] These, how celebrated soever they may be for their clearness and certainty of demonstration, which is hardly anywhere else to be found, cannot nevertheless be supposed altogether free from mistakes, if in their principles there lurks some secret error which is common to the professors of those sciences with the rest of mankind. Mathematicians, though they deduce their theorems from a great height of evidence, yet their first principles are limited by the consideration of quantity; and they do not ascend into any inquiry concerning those transcendental maxims which influence all the particular sciences, each part whereof, mathematics not excepted, does consequently participate of the errors involved in them. That the principles laid down by mathematicians are true, and their way of deduction from those principles clear and incontestable, we do not deny; but we hold there may be certain erroneous maxims of greater extent than the object of mathematics, and for that reason not expressly mentioned, though tacitly supposed throughout the whole progress of that science; and that the ill effects of those secret, unexamined errors are diffused through all the branches thereof. To be plain, we suspect the mathematicians are as well as other men concerned in the errors arising from the doctrine of abstract general ideas and the existence of objects without the mind.

119. Arithmetic has been thought to have for its object abstract ideas of *number;* of which to understand the properties and mutual habitudes is supposed no mean part of speculative knowledge. The opinion of the pure and intellectual nature of numbers in abstract has made them in esteem with those philosophers who seem to have affected an uncommon fineness and elevation of thought. It has set a price on the most trifling numerical speculations which in practice are of no use but serve only for amusement, and has therefore so far infected the minds of some that they have dreamed of mighty mysteries involved in numbers and attempted the

[19] [See also *The Analyst* (1734).]

explication of natural things by them. But, if we inquire into our own thoughts and consider what has been premised, we may perhaps entertain a low opinion of those high flights and abstractions, and look on all inquiries about numbers only as so many *difficiles nugae,* so far as they are not subservient to practice and promote the benefit of life.

120. Unity in abstract we have before considered in sec. 13, from which and what has been said in the Introduction, it plainly follows there is not any such idea. But, number being defined a "collection of units," we may conclude that, if there be no such thing as unity or unit in abstract, there are no ideas of number in abstract denoted by the numerical names and figures. The theories therefore in arithmetic, if they are abstracted from the names and figures, as likewise from all use and practice, as well as from the particular things numbered, can be supposed to have nothing at all for their object; hence we may see how entirely the science of numbers is subordinate to practice, and how jejune and trifling it becomes when considered as a matter of mere speculation.

121. However, since there may be some who, deluded by the specious show of discovering abstracted verities, waste their time in arithmetical theorems and problems which have not any use, it will not be amiss if we more fully consider and expose the vanity of that pretense; and this will plainly appear by taking a view of arithmetic in its infancy, and observing what it was that originally put men on the study of that science, and to what scope they directed it. It is natural to think that at first, men, for ease of memory and help of computation, made use of counters, or in writing of single strokes, points, or the like, each whereof was made to signify a unit, that is, some one thing of whatever kind they had occasion to reckon. Afterwards they found out the more compendious ways of making one character stand in place of several strokes or points. And, lastly, the notation of the Arabians or Indians came into use, wherein, by the repetition of a few characters or figures, and varying the signification of each figure according to the place it obtains, all numbers

may be most aptly expressed; which seems to have been done in imitation of language, so that an exact analogy is observed betwixt the notation by figures and names, the nine simple figures answering the nine first numeral names and places in the former, corresponding to denominations in the latter. And agreeably to those conditions of the simple and local value of figures were contrived methods of finding, from the given figures or marks of the parts, what figures and how placed are proper to denote the whole, or vice versa. And having found the sought figures, the same rule or analogy being observed throughout, it is easy to read them into words; and so the number becomes perfectly known. For then the number of any particular things is said to be known, when we know the name or figures (with their due arrangement) that according to the standing analogy belong to them. For, these signs being known, we can by the operations of arithmetic know the signs of any part of the particular sums signified by them; and, thus computing in signs (because of the connection established betwixt them and the distinct multitudes of things whereof one is taken for a unit), we may be able rightly to sum up, divide, and proportion the things themselves that we intend to number.

122. In arithmetic, therefore, we regard not the *things,* but the *signs,* which nevertheless are not regarded for their own sake, but because they direct us how to act with relation to things, and dispose rightly of them. Now, agreeable to what we have before observed of words in general (sec. 19, Introd.) it happens here likewise that abstract ideas are thought to be signified by numeral names or characters, while they do not suggest ideas of particular things to our minds. I shall not at present enter into a more particular dissertation on this subject, but only observe that it is evident from what has been said, those things which pass for abstract truths and theorems concerning numbers are in reality conversant about no object distinct from particular numerable things, except only names and characters which originally came to be considered on no other account but their being signs, or capable to represent

aptly whatever particular things men had need to compute. Whence it follows that to study them for their own sake would be just as wise, and to as good purpose as if a man, neglecting the true use or original intention and subservience of language, should spend his time in impertinent criticisms upon words, or reasonings and controversies purely verbal.

123. From numbers we proceed to speak of *extension*, which, considered as relative, is the object of geometry. The *infinite* divisibility of *finite* extension, though it is not expressly laid down either as an axiom or theorem in the elements of that science, yet is throughout the same everywhere supposed and thought to have so inseparable and essential a connection with the principles and demonstrations in geometry that mathematicians never admit it into doubt, or make the least question of it. And, as this notion is the source from whence do spring all those amusing geometrical paradoxes which have such a direct repugnancy to the plain common sense of mankind, and are admitted with so much reluctance into a mind not yet debauched by learning; so is it the principal occasion of all that nice and extreme subtlety which renders the study of mathematics so difficult and tedious. Hence, if we can make it appear that no finite extension contains innumerable parts, or is infinitely divisible, it follows that we shall at once clear the science of geometry from a great number of difficulties and contradictions which have ever been esteemed a reproach to human reason, and withal make the attainment thereof a business of much less time and pains than it hitherto has been.

124. Every particular finite extension which may possibly be the object of our thought is an *idea* existing only in the mind, and consequently each part thereof must be perceived. If, therefore, I cannot perceive innumerable parts in any finite extension that I consider, it is certain they are not contained in it; but it is evident that I cannot distinguish innumerable parts in any particular line, surface, or solid, which I either perceive by sense, or figure to myself in my mind: wherefore I conclude they are not contained in it.

Nothing can be plainer to me than that the extensions I have in view are no other than my own ideas; and it is no less plain that I cannot resolve any one of my ideas into an infinite number of other ideas, that is, that they are not infinitely divisible. If by "finite extension" be meant something distinct from a finite idea, I declare I do not know what that is, and so cannot affirm or deny anything of it. But if the terms "extension," "parts," and the like, are taken in any sense conceivable, that is, for ideas, then to say a finite quantity or extension consists of parts infinite in number is so manifest a contradiction that everyone at first sight acknowledges it to be so; and it is impossible it should ever gain the assent of any reasonable creature who is not brought to it by gentle and slow degrees, as a converted gentile to the belief of transubstantiation. Ancient and rooted prejudices do often pass into principles; and those propositions which once obtain the force and credit of a *principle* are not only themselves, but likewise whatever is deducible from them, thought privileged from all examination. And there is no absurdity so gross which, by this means, the mind of man may not be prepared to swallow.

125. He whose understanding is prepossessed with the doctrine of abstract general ideas may be persuaded that (whatever be thought of the ideas of sense) extension in *abstract* is infinitely divisible. And one who thinks the objects of sense exist without the mind will perhaps in virtue thereof be brought to admit that a line but an inch long may contain innumerable parts—really existing, though too small to be discerned. These errors are grafted as well in the minds of geometricians as of other men, and have a like influence on their reasonings; and it were no difficult thing to show how the arguments from geometry made use of to support the infinite divisibility of extension are bottomed on them. At present we shall only observe in general whence it is that the mathematicians are all so fond and tenacious of this doctrine.

126. It has been observed in another place that the theorems and demonstrations in geometry are conversant about

universal ideas (sec. 15, Introd.); where it is explained in what sense this ought to be understood, to wit, that the particular lines and figures included in the diagram are supposed to stand for innumerable others of different sizes; or, in other words, the geometer considers them abstracting from their magnitude—which does not imply that he forms an abstract idea, but only that he cares not what the particular magnitude is, whether great or small, but looks on that as a thing indifferent to the demonstration. Hence it follows that a line in the scheme but an inch long must be spoken of as though it contained ten thousand parts, since it is regarded not in itself, but as it is universal; and it is universal only in its signification, whereby it represents innumerable lines greater than itself, in which may be distinguished ten thousand parts or more, though there may not be above an inch in it. After this manner, the properties of the lines signified are (by a very usual figure) transferred to the sign, and thence, through mistake, thought to appertain to it considered in its own nature.

127. Because there is no number of parts so great but it is possible there may be a line containing more, the inch-line is said to contain parts more than any assignable number; which is true, not of the inch taken absolutely, but only for the things signified by it. But men, not retaining that distinction in their thoughts, slide into a belief that the small particular line described on paper contains in itself parts innumerable. There is no such thing as the ten thousandth part of an inch; but there is of a mile or diameter of the earth, which may be signified by that inch. When therefore I delineate a triangle on paper, and take one side not above an inch, for example, in length to be the radius, this I consider as divided into ten thousand or one hundred thousand parts or more; for, though the ten thousandth part of that line considered in itself is nothing at all, and consequently may be neglected without any error or inconvenience, yet these described lines, being only marks standing for greater quantities, whereof it may be the ten thousandth part is very considerable, it follows that,

to prevent notable errors in practice, the radius must be taken of ten thousand parts or more.

128. From what has been said the reason is plain why, to the end any theorem may become universal in its use, it is necessary we speak of the lines described on paper as though they contained parts which really they do not. In doing of which, if we examine the matter thoroughly, we shall perhaps discover that we cannot conceive an inch itself as consisting of, or being divisible into, a thousand parts, but only some other line which is far greater than an inch, and represented by it; and that when we say a line is "infinitely divisible" we must mean a line which is infinitely great. What we have here observed seems to be the chief cause why to suppose the infinite divisibility of finite extension has been thought necessary in geometry.

129. The several absurdities and contradictions which flowed from this false principle might, one would think, have been esteemed so many demonstrations against it. But, by I know not what logic, it is held that proofs a posteriori are not to be admitted against propositions relating to infinity, as though it were not impossible even for an infinite mind to reconcile contradictions; or as if anything absurd and repugnant could have a necessary connection with truth or flow from it. But whoever considers the weakness of this pretense will think it was contrived on purpose to humor the laziness of the mind which had rather acquiesce in an indolent skepticism than be at the pains to go through with a severe examination of those principles it has ever embraced for true.

130. Of late the speculations about infinites have run so high, and grown to such strange notions, as have occasioned no small scruples and disputes among the geometers of the present age. Some there are of great note who, not content with holding that finite lines may be divided into an infinite number of parts, do yet further maintain that each of those infinitesimals is itself subdivisible into an infinity of other parts or infinitesimals of a second order, and so on ad infinitum. These, I say, assert there are infinitesimals of infinitesimals of

infinitesimals, without ever coming to an end: so that according to them an inch does not barely contain an infinite number of parts, but an infinity of an infinity of an infinity ad infinitum of parts. Others there be who hold all orders of infinitesimals below the first to be nothing at all; thinking it with good reason absurd to imagine there is any positive quantity or part of extension which, though multiplied infinitely, can ever equal the smallest given extension. And yet on the other hand it seems no less absurd to think the square, cube, or other power of a positive real root should itself be nothing at all; which they who hold infinitesimals of the first order, denying all of the subsequent orders, are obliged to maintain.

131. Have we not therefore reason to conclude that they are *both* in the wrong, and that there is in effect no such thing as parts infinitely small, or an infinite number of parts contained in any finite quantity? But you will say that if this doctrine obtains it will follow the very foundations of geometry are destroyed, and those great men who have raised that science to so astonishing a height have been all the while building a castle in the air. To this it may be replied that whatever is useful in geometry and promotes the benefit of human life does still remain firm and unshaken on our principles; that science considered as practical will rather receive advantage than any prejudice from what has been said. But to set this in a due light may be the subject of a distinct inquiry. For the rest, though it should follow that some of the more intricate and subtle parts of speculative mathematics may be pared off without any prejudice to truth, yet I do not see what damage will be thence derived to mankind. On the contrary, it were highly to be wished that men of great abilities and obstinate application would draw off their thoughts from those amusements, and employ them in the study of such things as lie nearer the concerns of life, or have a more direct influence on the manners.

132. If it be said that several theorems undoubtedly true are discovered by methods in which infinitesimals are made use of, which could never have been if their existence included

a contradiction in it, I answer that upon a thorough examination it will not be found that in any instance it is necessary to make use of or conceive infinitesimal parts of finite lines, or even quantities less than the *minimum sensibile;* nay, it will be evident this is never done, it being impossible.

133. By what we have premised it is plain that very numerous and important errors have taken their rise from those false principles which were impugned in the foregoing parts of this treatise; and the opposites of those erroneous tenets at the same time appear to be most fruitful principles, from whence do flow innumerable consequences highly advantageous to true philosophy, as well as to religion. Particularly *matter,* or *the absolute existence of corporeal objects,* has been shown to be that wherein the most avowed and pernicious enemies of all knowledge, whether human or divine, have ever placed their chief strength and confidence. And surely, if by distinguishing the real existence of unthinking things from their being perceived, and allowing them a subsistence of their own out of the minds of spirits, no one thing is explained in nature, but, on the contrary, a great many inexplicable difficulties arise; if the supposition of matter is barely precarious, as not being grounded on so much as one single reason; if its consequences cannot endure the light of examination and free inquiry, but screen themselves under the dark and general pretense of "infinites being incomprehensible"; if withal the removal of this *matter* be not attended with the least evil consequence; if it be not even missed in the world, but everything as well, nay, much easier conceived without it; if, lastly, both skeptics and atheists are forever silenced upon supposing only spirits and ideas, and this scheme of things is perfectly agreeable both to reason and religion: methinks we may expect it should be admitted and firmly embraced, though it were proposed only as a *hypothesis,* and the existence of matter had been allowed possible, which yet I think we have evidently demonstrated that it is not.

134. True it is that, in consequence of the foregoing principles, several disputes and speculations which are esteemed

no mean parts of learning are rejected as useless. But, how great a prejudice soever against our notions this may give to those who have already been deeply engaged and made large advances in studies of that nature, yet by others we hope it will not be thought any just ground of dislike to the principles and tenets herein laid down that they abridge the labor of study, and make human sciences more clear, compendious, and attainable than they were before.

135. Having dispatched what we intended to say concerning the knowledge of *ideas,* the method we proposed leads us in the next place to treat of *spirits*—with regard to which, perhaps, human knowledge is not so deficient as is vulgarly imagined. The great reason that is assigned for our being thought ignorant of the nature of spirits is our not having an *idea* of it. But surely it ought not to be looked on as a defect in a human understanding that it does not perceive the idea of spirit if it is manifestly impossible there should be any such idea. And this, if I mistake not, has been demonstrated in section 27; to which I shall here add that a spirit has been shown to be the only substance or support wherein the unthinking beings or ideas can exist; but that this *substance* which supports or perceives ideas should itself be an idea or like an idea is evidently absurd.

136. It will perhaps be said that we want a sense (as some have imagined) proper to know substances withal, which, if we had, we might know our own soul as we do a triangle. To this I answer, that, in case we had a new sense bestowed upon us, we could only receive thereby some new sensations or ideas of sense. But I believe nobody will say that what he means by the terms "soul" and "substance" is only some particular sort of idea or sensation. We may therefore infer, that all things duly considered, it is not more reasonable to think our faculties defective in that they do not furnish us with an idea of spirit or active thinking substance than it would be if we should blame them for not being able to comprehend a *round square.*

137. From the opinion that spirits are to be known after

the manner of an idea or sensation have risen many absurd and heterodox tenets, and much skepticism about the nature of the soul. It is even probable that this opinion may have produced a doubt in some whether they had any soul at all distinct from their body, since upon inquiry they could not find they had an idea of it. That an *idea* which is inactive, and the existence whereof consists in being perceived, should be the image or likeness of an agent subsisting by itself seems to need no other refutation than barely attending to what is meant by those words. But perhaps you will say that though an idea cannot resemble a spirit in its thinking, acting, or subsisting by itself, yet it may in some other respects; and it is not necessary that an idea or image be in all respects like the original.

138. I answer, if it does not in those mentioned, it is impossible it should represent it in any other thing. Do but leave out the power of willing, thinking, and perceiving ideas, and there remains nothing else wherein the idea can be like a spirit. For by the word "spirit" we mean only that which thinks, wills, and perceives; this, and this alone, constitutes the signification of that term. If therefore it is impossible that any degree of those powers should be represented in an idea, it is evident there can be no idea of a spirit.

139. But it will be objected that, if there is no idea signified by the terms "soul," "spirit," and "substance," they are wholly insignificant or have no meaning in them. I answer, those words do mean or signify a real thing, which is neither an idea nor like an idea, but that which perceives ideas, and wills, and reasons about them. What I am myself, that which I denote by the term "I," is the same with what is meant by "soul," or "spiritual substance." If it be said that this is only quarreling at a word, and that, since the immediate significations of other names are by common consent called "ideas," no reason can be assigned why that which is signified by the name "spirit" or "soul" may not partake in the same appellation. I answer, all the unthinking objects of the mind agree in that they are entirely passive, and their existence consists only in

being perceived; whereas a soul or spirit is an active being whose existence consists, not in being perceived, but in perceiving ideas and thinking. It is therefore necessary, in order to prevent equivocation and confounding natures perfectly disagreeing and unlike, that we distinguish between *spirit* and *idea*. See sec. 27.

140. In a large sense, indeed, we may be said to have an idea [or rather a notion] of *spirit;* that is, we understand the meaning of the word, otherwise we could not affirm or deny anything of it. Moreover, as we conceive the ideas that are in the minds of other spirits by means of our own, which we suppose to be resemblances of them, so we know other spirits by means of our own soul—which in that sense is the image or idea of them; it having a like respect to other spirits that blueness or heat by me perceived has to those ideas perceived by another.

141. It must not be supposed that they who assert the natural immortality of the soul are of opinion that it is absolutely incapable of annihilation even by the infinite power of the Creator who first gave it being, but only that it is not liable to be broken or dissolved by the ordinary laws of nature or motion. They indeed who hold the soul of man to be only a thin vital flame, or system of animal spirits, make it perishing and corruptible as the body; since there is nothing more easily dissipated than such a being, which it is naturally impossible should survive the ruin of the tabernacle wherein it is enclosed. And this notion has been greedily embraced and cherished by the worst part of mankind, as the most effectual antidote against all impressions of virtue and religion. But it has been made evident that bodies, of what frame or texture soever, are barely passive ideas in the mind, which is more distant and heterogeneous from them than light is from darkness. We have shown that the soul is indivisible, incorporeal, unextended, and it is consequently incorruptible. Nothing can be plainer than that the motions, changes, decays, and dissolutions which we hourly see befall natural bodies (and which is what we mean by "the course of nature") cannot pos-

sibly affect an active, simple, uncompounded substance; such a being therefore is indissoluble by the force of nature; that is to say, the soul of man is naturally immortal.

142. After what has been said, it is, I suppose, plain that our souls are not to be known in the same manner as senseless, inactive objects, or by way of *idea*. *Spirits* and *ideas* are things so wholly different that when we say "they exist," "they are known," or the like, these words must not be thought to signify anything common to both natures. There is nothing alike or common in them: and to expect that by any multiplication or enlargement of our faculties we may be enabled to know a spirit as we do a triangle seems as absurd as if we should hope to see a sound. This is inculcated because I imagine it may be of moment toward clearing several important questions and preventing some very dangerous errors concerning the nature of the soul. [We may not, I think, strictly be said to have an *idea* of an active being, or of an action, although we may be said to have a *notion* of them. I have some knowledge or notion of my mind, and its acts about ideas, inasmuch as I know or understand what is meant by those words. What I know, that I have some notion of. I will not say that the terms "idea" and "notion" may not be used convertibly, if the world will have it so; but yet it conduces to clearness and propriety that we distinguish things very different by different names. It is also to be remarked that, all relations including an act of the mind, we cannot so properly be said to have an idea, but rather a notion of the relations or habitudes between things. But if, in the modern way, the word "idea" is extended to spirits, and relations, and acts, this is, after all, an affair of verbal concern.]

143. It will not be amiss to add that the doctrine of *abstract ideas* has had no small share in rendering those sciences intricate and obscure which are particularly conversant about spiritual things. Men have imagined they could frame abstract notions of the powers and acts of the mind and consider them prescinded as well from the mind or spirit itself as from their respective objects and effects. Hence a great number of

dark and ambiguous terms, presumed to stand for abstract notions, have been introduced into metaphysics and morality, and from these have grown infinite distractions and disputes amongst the learned.

144. But nothing seems more to have contributed toward engaging men in controversies and mistakes with regard to the nature and operations of the mind than the being used to speak of those things in terms borrowed from sensible ideas. For example, the will is termed "the motion of the soul": this infuses a belief that the mind of man is as a ball in motion, impelled and determined by the objects of sense, as necessarily as that is by the stroke of a racket. Hence arise endless scruples and errors of dangerous consequence in morality. All which, I doubt not, may be cleared, and truth appear plain, uniform, and consistent, could but philosophers be prevailed on to retire into themselves, and attentively consider their own meaning.

145. From what has been said it is plain that we cannot know the existence of other spirits otherwise than by their operations, or the ideas by them excited in us. I perceive several motions, changes, and combinations of ideas that inform me there are certain particular agents, like myself, which accompany them and concur in their production. Hence, the knowledge I have of other spirits is not immediate, as is the knowledge of my ideas, but depending on the intervention of ideas, by me referred to agents or spirits distinct from myself, as effects or concomitant signs.[20]

146. But though there be some things which convince us human agents are concerned in producing them, yet it is evident to everyone that those things which are called "the works of nature," that is, the far greater part of the ideas or sensations perceived by us, are not produced by, or dependent on, the wills of men. There is therefore some other spirit that causes them; since it is repugnant that they should subsist by themselves. See sec. 29. But, if we attentively consider the constant regularity, order, and concatenation of natural

[20] [See also *Alciphron*, Dialogue IV.]

things, the surprising magnificence, beauty, and perfection of the larger, and the exquisite contrivance of the smaller parts of the creation, together with the exact harmony and correspondence of the whole, but above all the never-enough-admired laws of pain and pleasure, and the instincts or natural inclinations, appetites, and passions of animals; I say if we consider all these things, and at the same time attend to the meaning and import of the attributes: one, eternal, infinitely wise, good, and perfect, we shall clearly perceive that they belong to the aforesaid spirit, "who works all in all," and "by whom all things consist."

147. Hence it is evident that God is known as certainly and immediately as any other mind or spirit whatsoever distinct from ourselves. We may even assert that the existence of God is far more evidently perceived than the existence of men; because the effects of nature are infinitely more numerous and considerable than those ascribed to human agents. There is not any one mark that denotes a man, or effect produced by him, which does not more strongly evince the being of that spirit who is the Author of Nature. For it is evident that in affecting other persons the will of man has no other object than barely the motion of the limbs of his body; but that such a motion should be attended by, or excite any idea in the mind of another, depends wholly on the will of the Creator. He alone it is who, "upholding all things by the word of his power," maintains that intercourse between spirits whereby they are able to perceive the existence of each other. And yet this pure and clear light which enlightens everyone is itself invisible.

148. It seems to be a general pretense of the unthinking herd that they cannot *see* God. Could we but see him, say they, as we see a man, we should believe that he is, and, believing, obey his commands. But alas, we need only open our eyes to see the sovereign Lord of all things, with a more full and clear view than we do any one of our fellow creatures. Not that I imagine we see God (as some will have it) by a direct and immediate view; or see corporeal things, not by

themselves, but by seeing that which represents them in the essence [21] of God, which doctrine is, I must confess, to me incomprehensible. But I shall explain my meaning: a human spirit or person is not perceived by sense, as not being an idea; when therefore we see the color, size, figure, and motions of a man, we perceive only certain sensations or ideas excited in our own minds; and these being exhibited to our view in sundry distinct collections, serve to mark out unto us the existence of finite and created spirits like ourselves. Hence it is plain we do not see a man—if by "man" is meant that which lives, moves, perceives, and thinks as we do—but only such a certain collection of ideas as directs us to think there is a distinct principle of thought and motion, like to ourselves, accompanying and represented by it. And after the same manner we see God; all the difference is that, whereas some one finite and narrow assemblage of ideas denotes a particular human mind, whithersoever we direct our view, we do at all times and in all places perceive manifest tokens of the divinity: everything we see, hear, feel, or anywise perceive by sense, being a sign or effect of the power of God; as is our perception of those very motions which are produced by men.

149. It is therefore plain that nothing can be more evident to anyone that is capable of the least reflection than the existence of God, or a spirit who is intimately present to our minds, producing in them all that variety of ideas or sensations which continually affect us, on whom we have an absolute and entire dependence, in short "in whom we live, and move, and have our being." That the discovery of this great truth, which lies so near and obvious to the mind, should be attained to by the reason of so very few, is a sad instance of the stupidity and inattention of men who, though they are surrounded with such clear manifestations of the Deity, are yet so little affected by them that they seem, as it were, blinded with excess of light.

150. But you will say, has nature no share in the production

[21] [The reference is to Malebranche's view that we directly know the Ideas of all things in God. See note 13, p. 55, and *Dialogues*, II, sec. 4.]

of natural things, and must they be all ascribed to the immediate and sole operation of God? I answer, if by "nature" is meant only the visible *series* of effects or sensations imprinted on our minds, according to certain fixed and general laws, then it is plain that nature, taken in this sense, cannot produce anything at all. But, if by "nature" is meant some being distinct from God, as well as from the laws of nature, and things perceived by sense, I must confess that word is to me an empty sound without any intelligible meaning annexed to it. Nature, in this acceptation, is a vain chimera, introduced by those heathens who had not just notions of the omnipresence and infinite perfection of God. But it is more unaccountable that it should be received among Christians, professing belief in the Holy Scriptures, which constantly ascribe those effects to the immediate hand of God that heathen philosophers are wont to impute to nature. "The Lord he causeth the vapours to ascend; he maketh lightnings with rain; he bringeth forth the wind out of his treasures." Jerem. 10:13. "He turneth the shadow of death into the morning, and maketh the day dark with night." Amos 5:8. "He visiteth the earth, and maketh it soft with showers: He blesseth the springing thereof, and crowneth the year with his goodness; so that the pastures are clothed with flocks, and the valleys are covered over with corn." See Psalm 65. But notwithstanding that this is the constant language of Scripture, yet we have I know not what aversion from believing that God concerns himself so nearly in our affairs. Fain would we suppose him at a great distance off, and substitute some blind, unthinking deputy in his stead, though (if we may believe Saint Paul) "he be not far from every one of us."

151. It will, I doubt not, be objected that the slow and gradual methods observed in the production of natural things do not seem to have for their cause the immediate hand of an Almighty Agent. Besides, monsters, untimely births, fruits blasted in the blossom, rains failing in desert places, miseries incident to human life, and the like, are so many arguments that the whole frame of nature is not immediately actuated

and superintended by a spirit of infinite wisdom and goodness. But the answer to this objection is in a good measure plain from sec. 62; it being visible that the aforesaid methods of nature are absolutely necessary, in order to working by the most simple and general rules, and after a steady and consistent manner; which argues both the wisdom and goodness of God. Such is the artificial contrivance of this mighty machine of nature that, whilst its motions and various phenomena strike on our senses, the hand which actuates the whole is itself unperceivable to men of flesh and blood. "Verily" (says the prophet) "thou art a God that hidest thyself." Isaiah 45:15. But, though God conceal himself from the eyes of the sensual and lazy, who will not be at the least expense of thought, yet to an unbiased and attentive mind nothing can be more plainly legible than the intimate presence of an all-wise Spirit, who fashions, regulates, and sustains the whole system of being. It is clear, from what we have elsewhere observed, that the operating according to general and stated laws is so necessary for our guidance in the affairs of life, and letting us into the secret of nature, that without it all reach and compass of thought, all human sagacity and design, could serve to no manner of purpose; it were even impossible there should be any such faculties or powers in the mind. See sec. 31. Which one consideration abundantly outbalances whatever particular inconveniences may thence arise.

152. We should further consider that the very blemishes and defects of nature are not without their use, in that they make an agreeable sort of variety and augment the beauty of the rest of the creation, as shades in a picture serve to set off the brighter and more enlightened parts. We would likewise do well to examine whether our taxing the waste of seeds and embryos, and accidental destruction of plants and animals, before they come to full maturity, as an imprudence in the Author of Nature, be not the effect of prejudice contracted by our familiarity with impotent and saving mortals. In man indeed a thrifty management of those things which he cannot procure without much pains and industry may be

esteemed wisdom. But we must not imagine that the inexplicably fine machine of an animal or vegetable costs the great Creator any more pains or trouble in its production than a pebble does; nothing being more evident than that an omnipotent spirit can indifferently produce everything by a mere fiat or act of his will. Hence, it is plain that the splendid profusion of natural things should not be interpreted weakness or prodigality in the agent who produces them, but rather be looked on as an argument of the riches of his power.

153. As for the mixture of pain or uneasiness which is in the world, pursuant to the general laws of nature, and the actions of finite, imperfect spirits, this, in the state we are in at present, is indispensably necessary to our well-being. But our prospects are too narrow. We take, for instance, the idea of some one particular pain into our thoughts, and account it *evil;* whereas, if we enlarge our view, so as to comprehend the various ends, connections, and dependencies of things, on what occasions and in what proportions we are affected with pain and pleasure, the nature of human freedom, and the design with which we are put into the world; we shall be forced to acknowledge that those particular things which, considered in themselves, appear to be evil, have the nature of good, when considered as linked with the whole system of beings.

154. From what has been said, it will be manifest to any considering person, that it is merely for want of attention and comprehensiveness of mind that there are any favorers of atheism or the Manichaean heresy [22] to be found. Little and

---

[22] [Manichaeism became one of the great religions. Founded by Mani of Persia in the third century, it spread rapidly in the Roman Empire and retained its vigor well into the Middle Ages. It had a wide and deep influence on Christianity. St. Augustine was a follower in his youth but later opposed it. The Albigenses in southern France, who were persecuted in 1207 by Innocent III, shared its views. A fusion of many religions, its central teaching is that the universe is controlled by two antagonistic powers, light or goodness (God's kingdom) and darkness or evil. Evil is thus an ultimate and ineradicable fact. Satan, the prince of darkness, is coeternal with God.]

unreflecting souls may indeed burlesque the works of Providence the beauty and order whereof they have not capacity, or will not be at the pains to comprehend; but those who are masters of any justness and extent of thought, and are withal used to reflect, can never sufficiently admire the divine traces of wisdom and goodness that shine throughout the economy of nature. But what truth is there which shines so strongly on the mind that by an aversion of thought, a willful shutting of the eyes, we may not escape seeing it? Is it therefore to be wondered at if the generality of men, who are ever intent on business or pleasure, and little used to fix or open the eye of their mind, should not have all that conviction and evidence of the being of God which might be expected in reasonable creatures?

155. We should rather wonder that men can be found so stupid as to neglect, than that neglecting they should be unconvinced of such an evident and momentous truth. And yet it is to be feared that too many of parts and leisure, who live in Christian countries, are, merely through a supine and dreadful negligence, sunk into a sort of atheism. Since it is downright impossible that a soul pierced and enlightened with a thorough sense of the omnipresence, holiness, and justice of that Almighty Spirit should persist in a remorseless violation of his laws. We ought, therefore, earnestly to meditate and dwell on those important points; that so we may attain conviction without all scruple "that the eyes of the Lord are in every place beholding the evil and the good; that he is with us and keepth us in all places whither we go, and giveth us bread to eat and raiment to put on"; that he is present and conscious to our innermost thoughts; and that we have a most absolute and immediate dependence on him. A clear view of which great truths cannot choose but fill our hearts with an awful circumspection and holy fear, which is the strongest incentive to *virtue* and the best guard against *vice*.

156. For, after all, what deserves the first place in our studies is the consideration of God and our duty; which to

promote, as it was the main drift and design of my labors, so shall I esteem them altogether useless and ineffectual if, by what I have said, I cannot inspire my readers with a pious sense of the presence of God; and, having shown the falseness or vanity of those barren speculations which make the chief employment of learned men, the better dispose them to reverence and embrace the salutary truths of the Gospel, which to know and to practice is the highest perfection of human nature.

THREE DIALOGUES BETWEEN HYLAS AND PHILONOUS

THE DESIGN OF WHICH IS PLAINLY TO DEMONSTRATE THE REALITY AND PERFECTION OF HUMAN KNOWLEDGE, THE INCORPOREAL NATURE OF THE SOUL, AND THE IMMEDIATE PROVIDENCE OF A DEITY: IN OPPOSITION TO SKEPTICS AND ATHEISTS. ALSO TO OPEN A METHOD FOR RENDERING THE SCIENCES MORE EASY, USEFUL, AND COMPENDIOUS.

THE PREFACE[1]

Though it seems the general opinion of the world, no less than the design of Nature and Providence, that the end of speculation be practice or the improvement and regulation of our lives and actions; yet those who are most addicted to speculative studies seem as generally of another mind. And, indeed, if we consider the pains that have been taken to perplex the plainest things—that distrust of the senses, those doubts and scruples, those abstractions and refinements that occur in the very entrance of the sciences—it will not seem strange that men of leisure and curiosity should lay themselves out in fruitless disquisitions without descending to the practical parts of life, or informing themselves in the more necessary and important parts of knowledge.

Upon the common principles of philosophers we are not assured of the existence of things from their being perceived. And we are taught to distinguish their real nature from that which falls under our senses. Hence arise skepticism and paradoxes. It is not enough that we see and feel, that we taste and smell a thing: its true nature, its absolute external entity, is still concealed. For, though it be the fiction of our own brain, we have made it inaccessible to all our faculties. Sense is fallacious, reason defective. We spend our lives in doubting of those things which other men evidently know, and believing those things which they laugh at and despise.

In order, therefore, to divert the busy mind of man from vain researches, it seemed necessary to inquire into the source of its perplexities and, if possible, to lay down such principles as, by an easy solution of them, together with their own native evidence, may at once recommend themselves for genuine to the mind, and rescue it from those endless pursuits it is en-

[1] [This Preface was not included in the 1734 edition.]

gaged in. Which with a plain demonstration of the immediate providence of an all-seeing God and the natural immortality of the soul should seem the readiest preparation, as well as the strongest motive, to the study and practice of virtue.

This design I proposed in the First Part of a treatise concerning the *Principles of Human Knowledge,* published in the year 1710. But, before I proceed to publish the Second Part, I thought it requisite to treat more clearly and fully of certain principles laid down in the First and to place them in a new light. Which is the business of the following *Dialogues.*

In this treatise, which does not presuppose in the reader any knowledge of what was contained in the former, it has been my aim to introduce the notions I advance into the mind in the most easy and familiar manner, especially because they carry with them a great opposition to the prejudices of philosophers which have so far prevailed against the common sense and natural notions of mankind.

If the principles which I here endeavor to propagate are admitted for true, the consequences which, I think, evidently flow from thence are that atheism and skepticism will be utterly destroyed, many intricate points made plain, great difficulties solved, several useless parts of science retrenched, speculation referred to practice, and men reduced from paradoxes to common sense.

And, although it may, perhaps, seem an uneasy reflection to some that, when they have taken a circuit through so many refined and unvulgar notions, they should at last come to think like other men, yet, methinks, this return to the simple dictates of nature, after having wandered through the wild mazes of philosophy, is not unpleasant. It is like coming home from a long voyage: a man reflects with pleasure on the many difficulties and perplexities he has passed through, sets his heart at ease, and enjoys himself with more satisfaction for the future.

As it was my intention to convince skeptics and infidels by reason, so it has been my endeavor strictly to observe the most rigid laws of reasoning. And to an impartial reader I hope it will be manifest that the sublime notion of a God and the comfortable expectation of immortality do naturally arise from a close and methodical application of thought—whatever may be the result of that loose, rambling way, not altogether improperly termed "Freethinking," by certain libertines in thought who can no more endure the restraints of logic than those of religion or government.

It will, perhaps, be objected to my design that, so far as it tends to ease the mind of difficult and useless inquiries, it can affect only a few speculative persons; but if, by their speculations rightly placed, the study of morality and the law of nature were brought more into fashion among men of parts and genius, the discouragements that draw to skepticism removed, the measures of right and wrong accurately defined, and the principles of natural religion reduced into regular systems, as artfully disposed and clearly connected as those of some other sciences—there are grounds to think these effects would not only have a gradual influence in repairing the too much defaced sense of virtue in the world, but also, by showing that such parts of revelation as lie within the reach of human inquiry are most agreeable to right reason, would dispose all prudent, unprejudiced persons to a modest and wary treatment of those sacred mysteries which are above the comprehension of our faculties.

It remains that I desire the reader to withhold his censure of these *Dialogues* till he has read them through. Otherwise he may lay them aside, in a mistake of their design or on account of difficulties or objections which he would find answered in the sequel. A treatise of this nature would require to be once read over coherently in order to comprehend its design, the proofs, solution of difficulties, and the connection and disposition of its parts. If it be thought to deserve a second reading, this, I imagine, will make the entire scheme very plain, especially if recourse be had to an essay I wrote some years since upon *Vision,* and the *Treatise Concerning the Principles of Human Knowledge*—wherein divers notions advanced in these *Dialogues* are further pursued or placed in different lights, and other points handled which naturally tend to confirm and illustrate them.

THREE DIALOGUES
BETWEEN HYLAS AND PHILONOUS

IN OPPOSITION TO SKEPTICS AND ATHEISTS

THE FIRST DIALOGUE

[1.] *Philonous.* Good morrow, Hylas. I did not expect to find you abroad so early.

Hylas. It is indeed something unusual; but my thoughts were so taken up with a subject I was discoursing of last night that, finding I could not sleep, I resolved to rise and take a turn in the garden.

Phil. It happened well, to let you see what innocent and agreeable pleasures you lose every morning. Can there be a pleasanter time of the day or a more delightful season of the year? That purple sky, these wild but sweet notes of birds, the fragrant bloom upon the trees and flowers, the gentle influence of the rising sun—these and a thousand nameless beauties of nature inspire the soul with secret transports; its faculties, too, being at this time fresh and lively, are fit for those meditations which the solitude of a garden and tranquility of the morning naturally dispose us to. But I am afraid I interrupt your thoughts, for you seemed very intent on something.

Hyl. It is true, I was, and shall be obliged to you if you will permit me to go on in the same vein; not that I would by any means deprive myself of your company, for my thoughts always flow more easily in conversation with a friend than when I am alone; but my request is that you would suffer me to impart my reflections to you.

Phil. With all my heart, it is what I should have requested myself if you had not prevented me.

Hyl. I was considering the odd fate of those men who have

in all ages, through an affectation of being distinguished from the vulgar, or some unaccountable turn of thought, pretended either to believe nothing at all or to believe the most extravagant things in the world. This, however, might be borne if their paradoxes and skepticism did not draw after them some consequences of general disadvantage to mankind. But the mischief lies here: that when men of less leisure see them who are supposed to have spent their whole time in the pursuits of knowledge professing an entire ignorance of all things or advancing such notions as are repugnant to plain and commonly received principles, they will be tempted to entertain suspicions concerning the most important truths, which they had hitherto held sacred and unquestionable.

Phil. I entirely agree with you as to the ill tendency of the affected doubts of some philosophers and fantastical conceits of others. I am even so far gone of late in this way of thinking that I have quitted several of the sublime notions I had got in their schools for vulgar opinions. And I give it you on my word, since this revolt from metaphysical notions to the plain dictates of nature and common sense, I find my understanding strangely enlightened, so that I can now easily comprehend a great many things which before were all mystery and riddle.

Hyl. I am glad to find there was nothing in the accounts I heard of you.

Phil. Pray, what were those?

Hyl. You were represented in last night's conversation as one who maintained the most extravagant opinion that ever entered into the mind of man, to wit, that there is no such thing as *material substance* in the world.

Phil. That there is no such thing as what philosophers call "material substance," I am seriously persuaded; but if I were made to see anything absurd or skeptical in this, I should then have the same reason to renounce this that I imagine I have now to reject the contrary opinion.

Hyl. What! Can anything be more fantastical, more repugnant to common sense or a more manifest piece of skepticism than to believe there is no such thing as matter?

Phil. Softly, good Hylas. What if it should prove that you, who hold there is, are, by virtue of that opinion, a greater skeptic and maintain more paradoxes and repugnancies to common sense than I who believe no such thing?

Hyl. You may as soon persuade me the part is greater than the whole, as that, in order to avoid absurdity and skepticism, I should ever be obliged to give up my opinion in this point.

Phil. Well, then, are you content to admit that opinion for true which, upon examination, shall appear most agreeable to common sense and remote from skepticism?

Hyl. With all my heart. Since you are for raising disputes about the plainest things in nature, I am content for once to hear what you have to say.

Phil. Pray, Hylas, what do you mean by a "skeptic"?

Hyl. I mean what all men mean, one that doubts of everything.

Phil. He then who entertains no doubt concerning some particular point, with regard to that point cannot be thought a skeptic.

Hyl. I agree with you.

Phil. Whether does doubting consist in embracing the affirmative or negative side of a question?

Hyl. In neither; for whoever understands English cannot but know that "doubting" signifies a suspense between both.

Phil. He then that denies any point can no more be said to doubt of it than he who affirms it with the same degree of assurance.

Hyl. True.

Phil. And, consequently, for such his denial is no more to be esteemed a skeptic than the other.

Hyl. I acknowledge it.

Phil. How comes it to pass then, Hylas, that you pronounce me a skeptic because I deny what you affirm, to wit, the existence of matter? Since, for aught you can tell, I am as peremptory in my denial as you in your affirmation.

Hyl. Hold, Philonous, I have been a little out in my definition; but every false step a man makes in discourse is not to be insisted on. I said indeed that a "skeptic" was one who doubted of everything; but I should have added: or who denies the reality and truth of things.

Phil. What things? Do you mean the principles and theorems of sciences? But these you know are universal intellectual notions, and consequently independent of matter; the denial therefore of this does not imply the denying them.

Hyl. I grant it. But are there no other things? What think you of distrusting the senses, of denying the real existence of sensible things, or pretending to know nothing of them. Is not this sufficient to denominate a man a skeptic?

Phil. Shall we therefore examine which of us it is that denies the reality of sensible things or professes the greatest ignorance of them, since, if I take you rightly, he is to be esteemed the greatest skeptic?

Hyl. That is what I desire.

* * *

[2.] *Phil.* What mean you by "sensible things"?

Hyl. Those things which are perceived by the senses. Can you imagine that I mean anything else?

Phil. Pardon me, Hylas, if I am desirous clearly to apprehend your notions, since this may much shorten our inquiry. Suffer me then to ask you this further question. Are those things only perceived by the senses which are perceived immediately? Or may those things properly be said to be "sensible" which are perceived mediately, or not without the intervention of others?

Hyl. I do not sufficiently understand you.

Phil. In reading a book, what I immediately perceive are the letters, but mediately, or by means of these, are suggested to my mind the notions of God, virtue, truth, etc. Now, that the letters are truly sensible things, or perceived by sense, there is no doubt; but I would know whether you take the things suggested by them to be so too.

Hyl. No, certainly; it were absurd to think God or virtue sensible things, though they may be signified and suggested to the mind by sensible marks with which they have an arbitrary connection.

Phil. It seems then, that by "sensible things" you mean those only which can be perceived immediately by sense.

Hyl. Right.

Phil. Does it not follow from this that, though I see one part of the sky red, and another blue, and that my reason does thence evidently conclude there must be some cause of that diversity of colors, yet that cause cannot be said to be a sensible thing or perceived by the sense of seeing?

Hyl. It does.

Phil. In like manner, though I hear variety of sounds, yet I cannot be said to hear the causes of those sounds.

Hyl. You cannot.

Phil. And when by my touch I perceive a thing to be hot and heavy, I cannot say, with any truth or propriety, that I feel the cause of its heat or weight.

Hyl. To prevent any more questions of this kind, I tell you once for all that by "sensible things" I mean those only which are perceived by sense, and that in truth the senses perceive nothing which they do not perceive immediately, for they make no inferences. The deducing therefore of causes or occasions from effects and appearances, which alone are perceived by sense, entirely relates to reason.

Phil. This point then is agreed between us—that *sensible things are those only which are immediately perceived by sense.* You will further inform me whether we immediately perceive by sight anything besides light and colors and figures; or by hearing, anything but sounds; by the palate, anything besides tastes; by the smell, besides odors; or by the touch, more than tangible qualities.

Hyl. We do not.

Phil. It seems, therefore, that if you take away all sensible qualities, there remains nothing sensible?

Hyl. I grant it.

Phil. Sensible things therefore are nothing else but so many sensible qualities or combinations of sensible qualities?

Hyl. Nothing else.

[3.] *Phil.* Heat is then a sensible thing?

Hyl. Certainly.

Phil. Does the reality of sensible things consist in being perceived, or is it something distinct from their being perceived, and that bears no relation to the mind?

Hyl. To *exist* is one thing, and to be *perceived* is another.

Phil. I speak with regard to sensible things only; and of these I ask, whether by their real existence you mean a subsistence exterior to the mind and distinct from their being perceived?

Hyl. I mean a real absolute being, distinct from and without any relation to their being perceived.

Phil. Heat therefore, if it be allowed a real being, must exist without the mind?

Hyl. It must.

Phil. Tell me, Hylas, is this real existence equally compatible to all degrees of heat, which we perceive, or is there any reason why we should attribute it to some and deny it to others? And if there be, pray let me know that reason.

Hyl. Whatever degree of heat we perceive by sense, we may be sure the same exists in the object that occasions it.

Phil. What! the greatest as well as the least?

Hyl. I tell you, the reason is plainly the same in respect of both: they are both perceived by sense; nay, the greater degree of heat is more sensibly perceived; and consequently, if there is any difference, we are more certain of its real existence than we can be of the reality of a lesser degree.

Phil. But is not the most vehement and intense degree of heat a very great pain?

Hyl. No one can deny it.

Phil. And is any unperceiving thing capable of pain or pleasure?

Hyl. No, certainly.

Phil. Is your material substance a senseless being or a being endowed with sense and perception?

Hyl. It is senseless, without doubt.

Phil. It cannot, therefore, be the subject of pain?

Hyl. By no means.

Phil. Nor, consequently, of the greatest heat perceived by sense, since you acknowledge this to be no small pain?

Hyl. I grant it.

Phil. What shall we say then of your external object: is it a material substance, or no?

Hyl. It is a material substance with the sensible qualities inhering in it.

Phil. How then can a great heat exist in it, since you own it cannot in a material substance? I desire you would clear this point.

Hyl. Hold, Philonous, I fear I was out in yielding intense heat to be a pain. It should seem rather that pain is something distinct from heat, and the consequence or effect of it.

Phil. Upon putting your hand near the fire, do you perceive one simple uniform sensation or two distinct sensations?

Hyl. But one simple sensation.

Phil. Is not the heat immediately perceived?

Hyl. It is.

Phil. And the pain?

Hyl. True.

Phil. Seeing therefore they are both immediately perceived at the same time, and the fire affects you only with one simple or uncompounded idea, it follows that this same simple idea is both the intense heat immediately perceived and the pain; and, consequently, that the intense heat immediately perceived is nothing distinct from a particular sort of pain.

Hyl. It seems so.

Phil. Again, try in your thoughts, Hylas, if you can conceive a vehement sensation to be without pain or pleasure.

Hyl. I cannot.

Phil. Or can you frame to yourself an idea of sensible pain or pleasure, in general, abstracted from every particular idea of heat, cold, tastes, smells, etc.?

Hyl. I do not find that I can.

Phil. Does it not therefore follow that sensible pain is nothing distinct from those sensations or ideas—in an intense degree?

Hyl. It is undeniable; and, to speak the truth, I begin to suspect a very great heat cannot exist but in a mind perceiving it.

Phil. What! are you then in that *skeptical* state of suspense, between affirming and denying?

Hyl. I think I may be positive in the point. A very violent and painful heat cannot exist without the mind.

Phil. It has not therefore, according to you, any real being?

Hyl. I own it.

Phil. Is it therefore certain that there is no body in nature really hot?

Hyl. I have not denied there is any real heat in bodies. I only say there is no such thing as an intense real heat.

Phil. But did you not say before that all degrees of heat were equally real, or, if there was any difference, that the greater were more undoubtedly real than the lesser?

Hyl. True; but it was because I did not then consider the ground there is for distinguishing between them, which I now plainly see. And it is this: because intense heat is nothing else but a particular kind of painful sensation, and pain cannot exist but in a perceiving being, it follows that no intense heat can really exist in an unperceiving corporeal substance. But this is no reason why we should deny heat in an inferior degree to exist in such a substance.

Phil. But how shall we be able to discern those degrees of heat which exist only in the mind from those which exist without it?

Hyl. That is no difficult matter. You know the least pain cannot exist unperceived; whatever, therefore, degree of heat is a pain exists only in the mind. But as for all other degrees of heat nothing obliges us to think the same of them.

Phil. I think you granted before that no unperceiving being was capable of pleasure any more than of pain.

Hyl. I did.

Phil. And is not warmth, or a more gentle degree of heat than what causes uneasiness, a pleasure?

Hyl. What then?

Phil. Consequently, it cannot exist without the mind in any unperceiving substance, or body.

Hyl. So it seems.

Phil. Since, therefore, as well those degrees of heat that are not painful, as those that are, can exist only in a thinking substance, may we not conclude that external bodies are absolutely incapable of any degree of heat whatsoever?

Hyl. On second thoughts, I do not think it is so evident that warmth is a pleasure as that a great degree of heat is a pain.

Phil. I do not pretend that warmth is as great a pleasure as heat is a pain. But if you grant it to be even a small pleasure, it serves to make good my conclusion.

Hyl. I could rather call it an "indolence." It seems to be nothing more than a privation of both pain and pleasure. And that such a quality or state as this may agree to an unthinking substance, I hope you will not deny.

Phil. If you are resolved to maintain that warmth, or a gentle degree of heat, is no pleasure, I know not how to convince you otherwise than by appealing to your own sense. But what think you of cold?

Hyl. The same that I do of heat. An intense degree of cold is a pain; for to feel a very great cold is to perceive a great uneasiness; it cannot therefore exist without the mind; but a lesser degree of cold may, as well as a lesser degree of heat.

Phil. Those bodies, therefore, upon whose application to our own we perceive a moderate degree of heat must be concluded to have a moderate degree of heat or warmth in them; and those upon whose application we feel a like degree of cold must be thought to have cold in them.

Hyl. They must.

Phil. Can any doctrine be true that necessarily leads a man into an absurdity?

Hyl. Without doubt it cannot.

Phil. Is it not an absurdity to think that the same thing should be at the same time both cold and warm?

Hyl. It is.

Phil. Suppose now one of your hands hot, and the other cold, and that they are both at once put into the same vessel of water, in an intermediate state, will not the water seem cold to one hand, and warm to the other?

Hyl. It will.

Phil. Ought we not therefore, by your principles, to conclude it is really both cold and warm at the same time, that is, according to your own concession, to believe an absurdity?

Hyl. I confess it seems so.

Phil. Consequently, the principles themselves are false, since you have granted that no true principle leads to an absurdity.

Hyl. But, after all, can anything be more absurd than to say, "there is no heat in the fire"?

Phil. To make the point still clearer; tell me whether, in two cases exactly alike, we ought not to make the same judgment?

Hyl. We ought.

Phil. When a pin pricks your finger, does it not rend and divide the fibers of your flesh?

Hyl. It does.

Phil. And when a coal burns your finger, does it any more?

Hyl. It does not.

Phil. Since, therefore, you neither judge the sensation itself occasioned by the pin, nor anything like it to be in the pin, you should not, conformably to what you have now granted, judge the sensation occasioned by the fire, or anything like it, to be in the fire.

Hyl. Well, since it must be so, I am content to yield this point and acknowledge that heat and cold are only sensations existing in our minds. But there still remain qualities enough to secure the reality of external things.

Phil. But what will you say, Hylas, if it shall appear that the case is the same with regard to all other sensible qualities, and that they can no more be supposed to exist without the mind than heat and cold?

Hyl. Then, indeed, you will have done something to the purpose; but that is what I despair of seeing proved.

[4.] *Phil.* Let us examine them in order. What think you of tastes—do they exist without the mind, or no?

Hyl. Can any man in his senses doubt whether sugar is sweet, or wormwood bitter?

Phil. Inform me, Hylas. Is a sweet taste a particular kind of pleasure or pleasant sensation, or is it not?

Hyl. It is.

Phil. And is not bitterness some kind of uneasiness or pain?

Hyl. I grant it.

Phil. If, therefore, sugar and wormwood are unthinking corporeal substances existing without the mind, how can sweetness and bitterness, that is, pleasure and pain, agree to them?

Hyl. Hold, Philonous. I now see what it was [that] deluded me all this time. You asked whether heat and cold, sweetness and bitterness, were not particular sorts of pleasure and pain; to which I answered simply that they were. Whereas I should have thus distinguished: those qualities as perceived by us are pleasures or pains, but not as existing in the external objects. We must not therefore conclude absolutely that there is no heat in the fire or sweetness in the sugar, but only that heat or sweetness, as perceived by us, are not in the fire or sugar. What say you to this?

Phil. I say it is nothing to the purpose. Our discourse proceeded altogether concerning sensible things, which you defined to be "the things we immediately perceive by our senses." Whatever other qualities, therefore, you speak of, as distinct from these, I know nothing of them, neither do they at all belong to the point in dispute. You may, indeed, pretend to have discovered certain qualities which you do not perceive and assert those insensible qualities exist in fire and sugar. But what use can be made of this to your present purpose, I am at a loss to conceive. Tell me then once more, do you acknowledge that heat and cold, sweetness and bitterness (meaning those qualities which are perceived by the senses), do not exist without the mind?

Hyl. I see it is to no purpose to hold out, so I give up the cause as to those mentioned qualities, though I profess it sounds oddly to say that sugar is not sweet.

Phil. But, for your further satisfaction, take this along with you: that which at other times seems sweet shall, to a distempered palate, appear bitter. And nothing can be plainer than that divers persons perceive different tastes in the same food, since that which one man delights in, another abhors. And how could this be if the taste was something really inherent in the food?

Hyl. I acknowledge I know not how.

Phil. In the next place, odors are to be considered. And with regard to these I would fain know whether what has been said of tastes does not exactly agree to them? Are they not so many pleasing or displeasing sensations?

Hyl. They are.

Phil. Can you then conceive it possible that they should exist in an unperceiving thing?

Hyl. I cannot.

Phil. Or can you imagine that filth and ordure affect those brute animals that feed on them out of choice with the same smells which we perceive in them?

Hyl. By no means.

Phil. May we not therefore conclude of smells, as of the other forementioned qualities, that they cannot exist in any but a perceiving substance or mind?

Hyl. I think so.

Phil. Then as to sounds, what must we think of them, are they accidents really inherent in external bodies or not?

Hyl. That they inhere not in the sonorous bodies is plain from hence; because a bell struck in the exhausted receiver of an air pump sends forth no sound. The air, therefore, must be thought the subject of sound.

Phil. What reason is there for that, Hylas?

Hyl. Because, when any motion is raised in the air, we perceive a sound greater or lesser, in proportion to the air's motion; but without some motion in the air we never hear any sound at all.

Phil. And granting that we never hear a sound but when some motion is produced in the air, yet I do not see how you can infer from thence that the sound itself is in the air.

Hyl. It is this very motion in the external air that produces in the mind the sensation of sound. For, striking on the drum of the ear, it causes a vibration which by the auditory nerves being communicated to the brain, the soul is thereupon affected with the sensation called "sound."

Phil. What! is sound then a sensation?

Hyl. I tell you, as perceived by us it is a particular sensation in the mind.

Phil. And can any sensation exist without the mind?

Hyl. No, certainly.

Phil. How then can sound, being a sensation, exist in the air if by the "air" you mean a senseless substance existing without the mind?

Hyl. You must distinguish, Philonous, between sound as it is perceived by us, and as it is in itself; or (which is the same thing) between the sound we immediately perceive and that which exists without us. The former, indeed, is a particular kind of sensation, but the latter is merely a vibrative or undulatory motion in the air.

Phil. I thought I had already obviated that distinction by the answer I gave when you were applying it in a like case before. But, to say no more of that, are you sure then that sound is really nothing but motion?

Hyl. I am.

Phil. Whatever, therefore, agrees to real sound may with truth be attributed to motion?

Hyl. It may.

Phil. It is then good sense to speak of motion as of a thing that is "loud," "sweet," "acute," or "grave."

Hyl. I see you are resolved not to understand me. Is it not evident those accidents or modes belong only to sensible sound, or sound in the common acceptation of the word, but not to sound in the real and philosophic sense, which, as I just now told you, is nothing but a certain motion of the air?

Phil. It seems then there are two sorts of sound—the one vulgar, or that which is heard, the other philosophical and real?

Hyl. Even so.

Phil. And the latter consists in motion?

Hyl. I told you so before.

Phil. Tell me, Hylas, to which of the senses, think you, the idea of motion belongs? To the hearing?

Hyl. No, certainly; but to the sight and touch.

Phil. It should follow then that, according to you, real sounds may possibly be *seen* or *felt,* but never *heard.*

Hyl. Look you, Philonous, you may, if you please, make a jest of my opinion, but that will not alter the truth of things. I own, indeed, the inferences you draw me into sound something oddly, but common language, you know, is framed by, and for the use of, the vulgar. We must not therefore wonder if expressions adapted to exact philosophic notions seem uncouth and out of the way.

Phil. Is it come to that? I assure you I imagine myself to have gained no small point since you make so light of departing from common phrases and opinions, it being a main part of our inquiry to examine whose notions are widest of the common road and most repugnant to the general sense of the world. But can you think it no more than a philosophical paradox to say that "real sounds are never heard," and that the idea of them is obtained by some other sense? And is there nothing in this contrary to nature and the truth of things?

Hyl. To deal ingenuously, I do not like it. And, after the concessions already made, I had as well grant that sounds, too, have no real being without the mind.

[5.] *Phil.* And I hope you will make no difficulty to acknowledge the same of colors.

Hyl. Pardon me; the case of colors is very different. Can anything be plainer than that we see them on the objects?

Phil. The objects you speak of are, I suppose, corporeal substances existing without the mind?

Hyl. They are.

Phil. And have true and real colors inhering in them?

Hyl. Each visible object has that color which we see in it.

Phil. How! is there anything visible but what we perceive by sight?

Hyl. There is not.

Phil. And do we perceive anything by sense which we do not perceive immediately?

Hyl. How often must I be obliged to repeat the same thing? I tell you, we do not.

Phil. Have patience, good Hylas, and tell me once more whether there is anything immediately perceived by the senses except sensible qualities. I know you asserted there was not; but I would now be informed whether you still persist in the same opinion.

Hyl. I do.

Phil. Pray, is your corporeal substance either a sensible quality or made up of sensible qualities?

Hyl. What a question that is! Who ever thought it was?

Phil. My reason for asking was, because in saying "each visible object has that color which we see in it," you make visible objects to be corporeal substances, which implies either that corporeal substances are sensible qualities or else that there is something besides sensible qualities perceived by sight; but as this point was formerly agreed between us, and is still maintained by you, it is a clear consequence that your corporeal substance is nothing distinct from sensible qualities.

Hyl. You may draw as many absurd consequences as you please and endeavor to perplex the plainest things, but you shall never persuade me out of my senses. I clearly understand my own meaning.

Phil. I wish you would make me understand it, too. But, since you are unwilling to have your notion of corporeal substance examined, I shall urge that point no further. Only be pleased to let me know whether the same colors which we see exist in external bodies or some other.

Hyl. The very same.

Phil. What! are then the beautiful red and purple we see on yonder clouds really in them? Or do you imagine they have in themselves any other form than that of a dark mist or vapor?

Hyl. I must own, Philonous, those colors are not really in the clouds as they seem to be at this distance. They are only apparent colors.

Phil. "Apparent" call you them? How shall we distinguish these apparent colors from real?

Hyl. Very easily. Those are to be thought apparent which, appearing only at a distance, vanish upon a nearer approach.

Phil. And those, I suppose, are to be thought real which are discovered by the most near and exact survey.

Hyl. Right.

Phil. Is the nearest and exactest survey made by the help of a microscope or by the naked eye?

Hyl. By a microscope, doubtless.

Phil. But a microscope often discovers colors in an object different from those perceived by the unassisted sight. And, in case we had microscopes magnifying to any assigned degree, it is certain that no object whatsoever, viewed through them, would appear in the same color which it exhibits to the naked eye.

Hyl. And what will you conclude from all this? You cannot argue that there are really and naturally no colors on objects because by artificial managements they may be altered or made to vanish.

Phil. I think it may evidently be concluded from your own concessions that all the colors we see with our naked eyes are only apparent as those on the clouds, since they vanish upon a more close and accurate inspection which is afforded us by a microscope. Then, as to what you say by way of prevention: I ask you whether the real and natural state of an object is better discovered by a very sharp and piercing sight or by one which is less sharp?

Hyl. By the former without doubt.

Phil. Is it not plain from dioptrics that microscopes make the sight more penetrating and represent objects as they would appear to the eye in case it were naturally endowed with a most exquisite sharpness?

Hyl. It is.

Phil. Consequently, the microscopical representation is to be thought that which best sets forth the real nature of the thing, or what it is in itself. The colors, therefore, by it perceived are more genuine and real than those perceived otherwise.

Hyl. I confess there is something in what you say.

Phil. Besides, it is not only possible but manifest that there actually are animals whose eyes are by nature framed to perceive those things which by reason of their minuteness escape our sight. What think you of those inconceivably small animals perceived by glasses? Must we suppose they are all stark blind? Or, in case they see, can it be imagined their sight has not the same use in preserving their bodies from injuries which appears in that of all other animals? And if it has, is it not evident they must see particles less than their own bodies, which will present them with a far different view in each object from that which strikes our senses? Even our own eyes do not always represent objects to us after the same manner. In the jaundice everyone knows that all things seem yellow. Is it not therefore highly probable those animals in whose eyes we discern a very different texture from that of ours, and whose bodies abound with different humors, do not see the same colors in every object that we do? From all which should it not seem to follow that all colors are equally apparent, and that none of those which we perceive are really inherent in any outward object?

Hyl. It should.

Phil. The point will be past all doubt if you consider that, in case colors were real properties or affections inherent in external bodies, they could admit of no alteration without some change wrought in the very bodies themselves; but is it not evident from what has been said that, upon the use of microscopes, upon a change happening in the humors of the eye, or a variation of distance, without any manner of real alteration in the thing itself, the colors of any object are either changed or totally disappear? Nay, all other circumstances remaining the same, change but the situation of some objects and they shall present different colors to the eye. The same thing happens upon viewing an object in various degrees of light. And what is more known than that the same bodies appear differently colored by candlelight from what they do in the open day? Add to these the experiment of a prism which, separating the heterogeneous rays of light, alters the color of any object and will cause the whitest to appear of a deep blue or red to the naked eye. And now tell me whether you are still of opinion that every body has its true real color inhering in it; and if you think it has, I would fain know further from you what certain distance and position of the object, what peculiar texture and formation of the eye, what degree or kind of light is necessary for ascertaining that true color and distinguishing it from apparent ones.

Hyl. I own myself entirely satisfied that they are all equally apparent and that there is no such thing as color really inhering in external bodies, but that it is altogether in the light. And what confirms me in this opinion is that in proportion to the light colors are still more or less vivid; and if there be no light, then are there no colors perceived. Besides, allowing there are colors on external objects, yet, how is it possible for us to perceive them? For no external body affects the mind unless it acts first on our organs of sense. But the only action of bodies is motion, and motion cannot be communicated otherwise than by impulse. A distant object, therefore, cannot act on the eye, nor consequently make itself or its properties perceivable to the soul. Whence it plainly follows that it is immediately some contiguous substance which, operating on the eye, occasions a perception of colors; and such is light.

Phil. How! is light then a substance?

Hyl. I tell you, Philonous, external light is nothing but a thin fluid substance whose minute particles, being agitated with a brisk motion and in various manners reflected from the different surfaces of outward objects to the eyes, communicate different motions to the optic nerves; which, being propagated to the brain, cause therein various impressions, and these are attended with the sensations of red, blue, yellow, etc.

Phil. It seems, then, the light does no more than shake the optic nerves.

Hyl. Nothing else.

Phil. And, consequent to each particular motion of the nerves, the mind is affected with a sensation which is some particular color.

Hyl. Right.

Phil. And these sensations have no existence without the mind.

Hyl. They have not.

Phil. How then do you affirm that colors are in the light, since by "light" you understand a corporeal substance external to the mind?

Hyl. Light and colors, as immediately perceived by us, I grant cannot exist without the mind. But in themselves they are only the motions and configurations of certain insensible particles of matter.

Phil. Colors, then, in the vulgar sense, or taken for the immediate objects of sight, cannot agree to any but a perceiving substance.

Hyl. That is what I say.

Phil. Well then, since you give up the point as to those sensible qualities which are alone thought colors by all mankind besides, you may hold what you please with regard to those invisible ones of the philosophers. It is not my business to dispute about them; only I would advise you to bethink yourself whether, considering the inquiry we are upon, it be prudent for you to affirm—"the red and blue which we see are not real colors, but certain unknown motions and figures which no man ever did or can see are truly so." Are not these shocking notions, and are not they subject to as many ridiculous inferences as those you were obliged to renounce before in the case of sounds?

[6.] *Hyl.* I frankly own, Philonous, that it is in vain to stand out any longer. Colors, sounds, tastes, in a word, all those termed "secondary qualities," have certainly no existence without the mind. But by this acknowledgment I must not be supposed to derogate anything from the reality of matter or external objects; seeing it is no more than several philosophers maintain, who nevertheless are the farthest imaginable from denying matter. For the clearer understanding of this you must know sensible qualities are by philosophers divided into *primary* and *secondary*. The former are extension, figure, solidity, gravity, motion, and rest. And these they hold exist really in bodies. The latter are those above enumerated, or, briefly, all sensible qualities besides the primary, which they assert are only so many sensations or ideas existing nowhere but in the mind. But all this, I doubt not, you are already apprised of. For my part I have been a long time sensible there was such an opinion current among philosophers, but was never thoroughly convinced of its truth till now.

Phil. You are still then of opinion that *extension* and *figures* are inherent in external unthinking substances?

Hyl. I am.

Phil. But what if the same arguments which are brought against secondary qualities will hold good against these also?

Hyl. Why then I shall be obliged to think they too exist only in the mind.

Phil. Is it your opinion the very figure and extension which you perceive by sense exist in the outward object or material substance?

Hyl. It is.

Phil. Have all other animals as good grounds to think the same of the figure and extension which they see and feel?

Hyl. Without doubt, if they have any thought at all.

Phil. Answer me, Hylas. Think you the senses were bestowed upon all animals for their preservation and well-being in life? Or were they given to men alone for this end?

Hyl. I make no question but they have the same use in all other animals.

Phil. If so, is it not necessary they should be enabled by them to perceive their own limbs and those bodies which are capable of harming them?

Hyl. Certainly.

Phil. A mite therefore must be supposed to see his own foot, and things equal or even less than it, as bodies of some considerable dimension, though at the same time they appear to you scarce discernible or at best as so many visible points?

Hyl. I cannot deny it.

Phil. And to creatures less than the mite they will seem yet larger?

Hyl. They will.

Phil. Insomuch that what you can hardly discern will to another extremely minute animal appear as some huge mountain?

Hyl. All this I grant.

Phil. Can one and the same thing be at the same time in itself of different dimensions?

Hyl. That were absurd to imagine.

Phil. But from what you have laid down it follows that both the extension by you perceived and that perceived by the mite itself, as likewise all those perceived by lesser animals, are each of them the true extension of the mite's foot; that is to say, by your own principles you are led into an absurdity.

Hyl. There seems to be some difficulty in the point.

Phil. Again, have you not acknowledged that no real inherent property of any object can be changed without some change in the thing itself?

Hyl. I have.

Phil. But, as we approach to or recede from an object, the visible extension varies, being at one distance ten or a hundred times greater than at another. Does it not therefore follow from hence likewise that it is not really inherent in the object?

Hyl. I own I am at a loss what to think.

Phil. Your judgment will soon be determined if you will venture to think as freely concerning this quality as you have done concerning the rest. Was it not admitted as a good argument that neither heat nor cold was in the water because it seemed warm to one hand and cold to the other?

Hyl. It was.

Phil. Is it not the very same reasoning to conclude there is no extension or figure in an object because to one eye it shall seem little, smooth, and round, when at the same time it appears to the other great, uneven, and angular?

Hyl. The very same. But does this latter fact ever happen?

Phil. You may at any time make the experiment by looking with one eye bare, and with the other through a microscope.

Hyl. I know not how to maintain it, and yet I am loath to give up *extension;* I see so many odd consequences following upon such a concession.

Phil. Odd, say you? After the concessions already made, I hope you will stick at nothing for its oddness. But, on the other hand, should it not seem very odd if the general reasoning which includes all other sensible qualities did not also include extension? If it be allowed that no idea nor anything like an idea can exist in an unperceiving substance, then surely it follows that no figure or mode of extension, which we can either perceive or imagine, or have any idea of, can be really inherent in matter, not to mention the peculiar difficulty there must be in conceiving a material substance, prior to and distinct from extension, to be the *substratum* of extension. Be the sensible quality what it will—figure or sound or color—it seems alike impossible it should subsist in that which does not perceive it.

Hyl. I give up the point for the present, reserving still a right to retract my opinion in case I shall hereafter discover any false step in my progress to it.

[7.] *Phil.* That is a right you cannot be denied. Figures and extension being dispatched, we proceed next to *motion*. Can a real motion in any external body be at the same time both very swift and very slow?

Hyl. It cannot.

Phil. Is not the motion of a body swift in a reciprocal proportion to the time it takes up in describing any given space? Thus a body that describes a mile in an hour moves three times faster than it would in case it described only a mile in three hours.

Hyl. I agree with you.

Phil. And is not time measured by the succession of ideas in our minds?

Hyl. It is.

Phil. And is it not possible ideas should succeed one another twice as fast in your mind as they do in mine, or in that of some spirit of another kind?

Hyl. I own it.

Phil. Consequently, the same body may to another seem to perform its motion over any space in half the time that it does to you. And the same reasoning will hold as to any other proportion; that is to say, according to your principles (since the motions perceived are both really in the object) it is possible one and the same body shall be really moved the same way at once, both very swift and very slow. How is this consistent either with common sense or with what you just now granted?

Hyl. I have nothing to say to it.

Phil. Then as for *solidity;* either you do not mean any sensible quality by that word, and so it is beside our inquiry; or if you do, it must be either hardness or resistance. But both the one and the other are plainly relative to our senses: it being evident that what seems hard to one animal may appear soft to another who has greater force and firmness of limbs. Nor is it less plain that the resistance I feel is not in the body.

Hyl. I own the very sensation of resistance, which is all you immediately perceive, is not in the *body,* but the cause of that sensation is.

Phil. But the causes of our sensations are not things immediately perceived, and therefore not sensible. This point I thought had been already determined.

Hyl. I own it was; but you will pardon me if I seem a little embarrassed; I know not how to quit my old notions.

Phil. To help you out, do but consider that if *extension* be once acknowledged to have no existence without the mind, the same must necessarily be granted of motion, solidity, and gravity, since they all evidently suppose extension. It is therefore superfluous to inquire particularly concerning each of them. In denying extension, you have denied them all to have any real existence.

Hyl. I wonder, Philonous, if what you say be true, why those philosophers who deny the secondary qualities any real existence should yet attribute it to the primary. If there is no difference between them, how can this be accounted for?

Phil. It is not my business to account for every opinion of the philosophers. But, among other reasons which may be assigned for this, it seems probable that pleasure and pain being rather annexed to the former than the latter may be one. Heat and cold, tastes and smells have something more vividly pleasing or disagreeable than the ideas of extension, figure, and motion affect us with. And, it being too visibly absurd to hold that pain or pleasure can be in an unperceiving substance, men are more easily weaned from believing the external existence of the secondary than the primary qualities. You will be satisfied there is something in this if you recollect the difference you made between an intense and more moderate degree of heat, allowing the one a real existence while you denied it to the other. But, after all, there is no rational ground for that distinction, for surely an indifferent sensation is as truly a *sensation* as one more pleasing or painful, and consequently should not any more than they be supposed to exist in an unthinking subject.

[8.] *Hyl.* It is just come into my head, Philonous, that I have somewhere heard of a distinction between *absolute* and *sensible* extension. Now though it be acknowledged that *great* and *small,* consisting merely in the relation which other extended beings have to the parts of our own bodies, do not really inhere in the substances themselves, yet nothing obliges us to hold the same with regard to *absolute* extension, which is something abstracted from *great* and *small,* from this or that particular magnitude or figure. So likewise as to motion: *swift* and *slow* are altogether relative to the succession of ideas in our own minds. But it does not follow, because those modifications of motion exist not without the mind, that therefore absolute motion abstracted from them does not.

Phil. Pray what is it that distinguishes one motion, or one part of extension, from another? Is it not something sensible, as some degree of swiftness or slowness, some certain magnitude or figure peculiar to each?

Hyl. I think so.

Phil. These qualities, therefore, stripped of all sensible properties, are without all specific and numerical differences, as the schools call them.

Hyl. They are.

Phil. That is to say, they are extension in general, and motion in general.

Hyl. Let it be so.

Phil. But it is a universally received maxim that "everything which exists is particular." [2] How then can motion in general, or extension in general, exist in any corporeal substance?

Hyl. I will take time to solve your difficulty.

Phil. But I think the point may be speedily decided. Without doubt you can tell whether you are able to frame this or that idea. Now I am content to put our dispute on this issue. If you can frame in your thoughts a distinct abstract idea of motion or extension divested of all those sensible modes as swift and slow, great and small, round and square, and the like, which are acknowledged to exist only in the mind, I will then yield the point you contend for. But if you cannot, it will be unreasonable on your side to insist any longer upon what you have no notion of.

Hyl. To confess ingenuously, I cannot.

Phil. Can you even separate the ideas of extension and motion from the ideas of all those qualities which they who make the distinction term "secondary"?

Hyl. What! is it not an easy matter to consider extension

[2] [Cf. Locke, *Essay*, Bk. III, chap. 3, sec. 1: "All things that exist being particulars...."]

and motion by themselves, abstracted from all other sensible qualities? Pray how do the mathematicians treat of them?

Phil. I acknowledge, Hylas, it is not difficult to form general propositions and reasonings about those qualities without mentioning any other, and, in this sense, to consider or treat of them abstractedly. But how does it follow that, because I can pronounce the word "motion" by itself, I can form the idea of it in my mind exclusive of body? Or because theorems may be made of extension and figures, without any mention of *great* or *small*, or any other sensible mode or quality, that therefore it is possible such an abstract idea of extension, without any particular size or figure or sensible quality, should be distinctly formed and apprehended by the mind? Mathematicians treat of quantity without regarding what other sensible qualities it is attended with, as being altogether indifferent to their demonstrations. But when, laying aside the words, they contemplate the bare ideas, I believe you will find they are not the pure abstracted ideas of extension.[3]

Hyl. But what say you to *pure intellect?* May not abstracted ideas be framed by that faculty?

Phil. Since I cannot frame abstract ideas at all, it is plain I cannot frame them by the help of pure intellect, whatsoever faculty you understand by those words. Besides, not to inquire into the nature of pure intellect and its spiritual objects, as *virtue, reason, God,* or the like, thus much seems manifest that sensible things are only to be perceived by sense or represented by the imagination. Figures, therefore, and extension, being originally perceived by sense, do not belong to pure intellect; but, for your further satisfaction, try if you can frame the idea of any figure abstracted from all particularities of size or even from other sensible qualities.

Hyl. Let me think a little— I do not find that I can.

Phil. And can you think it possible that should really exist in nature which implies a repugnancy in its conception?

Hyl. By no means.

Phil. Since therefore it is impossible even for the mind to

[3] [Cf. *Principles,* Introduction, sec. 16, note 3.]

disunite the ideas of extension and motion from all other sensible qualities, does it not follow that where the one exist there necessarily the other exist likewise?

Hyl. It should seem so.

Phil. Consequently, the very same arguments which you admitted as conclusive against the secondary qualities are, without any further application of force, against the primary, too. Besides, if you will trust your senses, is it not plain all sensible qualities coexist, or to them appear as being in the same place? Do they ever represent a motion or figure as being divested of all other visible and tangible qualities?

Hyl. You need say no more on this head. I am free to own, if there be no secret error or oversight in our proceedings hitherto, that all sensible qualities are alike to be denied existence without the mind. But my fear is that I have been too liberal in my former concessions, or overlooked some fallacy or other. In short, I did not take time to think.

Phil. For that matter, Hylas, you may take what time you please in reviewing the progress of our inquiry. You are at liberty to recover any slips you might have made, or offer whatever you have omitted which makes for your first opinion.

[9.] *Hyl.* One great oversight I take to be this—that I did not sufficiently distinguish the *object* from the *sensation*. Now, though this latter may not exist without the mind, yet it will not thence follow that the former cannot.

Phil. What object do you mean? The object of the senses?

Hyl. The same.

Phil. It is then immediately perceived?

Hyl. Right.

Phil. Make me to understand the difference between what is immediately perceived and a sensation.

Hyl. The sensation I take to be an act of the mind perceiving; besides which there is something perceived, and this I call the "object." For example, there is red and yellow on that tulip. But then the act of perceiving those colors is in me only, and not in the tulip.

Phil. What tulip do you speak of? Is it that which you see?

Hyl. The same.

Phil. And what do you see besides color, figure, and extension?

Hyl. Nothing.

Phil. What you would say then is that the red and yellow are coexistent with the extension; is it not?

Hyl. That is not all; I would say they have a real existence without the mind, in some unthinking substance.

Phil. That the colors are really in the tulip which I see is manifest. Neither can it be denied that this tulip may exist independent of your mind or mine; but that any immediate object of the senses—that is, any idea, or combination of ideas—should exist in an unthinking substance, or exterior to all minds, is in itself an evident contradiction. Nor can I imagine how this follows from what you said just now, to wit, that the red and yellow were on the tulip *you saw,* since you do not pretend to *see* that unthinking substance.

Hyl. You have an artful way, Philonous, of diverting our inquiry from the subject.

Phil. I see you have no mind to be pressed that way. To return then to your distinction between *sensation* and *object;* if I take you right, you distinguish in every perception two things, the one an action of the mind, the other not.

Hyl. True.

Phil. And this action cannot exist in, or belong to, any unthinking thing, but whatever besides is implied in a perception may?

Hyl. That is my meaning.

Phil. So that if there was a perception without any act of the mind, it were possible such a perception should exist in an unthinking substance?

Hyl. I grant it. But it is impossible there should be such a perception.

Phil. When is the mind said to be active?

Hyl. When it produces, puts an end to, or changes anything.

Phil. Can the mind produce, discontinue, or change anything but by an act of the will?

Hyl. It cannot.

Phil. The mind therefore is to be accounted *active* in its perceptions so far forth as *volition* is included in them?

Hyl. It is.

Phil. In plucking this flower I am active, because I do it by the motion of my hand, which was consequent upon my volition; so likewise in applying it to my nose. But is either of these smelling?

Hyl. No.

Phil. I act, too, in drawing the air through my nose, because my breathing so rather than otherwise is the effect of my volition. But neither can this be called "smelling," for if it were I should smell every time I breathed in that manner?

Hyl. True.

Phil. Smelling then is somewhat consequent to all this?

Hyl. It is.

Phil. But I do not find my will concerned any further. Whatever more there is—as that I perceive such a particular smell, or any smell at all—this is independent of my will, and therein I am altogther passive. Do you find it otherwise with you, Hylas?

Hyl. No, the very same.

Phil. Then, as to seeing, is it not in your power to open your eyes or keep them shut, to turn them this or that way?

Hyl. Without doubt.

Phil. But does it in like manner depend on your will that in looking on this flower you perceive *white* rather than any other color? Or, directing your open eyes toward yonder part of the heaven, can you avoid seeing the sun? Or is light or darkness the effect of your volition?

Hyl. No, certainly.

Phil. You are then in these respects altogether passive?

Hyl. I am.

Phil. Tell me now whether *seeing* consists in perceiving light and colors or in opening and turning the eyes?

Hyl. Without doubt, in the former.

Phil. Since, therefore, you are in the very perception of light and colors altogether passive, what is become of that action you were speaking of as an ingredient in every sensation? And does it not follow from your own concessions that the perception of light and colors, including no action in it, may exist in an unperceiving substance? And is not this a plain contradiction?

Hyl. I know not what to think of it.

Phil. Besides, since you distinguish the *active* and *passive* in every perception, you must do it in that of pain. But how is it possible that pain, be it as little active as you please, should exist in an unperceiving substance? In short, do but consider the point and then confess ingenuously whether light and colors, tastes, sounds, etc., are not all equally passions or sensations in the soul. You may indeed call them "external objects" and give them in words what subsistence you please. But examine your own thoughts and then tell me whether it be not as I say?

[10.] *Hyl.* I acknowledge, Philonous, that, upon a fair observation of what passes in my mind, I can discover nothing else but that I am a thinking being affected with variety of sensations, neither is it possible to conceive how a sensation should exist in an unperceiving substance. But then, on the other hand, when I look on sensible things in a different view, considering them as so many modes and qualities, I find it necessary to suppose a material *substratum,* without which they cannot be conceived to exist.

Phil. "Material substratum" call you it? Pray, by which of your senses came you acquainted with that being?

Hyl. It is not itself sensible; its modes and qualities only being perceived by the senses.

Phil. I presume then it was by reflection and reason you obtained the idea of it?

Hyl. I do not pretend to any proper positive idea of it. However, I conclude it exists because qualities cannot be conceived to exist without a support.

Phil. It seems then you have only a relative notion of it, or that you conceive it not otherwise than by conceiving the relation it bears to sensible qualities?

Hyl. Right.

Phil. Be pleased, therefore, to let me know wherein that relation consists.

Hyl. Is it not sufficiently expressed in the term "substratum" or "substance"?

Phil. If so, the word "substratum" should import that it is spread under the sensible qualities or accidents?

Hyl. True.

Phil. And consequently under extension?

Hyl. I own it.

Phil. It is therefore somewhat in its own nature entirely distinct from extension?

Hyl. I tell you extension is only a mode, and matter is something that supports modes. And is it not evident the thing supported is different from the thing supporting?

Phil. So that something distinct from, and exclusive of, extension is supposed to be the *substratum* of extension?

Hyl. Just so.

Phil. Answer me, Hylas, can a thing be spread without extension, or is not the idea of extension necessarily included in *spreading*?

Hyl. It is.

Phil. Whatsoever therefore you suppose spread under anything must have in itself an extension distinct from the extension of that thing under which it is spread?

Hyl. It must.

Phil. Consequently, every corporeal substance being the *substratum* of extension must have in itself another extension by which it is qualified to be a *substratum,* and so on to infinity? And I ask whether this be not absurd in itself and repugnant to what you granted just now, to wit, that the *substratum* was something distinct from and exclusive of extension?

Hyl. Aye, but, Philonous, you take me wrong. I do not mean that matter is *spread* in a gross literal sense under extension. The word "substratum" is used only to express in general the same thing with "substance."

Phil. Well then, let us examine the relation implied in the term "substance." Is it not that it stands under accidents?

Hyl. The very same.

Phil. But that one thing may stand under or support another, must it not be extended?

Hyl. It must.

Phil. Is not therefore this supposition liable to the same absurdity with the former?

Hyl. You still take things in a strict literal sense; that is not fair, Philonous.

Phil. I am not for imposing any sense on your words; you are at liberty to explain them as you please. Only I beseech you, make me understand something by them. You tell me matter supports or stands under accidents. How! is it as your legs support your body?

Hyl. No; that is the literal sense.

Phil. Pray let me know any sense, literal or not literal, that you understand it in.— How long must I wait for an answer, Hylas?

Hyl. I declare I know not what to say. I once thought I understood well enough what was meant by matter's supporting accidents. But now, the more I think on it, the less can I comprehend it; in short, I find that I know nothing of it.

Phil. It seems then you have no idea at all, neither relative nor positive, of matter; you know neither what it is in itself nor what relation it bears to accidents?

Hyl. I acknowledge it.

Phil. And yet you asserted that you could not conceive how qualities or accidents should really exist without conceiving at the same time a material support of them?

Hyl. I did.

Phil. That is to say, when you conceive the real existence of qualities, you do withal conceive something which you cannot conceive?

[11.] *Hyl.* It was wrong I own. But still I fear there is some fallacy or other. Pray, what think you of this? It is just come into my head that the ground of all our mistake lies in your treating of each quality by itself. Now I grant that each quality cannot singly subsist without the mind. Color cannot without extension, neither can figure without some other sensible quality. But, as the several qualities united or blended together form entire sensible things, nothing hinders why such things may not be supposed to exist without the mind.

Phil. Either, Hylas, you are jesting or have a very bad memory. Though, indeed, we went through all the qualities by name one after another, yet my arguments, or rather your concessions, nowhere tended to prove that the secondary qualities did not subsist each alone by itself, but that they were not *at all* without the mind. Indeed, in treating of figure and motion we concluded they could not exist without the mind, because it was impossible even in thought to separate them from all secondary qualities, so as to conceive them existing by themselves. But then this was not the only argument made use of upon that occasion. But (to pass by all that has been hitherto said and reckon it for nothing, if you will have it so) I am content to put the whole upon this issue. If you can conceive it possible for any mixture or combination of qualities, or any sensible object whatever, to exist without the mind, then I will grant it actually to be so.

Hyl. If it comes to that the point will soon be decided. What more easy than to conceive a tree or house existing by itself, independent of, and unperceived by, any mind whatsoever? I do at this present time conceive them existing after that manner.

Phil. How say you, Hylas, can you see a thing which is at the same time unseen?

Hyl. No, that were a contradiction.

Phil. Is it not as great a contradiction to talk of *conceiving* a thing which is *unconceived*?

Hyl. It is.

Phil. The tree or house, therefore, which you think of is conceived by you?

Hyl. How should it be otherwise?

Phil. And what is conceived is surely in the mind?

Hyl. Without question, that which is conceived is in the mind.

Phil. How then came you to say you conceived a house or tree existing independent and out of all minds whatsoever?

Hyl. That was I own an oversight, but stay, let me consider what led me into it.—It is a pleasant mistake enough. As I was thinking of a tree in a solitary place where no one was present to see it, methought that was to conceive a tree as existing unperceived or unthought of, not considering that I myself conceived it all the while. But now I plainly see that all I can do is to frame ideas in my own mind. I may indeed conceive in my own thoughts the idea of a tree, or a house, or a mountain, but that is all. And this is far from proving that I can conceive them *existing out of the minds of all spirits.*

Phil. You acknowledge then that you cannot possibly conceive how any one corporeal sensible thing should exist otherwise than in a mind?

Hyl. I do.

Phil. And yet you will earnestly contend for the truth of that which you cannot so much as conceive?

[12.] *Hyl.* I profess I know not what to think; but still there are some scruples remain with me. Is it not certain I see things at a distance? Do we not perceive the stars and moon, for example, to be a great way off? Is not this, I say, manifest to the senses?

Phil. Do you not in a dream, too, perceive those or the like objects?

Hyl. I do.

Phil. And have they not then the same appearance of being distant?

Hyl. They have.

Phil. But you do not thence conclude the apparitions in a dream to be without the mind?

Hyl. By no means.

Phil. You ought not therefore to conclude that sensible objects are without the mind, from their appearance or manner wherein they are perceived.

Hyl. I acknowledge it. But does not my sense deceive me in those cases?

Phil. By no means. The idea or thing which you immediately perceive, neither sense nor reason informs you that it actually exists without the mind. By sense you only know that you are affected with such certain sensations of light and colors, etc. And these you will not say are without the mind.

Hyl. True, but, besides all that, do you not think the sight suggests something of *outness* or *distance*?

Phil. Upon approaching a distant object, do the visible size and figure change perpetually or do they appear the same at all distances?

Hyl. They are in a continual change.

Phil. Sight, therefore, does not suggest or any way inform you that the visible object you immediately perceive exists at a distance,[4] or will be perceived when you advance farther onward, there being a continued series of visible objects succeeding each other during the whole time of your approach.

Hyl. It does not; but still I know, upon seeing an object, what object I shall perceive after having passed over a certain distance; no matter whether it be exactly the same or no, there is still something of distance suggested in the case.

Phil. Good Hylas, do but reflect a little on the point, and then tell me whether there be any more in it than this. From the ideas you actually perceive by sight, you have by experience learned to collect what other ideas you will (according to the standing order of nature) be affected with, after such a certain succession of time and motion.

Hyl. Upon the whole, I take it to be nothing else.

[4] See the *Essay Towards a New Theory of Vision;* and its Vindication [*The Theory of Vision, or Visual Language Vindicated and Explained*].

Phil. Now is it not plain that if we suppose a man born blind was on a sudden made to see, he could at first have no experience of what may be suggested by sight?

Hyl. It is.

Phil. He would not then, according to you, have any notion of distance annexed to the things he saw, but would take them for a new set of sensations existing only in his mind?

Hyl. It is undeniable.

Phil. But to make it still more plain: is not *distance* a line turned endwise to the eye?

Hyl. It is.

Phil. And can a line so situated be perceived by sight?

Hyl. It cannot.

Phil. Does it not therefore follow that distance is not properly and immediately perceived by sight?

Hyl. It should seem so.

Phil. Again, is it your opinion that colors are at a distance?

Hyl. It must be acknowledged they are only in the mind.

Phil. But do not colors appear to the eye as coexisting in the same place with extension and figures?

Hyl. They do.

Phil. How can you then conclude from sight that figures exist without, when you acknowledge colors do not; the sensible appearance being the very same with regard to both?

Hyl. I know not what to answer.

Phil. But allowing that distance was truly and immediately perceived by the mind, yet it would not thence follow it existed out of the mind. For whatever is immediately perceived is an idea; and can any *idea* exist out of the mind?

[13.] *Hyl.* To suppose that were absurd; but, inform me, Philonous, can we perceive or know nothing besides our ideas?

Phil. As for the rational deducing of causes from effects, that is beside our inquiry. And by the senses you can best tell whether you perceive anything which is not immediately perceived. And I ask you whether the things immediately perceived are other than your own sensations or ideas? You have indeed more than once, in the course of this conversation, declared yourself on those points, but you seem, by this last question, to have departed from what you then thought.

Hyl. To speak the truth, Philonous, I think there are two kinds of objects: the one perceived immediately, which are likewise called "ideas"; the other are real things or external objects, perceived by the mediation of ideas which are their images and representations. Now I own ideas do not exist without the mind, but the latter sort of objects do. I am sorry I did not think of this distinction sooner; it would probably have cut short your discourse.

Phil. Are those external objects perceived by sense or by some other faculty?

Hyl. They are perceived by sense.

Phil. How! is there anything perceived by sense which is not immediately perceived?

Hyl. Yes, Philonous, in some sort there is. For example, when I look on a picture or statue of Julius Caesar, I may be said, after a manner, to perceive him (though not immediately) by my senses.

Phil. It seems then you will have our ideas, which alone are immediately perceived, to be pictures of external things: and that these also are perceived by sense inasmuch as they have a conformity or resemblance to our ideas?

Hyl. That is my meaning.

Phil. And in the same way that Julius Caesar, in himself invisible, is nevertheless perceived by sight, real things, in themselves imperceptible, are perceived by sense.

Hyl. In the very same.

Phil. Tell me, Hylas, when you behold the picture of Julius Caesar, do you see with your eyes any more than some colors and figures, with a certain symmetry and composition of the whole?

Hyl. Nothing else.

Phil. And would not a man who had never known anything of Julius Caesar see as much?

Hyl. He would.

Phil. Consequently, he has his sight and the use of it in as perfect a degree as you?

Hyl. I agree with you.

Phil. Whence comes it then that your thoughts are directed to the Roman emperor, and his are not? This cannot proceed from the sensations or ideas of sense by you then perceived, since you acknowledge you have no advantage over him in that respect. It should seem therefore to proceed from reason and memory, should it not?

Hyl. It should.

Phil. Consequently, it will not follow from that instance that anything is perceived by sense which is not immediately perceived. Though I grant we may, in one acceptation, be said to perceive sensible things mediately by sense—that is, when, from a frequently perceived connection, the immediate perception of ideas by one sense suggests to the mind others, perhaps belonging to another sense, which are wont to be connected with them. For instance, when I hear a coach drive along the streets, immediately I perceive only the sound; but from the experience I have had that such a sound is connected with a coach, I am said to hear the coach. It is nevertheless evident that, in truth and strictness, nothing can be *heard* but *sound;* and the coach is not then properly perceived by sense, but suggested from experience. So likewise when we are said to see a red-hot bar of iron; the solidity and heat of the iron are not the objects of sight, but suggested to the imagination by the color and figure which are properly perceived by that sense. In short, those things alone are actually and strictly perceived by any sense which would have been perceived in case that same sense had then been first conferred on us. As for other things, it is plain they are only suggested to the mind by experience grounded on former perceptions. But, to return to your comparison of Caesar's picture, it is plain, if you keep to that, you must hold the real things or archetypes of our ideas are not perceived by sense, but by some internal faculty of the soul, as reason or memory. I would, therefore, fain know what arguments you can draw from reason for the existence of what you call "real things" or "material objects," or whether you remember to have seen them formerly as they are in themselves, or if you have heard or read of anyone that did.

Hyl. I see, Philonous, you are disposed to raillery; but that will never convince me.

Phil. My aim is only to learn from you the way to come at the knowledge of *material beings*. Whatever we perceive is perceived either immediately or mediately—by sense, or by reason and reflection. But, as you have excluded sense, pray show me what reason you have to believe their existence, or what *medium* you can possibly make use of to prove it, either to mine or your own understanding.

Hyl. To deal ingenuously, Philonous, now I consider the point, I do not find I can give you any good reason for it. But this much seems pretty plain, that it is at least possible such things may really exist. And as long as there is no absurdity in supposing them, I am resolved to believe as I did, till you bring good reasons to the contrary.

Phil. What! is it come to this, that you only believe the existence of material objects, and that your belief is founded barely on the possibility of its being true? Then you will have me bring reasons against it, though another would think it reasonable the proof should lie on him who holds the affirmative. And, after all, this very point which you are now resolved to maintain, without any reason, is in effect what you have more than once during this discourse seen good reason to give up. But to pass over all this—if I understand you rightly, you say our ideas do not exist without the mind, but that they are copies, images, or representations of certain originals that do?

Hyl. You take me right.

Phil. They are then like external things?

Hyl. They are.

Phil. Have those things a stable and permanent nature, independent of our senses, or are they in a perpetual change, upon our producing any motions in our bodies, suspending, exerting, or altering our faculties or organs of sense?

Hyl. Real things, it is plain, have a fixed and real nature, which remains the same notwithstanding any change in our senses or in the posture and motion of our bodies; which indeed may affect the ideas in our minds, but it were absurd to think they had the same effect on things existing without the mind.

Phil. How then is it possible that things perpetually fleeting and variable as our ideas should be copies or images of anything fixed and constant? Or, in other words, since all sensible qualities, as size, figure, color, etc., that is, our ideas, are continually changing upon every alteration in the distance, medium, or instruments of sensation—how can any determinate material objects be properly represented or painted forth by several distinct things each of which is so different from and unlike the rest? Or, if you say it resembles some one only of our ideas, how shall we be able to distinguish the true copy from all the false ones?

Hyl. I profess, Philonous, I am at a loss. I know not what to say to this.

Phil. But neither is this all. Which are material objects in themselves—perceptible or imperceptible?

Hyl. Properly and immediately nothing can be perceived but ideas. All material things, therefore, are in themselves insensible and to be perceived only by their ideas.

Phil. Ideas then are sensible, and their archetypes or originals insensible?

Hyl. Right.

Phil. But how can that which is sensible be like that which is insensible? Can a real thing, in itself *invisible,* be like a *color,* or a real thing which is not *audible* be like a *sound?* In a word, can anything be like a sensation or idea, but another sensation or idea?

Hyl. I must own, I think not.

Phil. Is it possible there should be any doubt on the point? Do you not perfectly know your own ideas?

Hyl. I know them perfectly, since what I do not perceive or know can be no part of my idea.

Phil. Consider, therefore, and examine them, and then tell me if there be anything in them which can exist without the mind, or if you can conceive anything like them existing without the mind?

Hyl. Upon inquiry I find it is impossible for me to conceive or understand how anything but an idea can be like an idea. And it is most evident that *no idea can exist without the mind.*

[14.] *Phil.* You are, therefore, by your principles forced to deny the reality of sensible things, since you made it to consist in an absolute existence exterior to the mind. That is to say, you are a downright skeptic. So I have gained my point, which was to show your principles led to skepticism.

Hyl. For the present I am, if not entirely convinced, at least silenced.

Phil. I would fain know what more you would require in order to a perfect conviction. Have you not had the liberty of explaining yourself all manner of ways? Were any little slips in discourse laid hold and insisted on? Or were you not allowed to retract or reinforce anything you had offered, as best served your purpose? Has not everything you could say been heard and examined with all the fairness imaginable? In a word, have you not in every point been convinced out of your own mouth? And, if you can at present discover any flaw in any of your former concessions, or think of any remaining subterfuge, any new distinction, color, or comment whatsoever, why do you not produce it?

Hyl. A little patience, Philonous. I am at present so amazed to see myself ensnared, and as it were imprisoned in the labyrinths you have drawn me into, that on the sudden it cannot be expected I should find my way out. You must give me time to look about me and recollect myself.

Phil. Hark; is not this the college bell?

Hyl. It rings for prayers.

Phil. We will go in then, if you please, and meet here again tomorrow morning. In the meantime, you may employ your thoughts on this morning's discourse and try if you can find any fallacy in it, or invent any new means to extricate yourself.

Hyl. Agreed.

THE SECOND DIALOGUE

[1.] *Hylas.* I beg your pardon, Philonous, for not meeting you sooner. All this morning my head was so filled with our late conversation that I had not leisure to think of the time of the day, or indeed of anything else.

Philonous. I am glad you were so intent upon it, in hopes if there were any mistakes in your concessions, or fallacies in my reasonings from them, you will now discover them to me.

Hyl. I assure you I have done nothing ever since I saw you but search after mistakes and fallacies, and, with that view, have minutely examined the whole series of yesterday's discourse; but all in vain, for the notions it led me into, upon review, appear still more clear and evident; and the more I consider them, the more irresistibly do they force my assent.

Phil. And is not this, think you, a sign that they are genuine, that they proceed from nature and are conformable to right reason? Truth and beauty are in this alike, that the strictest survey sets them both off to advantage, while the false luster of error and disguise cannot endure being reviewed or too nearly inspected.

Hyl. I own there is a great deal in what you say. Nor can anyone be more entirely satisfied of the truth of those odd consequences so long as I have in view the reasonings that lead to them. But when these are out of my thoughts, there seems, on the other hand, something so satisfactory, so natural and intelligible in the modern way of explaining things that I profess I know not how to reject it.

Phil. I know not what way you mean.

Hyl. I mean the way of accounting for our sensations or ideas.

Phil. How is that?

Hyl. It is supposed the soul makes her residence in some part of the brain, from which the nerves take their rise, and are thence extended to all parts of the body; and that outward objects, by the different impressions they make on the organs of sense, communicate certain vibrative motions to the nerves, and these, being filled with spirits, propagate them to the brain or seat of the soul, which, according to the various impressions or traces thereby made in the brain, is variously affected with ideas.

Phil. And call you this an explication of the manner whereby we are affected with ideas?

Hyl. Why not, Philonous; have you anything to object against it?

Phil. I would first know whether I rightly understand your hypothesis. You make certain traces in the brain to be the causes or occasions of our ideas. Pray tell me whether by the "brain" you mean any sensible thing.

Hyl. What else think you I could mean?

Phil. Sensible things are all immediately perceivable; and those things which are immediately perceivable are ideas, and these exist only in the mind. This much you have, if I mistake not, long since agreed to.

Hyl. I do not deny it.

Phil. The brain therefore you speak of, being a sensible thing, exists only in the mind. Now I would fain know whether you think it reasonable to suppose that one idea or thing existing in the mind occasions all other ideas. And if you think so, pray how do you account for the origin of that primary idea or brain itself?

Hyl. I do not explain the origin of our ideas by that brain which is perceivable to sense, this being itself only a combination of sensible ideas, but by another which I imagine.

Phil. But are not things imagined as truly *in the mind* as things perceived?

Hyl. I must confess they are.

Phil. It comes, therefore, to the same thing; and you have been all this while accounting for ideas by certain motions or impressions in the brain, that is, by some alterations in an idea, whether sensible or imaginable it matters not.

Hyl. I begin to suspect my hypothesis.

Phil. Besides spirits, all that we know or conceive are our own ideas. When, therefore, you say all ideas are occasioned by impressions in the brain, do you conceive this brain or no? If you do, then you talk of ideas imprinted in an idea causing that same idea, which is absurd. If you do not conceive it, you talk unintelligibly, instead of forming a reasonable hypothesis.

Hyl. I now clearly see it was a mere dream. There is nothing in it.

Phil. You need not be much concerned at it, for, after all, this way of explaining things, as you called it, could never have satisfied any reasonable man. What connection is there between a motion in the nerves and the sensations of sound or color in the mind? Or how is it possible these should be the effect of that?

Hyl. But I could never think it had so little in it as now it seems to have.

Phil. Well then, are you at length satisfied that no sensible things have a real existence, and that you are in truth an arrant *skeptic*?

Hyl. It is too plain to be denied.

[2.] *Phil.* Look! are not the fields covered with a delightful verdure? Is there not something in the woods and groves, in the rivers and clear springs, that soothes, that delights, that transports the soul? At the prospect of the wide and deep ocean, or some huge mountain whose top is lost in the clouds, or of an old gloomy forest, are not our minds filled with a pleasing horror? Even in rocks and deserts is there not an agreeable wildness? How sincere a pleasure is it to behold the natural beauties of the earth! To preserve and renew our relish for them, is not the veil of night alternately drawn over her face, and does she not change her dress with the seasons? How aptly are the elements disposed! What variety and use in the meanest productions of nature! What delicacy, what beauty, what contrivance in animal and vegetable bodies! How exquisitely are all things suited, as well to their particular ends as to constitute apposite parts of the whole! And while they mutually aid and support, do they not also set off and illustrate each other? Raise now your thoughts from this ball of earth to all those glorious luminaries that adorn the high arch of heaven. The motion and situation of the planets, are they not admirable for use and order? Were those (miscalled "erratic") globes ever known to stray in their repeated journeys through the pathless void? Do they not measure areas round the sun ever proportioned to the times? So fixed, so immutable are the laws by which the unseen Author of Nature actuates the universe. How vivid and radiant is the luster of the fixed stars! How magnificent and rich that negligent profusion with which they appear to be scattered throughout the whole azure vault! Yet, if you take the telescope, it brings into your sight a new host of stars that escape the naked eye. Here they seem contiguous and minute, but to a nearer view, immense orbs of light at various distances, far sunk in the abyss of space. Now you must call imagination to your aid. The feeble narrow sense cannot descry innumerable worlds revolving round the central fires, and in those worlds the energy of an all-perfect Mind displayed in endless forms. But neither sense nor imagination are big enough to comprehend the boundless extent with all its glittering furniture. Though the laboring mind exert and strain each power to its utmost reach, there still stands out ungrasped a surplusage immeasurable. Yet all the vast bodies that compose this mighty frame, how distant and remote soever, are by some secret mechanism, some divine art and force linked in a mutual dependence and intercourse with each other, even with this earth, which was almost slipt from my thoughts and lost in the crowd of worlds. Is not the whole system immense, beautiful, glorious beyond expression and beyond thought! What treatment, then, do those philosophers deserve who would deprive these noble and delightful scenes of all reality? How should those principles be entertained that lead us to think all the visible beauty of the creation a false imaginary glare? To be plain, can you expect this skepticism of yours will not be thought extravagantly absurd by all men of sense?

[3.] *Hyl.* Other men may think as they please, but for your part you have nothing to reproach me with. My comfort is you are as much a skeptic as I am.

Phil. There, Hylas, I must beg leave to differ from you.

Hyl. What! have you all along agreed to the premises, and do you now deny the conclusion and leave me to maintain those paradoxes by myself which you led me into? This surely is not fair.

Phil. I deny that I agreed with you in those notions that led to skepticism. You indeed said the *reality* of sensible things consisted in an *absolute existence* out of the minds of spirits, or distinct from their being perceived. And, pursuant to this notion of reality, you are obliged to deny sensible things any real existence; that is, according to your own definition, you profess yourself a skeptic. But I neither said nor thought the reality of sensible things was to be defined after that manner. To me it is evident, for the reasons you allow of, that sensible things cannot exist otherwise than in a mind or spirit. Whence I conclude, not that they have no real existence, but that, seeing they depend not on my thought and have an existence distinct from being perceived by me, *there must be some other mind wherein they exist.* As sure, therefore, as the sensible world really exists, so sure is there an infinite omnipresent Spirit, who contains and supports it.

Hyl. What! this is no more than I and all Christians hold; nay, and all others, too, who believe there is a God and that He knows and comprehends all things.

Phil. Aye, but here lies the difference. Men commonly believe that all things are known or perceived by God, because they believe the being of a God; whereas I, on the other side, immediately and necessarily conclude the being of a God, because all sensible things must be perceived by Him.

Hyl. But so long as we all believe the same thing, what matter is it how we come by that belief?

Phil. But neither do we agree in the same opinion. For philosophers, though they acknowledge all corporeal beings to be perceived by God, yet they attribute to them an absolute subsistence distinct from their being perceived by any mind whatever, which I do not. Besides, is there no difference between saying, "there is a God, therefore He perceives all things," and saying, "sensible things do really exist; and if they really exist, they are necessarily perceived by an infinite mind: therefore there is an infinite mind, or God"? This furnishes you with a direct and immediate demonstration, from a most evident principle, of the *being of a God*. Divines and philosophers had proved beyond all controversy, from the beauty and usefulness of the several parts of the creation, that it was the workmanship of God. But that—setting aside all help of astronomy and natural philosophy, all contemplation of the contrivance, order, and adjustment of things—an infinite mind should be necessarily inferred from the bare *existence* of the sensible world is an advantage peculiar to them only who have made this easy reflection, that the sensible world is that which we perceive by our several senses; and that nothing is perceived by the senses besides ideas; and that no idea or archetype of an idea can exist otherwise than in a mind. You may now, without any laborious search into the sciences, without any subtlety of reason or tedious length of discourse, oppose and baffle the most strenuous advocate for atheism, those miserable refuges, whether in an eternal succession of unthinking causes and effects or in a fortuitous concourse of atoms; those wild imaginations of Vanini,[5] Hobbes, and Spinoza; in a word, the whole system of atheism, is it not entirely overthrown by this single reflection on the repugnancy included in supposing the whole or any part, even the most rude and shapeless, of the visible world to exist without a mind? Let any one of those abettors of impiety but look into his own thoughts, and there try if he can conceive how so much as a rock, a desert, a chaos, or confused jumble of atoms, how anything at all, either sensible or imaginable, can exist independent of a mind, and he need go no further to be convinced of

---

[5] [Lucilio Vanini (1585–1619), Italian freethinker, author of *Ampitheatrum aeternae providentiae divino-magicum* (1615) and *De admirandis naturae reginae deaeque mortalium arcanis* (Paris, 1616), burned at the stake for his atheism.]

his folly. Can anything be fairer than to put a dispute on such an issue and leave it to a man himself to see if he can conceive, even in thought, what he holds to be true in fact, and from a notional to allow it a real existence?

[4.] *Hyl.* It cannot be denied there is something highly serviceable to religion in what you advance. But do you not think it looks very like a notion entertained by some eminent moderns,[6] of *seeing all things in God?*

Phil. I would gladly know that opinion; pray explain it to me.

Hyl. They conceive that the soul, being immaterial, is incapable of being united with material things so as to perceive them in themselves, but that she perceives them by her union with the substance of God, which, being spiritual, is therefore purely intelligible, or capable of being the immediate object of a spirit's thought. Besides, the divine essence contains in it perfections correspondent to each created being, and which are, for that reason, proper to exhibit or represent them to the mind.

Phil. I do not understand how our ideas, which are things altogether passive and inert, can be the essence or any part (or like any part) of the essence or substance of God, who is an impassive, indivisible, purely active being. Many more difficulties and objections there are which occur at first view against this hypothesis; but I shall only add that it is liable to all the absurdities of the common hypothesis, in making a created world exist otherwise than in the mind of a Spirit. Besides all which it has this peculiar to itself that it makes that material world serve to no purpose. And if it pass for a good argument against other hypotheses in the sciences that they suppose nature or the divine wisdom to make something in vain, or do that by tedious roundabout methods which might have been performed in a much more easy and compendious way, what shall we think of that hypothesis which supposes the whole world made in vain?

Hyl. But what say you, are not you too of opinion that we

[6] [I.e., Malebranche. See *Principles*, note 13, p. 55, and note 21, p. 96.]

see all things in God? If I mistake not, what you advance comes near it.

Phil. Few men think, yet all have opinions. Hence men's opinions are superficial and confused. It is nothing strange that tenets which in themselves are ever so different should nevertheless be confounded with each other by those who do not consider them attentively. I shall not therefore be surprised if some men imagine that I run into the enthusiasm of Malebranche, though in truth I am very remote from it. He builds on the most abstract general ideas, which I entirely disclaim. He asserts an absolute external world, which I deny. He maintains that we are deceived by our senses and know not the real natures or the true forms and figures of extended beings; of all which I hold the direct contrary. So that upon the whole there are no principles more fundamentally opposite than his and mine. It must be owned I entirely agree with what the Holy Scripture says, "That in God we live and move and have our being." But that we see things in His essence, after the manner above set forth, I am far from believing. Take here in brief my meaning: It is evident that the things I perceive are my own ideas, and that no idea can exist unless it be in a mind. Nor is it less plain that these ideas or things by me perceived, either themselves or their archetypes, exist independently of my mind; since I know myself not to be their author, it being out of my power to determine at pleasure what particular ideas I shall be affected with upon opening my eyes or ears. They must therefore exist in some other mind, whose will it is they should be exhibited to me. The things, I say, immediately perceived are ideas or, sensations, call them which you will. But how can any idea or sensation exist in, or be produced by, anything but a mind or spirit? This indeed is inconceivable; and to assert that which is inconceivable is to talk nonsense, is it not?

Hyl. Without doubt.

Phil. But, on the other hand, it is very conceivable that they should exist in and be produced by a spirit, since this is no more than I daily experience in myself, inasmuch as I perceive numberless ideas, and, by an act of my will, can form a great variety of them and raise them up in my imagination; though, it must be confessed, these creatures of the fancy are not altogether so distinct, so strong, vivid, and permanent as those perceived by my senses, which latter are called "real things." From all which I conclude, *there is a Mind which affects me every moment with all the sensible impressions I perceive.* And from the variety, order, and manner of these I conclude the Author of them to be *wise, powerful, and good beyond comprehension.* Mark it well; I do not say: "I see things by perceiving that which represents them in the intelligible Substance of God." This I do not understand; but I say: "the things by me perceived are known by the understanding and produced by the will of an infinite Spirit." And is not all this most plain and evident? Is there any more in it than what a little observation of our own minds, and that which passes in them, not only enables us to conceive but also obliges us to acknowledge?

[5.] *Hyl.* I think I understand you very clearly and own the proof you give of a Deity seems no less evident than it is surprising. But allowing that God is the supreme and universal cause of all things, yet may there not be still a third nature besides spirits and ideas? May we not admit a subordinate and limited cause of our ideas? In a word, may there not for all that be *matter?*

Phil. How often must I inculcate the same thing? You allow the things immediately perceived by sense to exist nowhere without the mind; but there is nothing perceived by sense which is not perceived immediately: therefore there is nothing sensible that exists without the mind. The matter, therefore, which you still insist on is something intelligible, I suppose something that may be discovered by reason, and not by sense.

Hyl. You are in the right.

Phil. Pray let me know what reasoning your belief of matter is grounded on, and what this matter is in your present sense of it.

Hyl. I find myself affected with various ideas whereof I know I am not the cause; neither are they the cause of themselves or of one another, or capable of subsisting by themselves, as being altogether inactive, fleeting, dependent beings. They have therefore some cause distinct from me and them, of which I pretend to know no more than that it is *the cause of my ideas.* And this thing, whatever it be, I call "matter."

Phil. Tell me, Hylas, has everyone a liberty to change the current proper signification annexed to a common name in any language? For example, suppose a traveler should tell you that in a certain country men pass unhurt through the fire; and, upon explaining himself, you found he meant by the word "fire" that which others call "water"; or, if he should assert that there are trees that walk upon two legs, meaning men by the term "trees." Would you think this reasonable?

Hyl. No, I should think it very absurd. Common custom is the standard of propriety in language. And for any man to affect speaking improperly is to pervert the use of speech, and can never serve to a better purpose than to protract and multiply disputes where there is no difference in opinion.

Phil. And does not "matter," in the common current acceptation of the word, signify an extended, solid, movable, unthinking, inactive substance?

Hyl. It does.

Phil. And has it not been made evident that no such substance can possibly exist? And though it should be allowed to exist, yet how can that which is *inactive* be a *cause,* or that which is *unthinking* be a *cause of thought*? You may, indeed, if you please, annex to the word "matter" a contrary meaning to what is vulgarly received, and tell me you understand by it an unextended, thinking, active being which is the cause of our ideas. But what else is this than to play with words and run into that very fault you just now condemned with so much reason? I do by no means find fault with your reasoning, in that you collect a cause from the phenomena; but I deny that the cause deducible by reason can properly be termed "matter."

Hyl. There is indeed something in what you say. But I am afraid you do not thoroughly comprehend my meaning. I would by no means be thought to deny that God, or an infinite Spirit, is the Supreme Cause of all things. All I contend for is that, subordinate to the Supreme Agent, there is a cause of a limited and inferior nature which concurs in the production of our ideas, not by any act of will or spiritual efficiency, but by that kind of action which belongs to matter, viz., motion.

Phil. I find you are at every turn relapsing into your old exploded conceit, of a movable and consequently an extended substance existing without the mind. What! have you already forgotten you were convinced, or are you willing I should repeat what has been said on that head? In truth, this is not fair dealing in you still to suppose the being of that which you have so often acknowledged to have no being. But, not to insist further on what has been so largely handled, I ask whether all your ideas are not perfectly passive and inert, including nothing of action in them?

Hyl. They are.

Phil. And are sensible qualities anything else but ideas?

Hyl. How often have I acknowledged that they are not.

Phil. But is not motion a sensible quality?

Hyl. It is.

Phil. Consequently, it is no action?

Hyl. I agree with you. And indeed it is very plain that when I stir my finger it remains passive, but my will which produced the motion is active.

Phil. Now I desire to know, in the first place, whether, motion being allowed to be no action, you can conceive any action besides volition; and, in the second place, whether to say something and conceive nothing be not to talk nonsense; and, lastly, whether, having considered the premises, you do not perceive that to suppose any efficient or active cause of our ideas other than *spirit* is highly absurd and unreasonable?

[6.] *Hyl.* I give up the point entirely. But, though matter may not be a cause, yet what hinders its being an *instrument* subservient to the Supreme Agent in the production of our ideas?

Phil. An instrument say you; pray what may be the figure, springs, wheels, and motions of that instrument?

Hyl. Those I pretend to determine nothing of, both the substance and its qualities being entirely unknown to me.

Phil. What! You are then of opinion it is made up of unknown parts, that it has unknown motions and an unknown shape?

Hyl. I do not believe that it has any figure or motion at all, being already convinced that no sensible qualities can exist in an unperceiving substance.

Phil. But what notion is it possible to frame of an instrument void of all sensible qualities, even extension itself?

Hyl. I do not pretend to have any notion of it.

Phil. And what reason have you to think this unknown, this inconceivable somewhat does exist? Is it that you imagine God cannot act as well without it, or that you find by experience the use of some such thing when you form ideas in your own mind?

Hyl. You are always teasing me for reasons of my belief. Pray what reasons have you not to believe it?

Phil. It is to me a sufficient reason not to believe the existence of anything if I see no reason for believing it. But, not to insist on reasons for believing, you will not so much as let me know what it is you would have me believe, since you say you have no manner of notion of it. After all, let me entreat you to consider whether it be like a philosopher, or even like a man of common sense, to pretend to believe you know not what, and you know not why.

Hyl. Hold, Philonous. When I tell you matter is an *instrument*, I do not mean altogether nothing. It is true I know not the particular kind of instrument, but, however, I have some notion of *instrument in general*, which I apply to it.

Phil. But what if it should prove that there is something, even in the most general notion of *instrument,* as taken in a distinct sense from *cause,* which makes the use of it inconsistent with the divine attributes?

Hyl. Make that appear and I shall give up the point.

Phil. What mean you by the general nature or notion of instrument?

Hyl. That which is common to all particular instruments composes the general notion.

Phil. Is it not common to all instruments that they are applied to the doing those things only which cannot be performed by the mere act of our wills? Thus, for instance, I never use an instrument to move my finger, because it is done by a volition. But I should use one if I were to remove part of a rock or tear up a tree by the roots. Are you of the same mind? Or can you show any example where an instrument is made use of in producing an effect immediately depending on the will of the agent?

Hyl. I own I cannot.

Phil. How, therefore, can you suppose that an all-perfect Spirit, on whose will all things have an absolute and immediate dependence, should need an instrument in His operations or, not needing it, make use of it? Thus it seems to me that you are obliged to own the use of a lifeless inactive instrument to be incompatible with the infinite perfection of God, that is, by your own confession, to give up the point.

Hyl. It does not readily occur what I can answer you.

Phil. But methinks you should be ready to own the truth when it has been fairly proved to you. We, indeed, who are beings of finite powers, are forced to make use of instruments. And the use of an instrument shows the agent to be limited by rules of another's prescription, and that he cannot obtain his end but in such a way and by such conditions. Whence it seems a clear consequence that the Supreme Unlimited Agent uses no tool or instrument at all. The will of an Omnipotent Spirit is no sooner exerted than executed, without the application of means, which, if they are employed by inferior agents, it is not upon account of any real efficacy that is in them, or necessary aptitude to produce any effect, but merely in compliance with the laws of nature or those conditions prescribed to them by the First Cause, who is Himself above all limitation or prescription whatsoever.

[7.] *Hyl.* I will no longer maintain that matter is an instrument. However, I would not be understood to give up its existence neither, since, notwithstanding what has been said, it may still be an *occasion*.

Phil. How many shapes is your matter to take? Or how often must it be proved not to exist before you are content to part with it? But to say no more of this (though by all the laws of disputation I may justly blame you for so frequently changing the signification of the principal term), I would fain know what you mean by affirming that matter is an occasion, having already denied it to be a cause. And when you have shown in what sense you understand occasion, pray, in the next place, be pleased to show me what reason induces you to believe there is such an occasion of our ideas?

Hyl. As to the first point: by "occasion" I mean an inactive unthinking being, at the presence whereof God excites ideas in our minds.

Phil. And what may be the nature of that inactive unthinking being?

Hyl. I know nothing of its nature.

Phil. Proceed then to the second point and assign some reason why we should allow an existence to this inactive, unthinking, unknown thing.

Hyl. When we see ideas produced in our minds after an orderly and constant manner, it is natural to think they have some fixed and regular occasions at the presence of which they are excited.

Phil. You acknowledge then God alone to be the cause of our ideas, and that He causes them at the presence of those occasions.

Hyl. That is my opinion.

Phil. Those things which you say are present to God, without doubt He perceives.

Hyl. Certainly; otherwise they could not be to Him an occasion of acting.

Phil. Not to insist now on your making sense of this hypothesis, or answering all the puzzling questions and difficulties it is liable to: I only ask whether the order and regularity observable in the series of our ideas, or the course of nature, be not sufficiently accounted for by the wisdom and power of God; and whether it does not derogate from those attributes to suppose He is influenced, directed, or put in mind, when and what He is to act, by an unthinking substance? And, lastly, whether, in case I granted all you contend for, it would make anything to your purpose, it not being easy to conceive how the external or absolute existence of an unthinking substance, distinct from its being perceived, can be inferred from my allowing that there are certain things perceived by the mind of God which are to Him the occasion of producing ideas in us?

Hyl. I am perfectly at a loss what to think, this notion of occasion seeming now altogether as groundless as the rest.

Phil. Do you not at length perceive that in all these different acceptations of matter you have been only supposing you know not what, for no manner of reason and to no kind of use?

[8.] *Hyl.* I freely own myself less fond of my notions since they have been so accurately examined. But still, methinks, I have some confused perception that there is such a thing as matter.

Phil. Either you perceive the being of matter immediately or mediately. If immediately, pray inform me by which of the senses you perceive it. If mediately, let me know by what reasoning it is inferred from those things which you perceive immediately. So much for the perception. Then for the matter itself, I ask whether it is object, substratum, cause, instrument, or occasion? You have already pleaded for each of these, shifting your notions and making matter to appear sometimes in one shape, then in another. And what you have offered has been disapproved and rejected by yourself. If you have anything new to advance I would gladly hear it.

Hyl. I think I have already offered all I had to say on those heads. I am at a loss what more to urge.

Phil. And yet you are loath to part with your old prejudice. But to make you quit it more easily, I desire that, besides what has been hitherto suggested, you will further consider whether, upon supposition that matter exists, you can possibly conceive how you should be affected by it? Or, supposing it did not exist, whether it be not evident you might for all that be affected with the same ideas you now are, and consequently have the very same reasons to believe its existence that you now can have?

Hyl. I acknowledge it is possible we might perceive all things just as we do now, though there was no matter in the world; neither can I conceive, if there be matter, how it should produce any idea in our minds. And I do further grant you have entirely satisfied me that it is impossible there should be such a thing as matter in any of the foregoing acceptations. But still I cannot help supposing that there is *matter* in some sense or other. What that is I do not indeed pretend to determine.

Phil. I do not expect you should define exactly the nature of that unknown being. Only be pleased to tell me whether it is a substance—and if so, whether you can suppose a substance without accidents; or in case you suppose it to have accidents or qualities, I desire you will let me know what those qualities are, at least what is meant by "matter's supporting them"?

[9.] *Hyl.* We have already argued on those points. I have no more to say to them. But, to prevent any further questions, let me tell you I at present understand by "matter" neither substance nor accident, thinking nor extended being, neither cause, instrument, nor occasion, but something entirely unknown, distinct from all these.

Phil. It seems then you include in your present notion of matter nothing but the general abstract idea of *entity*.

Hyl. Nothing else, save only that I superadd to this general idea the negation of all those particular things, qualities, or ideas that I perceive, imagine, or in anywise apprehend.

Phil. Pray where do you suppose this unknown matter to exist?

Hyl. Oh Philonous! now you think you have entangled me; for if I say it exists in place, then you will infer that it exists in the mind, since it is agreed that place or extension exists only in the mind; but I am not ashamed to own my ignorance. I know not where it exists; only I am sure it exists not in place. There is a negative answer for you. And you must expect no other to all the questions you put for the future about matter.

Phil. Since you will not tell me where it exists, be pleased to inform me after what manner you suppose it to exist, or what you mean by its "existence"?

Hyl. It neither thinks nor acts, neither perceives nor is perceived.

Phil. But what is there positive in your abstracted notion of its existence?

Hyl. Upon a nice observation, I do not find I have any positive notion or meaning at all. I tell you again, I am not ashamed to own my ignorance. I know not what is meant by its existence or how it exists.

Phil. Continue, good Hylas, to act the same ingenuous part and tell me sincerely whether you can frame a distinct idea of entity in general, prescinded from and exclusive of all thinking and corporeal beings, all particular things whatsoever.

Hyl. Hold, let me think a little— I profess, Philonous, I do not find that I can. At first glance methought I had some dilute and airy notion of pure entity in abstract, but, upon closer attention, it has quite vanished out of sight. The more I think on it, the more am I confirmed in my prudent resolution of giving none but negative answers and not pretending to the least degree of any positive knowledge or conception of matter, its *where*, its *how*, its *entity*, or anything belonging to it.

Phil. When, therefore, you speak of the existence of matter, you have not any notion in your mind?

Hyl. None at all.

Phil. Pray tell me if the case stands not thus: at first, from a belief of material substance, you would have it that the immediate objects existed without the mind; then, that they are archetypes; then, causes; next, instruments; then, occasions: lastly, s*omething in general,* which being interpreted proves *nothing.* So matter comes to nothing. What think you, Hylas, is not this a fair summary of your whole proceeding?

Hyl. Be that as it will, yet I still insist upon it, that our not being able to conceive a thing is no argument against its existence.

Phil. That from a cause, effect, operation, sign, or other circumstance there may reasonably be inferred the existence of a thing not immediately perceived; and that it were absurd for any man to argue against the existence of that thing, from his having no direct and positive notion of it, I freely own. But where there is nothing of all this, where neither reason nor revelation induces us to believe the existence of a thing where we have not even a relative notion of it, where an abstraction is made from perceiving and being perceived, from spirit and idea, lastly, where there is not so much as the most inadequate or faint idea pretended to, I will not, indeed, thence conclude against the reality of any notion or existence of anything; but my inference shall be that you mean nothing at all, that you employ words to no manner of purpose, without any design or signification whatsoever. And I leave it to you to consider how mere jargon should be treated.

Hyl. To deal frankly with you, Philonous, your arguments seem in themselves unanswerable, but they have not so great an effect on me as to produce that entire conviction, that hearty acquiescence, which attends demonstration. I find myself still relapsing into an obscure surmise of I know not what —*matter*.

Phil. But are you not sensible, Hylas, that two things must concur to take away all scruple and work a plenary assent in the mind? Let a visible object be set in never so clear a light, yet, if there is any imperfection in the sight, or if the eye is not directed toward it, it will not be distinctly seen. And though a demonstration be never so well grounded and fairly proposed, yet, if there is withal a stain of prejudice or a wrong bias on the understanding, can it be expected on a sudden to perceive clearly and adhere firmly to the truth? No, there is need of time and pains: the attention must be awakened and detained by a frequent repetition of the same thing placed oft in the same, oft in different lights. I have said it already, and find I must still repeat and inculcate, that it is an unaccountable license you take in pretending to maintain you know not what, for you know not what reason, to you know not what purpose. Can this be paralleled in any art or science, any sect or profession of men? Or is there anything so barefacedly groundless and unreasonable to be met with even in the lowest of common conversation? But, perhaps, you will still say, matter may exist, though at the same time you neither know what is meant by "matter" or by its "existence." This indeed is surprising, and the more so because it is altogether voluntary, you not being led to it by any one reason, for I challenge you to show me that thing in nature which needs matter to explain or account for it.

[10.] *Hyl.* The reality of things cannot be maintained without supposing the existence of matter. And is not this, think you, a good reason why I should be earnest in its defense?

Phil. The reality of things! What things, sensible or intelligible?

Hyl. Sensible things.

Phil. My glove, for example?

Hyl. That or any other thing perceived by the senses.

Phil. But to fix on some particular thing, is it not a sufficient evidence to me of the existence of this *glove* that I see it and feel it and wear it? Or, if this will not do, how is it possible I should be assured of the reality of this thing which I actually see in this place by supposing that some unknown thing, which I never did or can see, exists after an unknown manner, in an unknown place, or in no place at all? How can the supposed reality of that which is intangible be a proof that anything tangible really exists? Or of that which is invisible, that any visible thing or, in general, of anything which is imperceptible, that a perceptible exists? Do but explain this and I shall think nothing too hard for you.

[11.] *Hyl.* Upon the whole, I am content to own the existence of matter is highly improbable; but the direct and absolute impossibility of it does not appear to me.

Phil. But granting matter to be possible, yet, upon that account merely, it can have no more claim to existence than a golden mountain or a centaur.

Hyl. I acknowledge it, but still you do not deny it is possible; and that which is possible, for aught you know, may actually exist.

Phil. I deny it to be possible; and have, if I mistake not, evidently proved, from your own concessions, that it is not. In the common sense of the word "matter," is there any more implied than an extended, solid, figured, movable substance existing without the mind? And have not you acknowledged, over and over, that you have seen evident reason for denying the possibility of such a substance?

Hyl. True, but that is only one sense of the term "matter."

Phil. But is it not the only proper genuine received sense? And if matter in such a sense be proved impossible, may it not be thought with good grounds absolutely impossible? Else how could anything be proved impossible? Or, indeed, how could there be any proof at all one way or other to a man who takes the liberty to unsettle and change the common signification of words?

Hyl. I thought philosophers might be allowed to speak

more accurately than the vulgar, and were not always confined to the common acceptation of a term.

Phil. But this now mentioned is the common received sense among philosophers themselves. But, not to insist on that, have you not been allowed to take matter in what sense you pleased? And have you not used this privilege in the utmost extent, sometimes entirely changing, at others leaving out or putting into the definition of it whatever, for the present, best served your design, contrary to all the known rules of reason and logic? And has not this shifting, unfair method of yours spun out our dispute to an unnecessary length, matter having been particularly examined and by your own confession refuted in each of those senses? And can any more be required to prove the absolute impossibility of a thing than the proving it impossible in every particular sense that either you or anyone else understands it in?

Hyl. But I am not so thoroughly satisfied that you have proved the impossibility of matter in the last most obscure abstracted and indefinite sense.

Phil. When is a thing shown to be impossible?

Hyl. When a repugnancy is demonstrated between the ideas comprehended in its definition.

Phil. But where there are no ideas, there no repugnancy can be demonstrated between ideas?

Hyl. I agree with you.

Phil. Now, in that which you call the obscure indefinite sense of the word "matter," it is plain, by your own confession, there was included no idea at all, no sense except an unknown sense, which is the same thing as none. You are not, therefore, to expect I should prove a repugnancy between ideas where there are no ideas, or the impossibility of matter taken in an *unknown* sense, that is, no sense at all. My business was only to show you meant *nothing;* and this you were brought to own. So that, in all your various senses, you have been shown either to mean nothing at all or, if anything, an absurdity. And if this be not sufficient to prove the impossibility of a thing, I desire you will let me know what is.

Hyl. I acknowledge you have proved that matter is impossible, nor do I see what more can be said in defense of it. But, at the same time that I give up this, I suspect all my other notions. For surely none could be more seemingly evident than this once was; and yet it now seems as false and absurd as ever it did true before. But I think we have discussed the point sufficiently for the present. The remaining part of the day I would willingly spend in running over in my thoughts the several heads of this morning's conversation, and tomorrow shall be glad to meet you here again about the same time.

Phil. I will not fail to attend you.

THE THIRD DIALOGUE

[1.] *Philonous.* Tell me, Hylas, what are the fruits of yesterday's meditation? Has it confirmed you in the same mind you were in at parting, or have you since seen cause to change your opinion?

Hylas. Truly my opinion is that all our opinions are alike vain and uncertain. What we approve today, we condemn tomorrow. We keep a stir about knowledge and spend our lives in the pursuit of it, when, alas! we know nothing all the while; nor do I think it possible for us ever to know anything in this life. Our faculties are too narrow and too few. Nature certainly never intended us for speculation.

Phil. What! say you we can know nothing, Hylas?

Hyl. There is not that single thing in the world whereof we can know the real nature, or what it is in itself.

Phil. Will you tell me I do not really know what fire or water is?

Hyl. You may indeed know that fire appears hot, and water fluid; but this is no more than knowing what sensations are produced in your own mind upon the application of fire and water to your organs of sense. Their internal constitution, their true and real nature, you are utterly in the dark as to *that*.

Phil. Do I not know this to be a real stone that I stand on, and that which I see before my eyes to be a real tree?

Hyl. Know? No, it is impossible you or any man alive should know it. All you know is that you have such a certain idea or appearance in your own mind. But what is this to the real tree or stone? I tell you that color, figure, and hardness, which you perceive, are not the real natures of those things, or in the least like them. The same may be said of all other real things or corporeal substances which compose the world. They have, none of them, anything in themselves, like those sensible qualities by us perceived. We should not, therefore, pretend to affirm or know anything of them, as they are in their own nature.

Phil. But surely, Hylas, I can distinguish gold, for example, from iron; and how could this be if I knew not what either truly was?

Hyl. Believe me, Philonous, you can only distinguish between your own ideas. That yellowness, that weight, and other sensible qualities, think you they are really in the gold? They are only relative to the senses and have no absolute existence in nature. And in pretending to distinguish the species of real things by the appearances in your mind, you may perhaps act as wisely as he that should conclude two men were of a different species because their clothes were not of the same color.

Phil. It seems, then, we are altogether put off with the appearances of things, and those false ones, too. The very meat I eat, and the cloth I wear, have nothing in them like what I see and feel.

Hyl. Even so.

Phil. But is it not strange the whole world should be thus imposed on and so foolish as to believe their senses? And yet I know not how it is, but men eat, and drink, and sleep, and perform all the offices of life as comfortably and conveniently as if they really knew the things they are conversant about.

Hyl. They do so; but you know ordinary practice does not require a nicety of speculative knowledge. Hence the vulgar retain their mistakes, and for all that make a shift to bustle through the affairs of life. But philosophers know better things.

Phil. You mean they know that they *know nothing*.

Hyl. That is the very top and perfection of human knowledge.

Phil. But are you all this while in earnest, Hylas; and are you seriously persuaded that you know nothing real in the world? Suppose you are going to write, would you not call for pen, ink, and paper, like another man; and do you not know what it is you call for?

Hyl. How often must I tell you that I know not the real nature of any one thing in the universe? I may indeed upon occasion make use of pen, ink, and paper. But what any one of them is in its own true nature, I declare positively I know not. And the same is true with regard to every other corporeal thing. And what is more, we are not only ignorant of the true and real nature of things, but even of their existence. It cannot be denied that we perceive such certain appearances or ideas, but it cannot be concluded from thence that bodies really exist. Nay, now I think on it, I must, agreeably to my former concessions, further declare that it is impossible any real corporeal thing should exist in nature.

Phil. You amaze me. Was ever anything more wild and extravagant than the notions you now maintain? And is it not evident you are led into all these extravagances by the belief of *material substance*? This makes you dream of those unknown natures in everything. It is this occasions your distinguishing between the reality and sensible appearances of things. It is to this you are indebted for being ignorant of what everybody else knows perfectly well. Nor is this all: you are not only ignorant of the true nature of everything, but you know not whether any thing really exists or whether there are any true natures at all, forasmuch as you attribute to your material beings an absolute or external existence wherein you suppose their reality consists. And as you are forced in the end to acknowledge such an existence means either a direct repugnancy or nothing at all, it follows that you are obliged to pull down your own hypothesis of material substance and positively to deny the real existence of any part of the universe. And so you are plunged into the deepest and most deplorable skepticism that ever man was. Tell me, Hylas, is it not as I say?

[2.] *Hyl.* I agree with you. *Material substance* was no more than a hypothesis, and a false and groundless one, too. I will no longer spend my breath in defense of it. But whatever hypothesis you advance or whatsoever scheme of things you introduce in its stead, I doubt not it will appear every whit as false; let me but be allowed to question you upon it. That is, suffer me to serve you in your own kind, and I warrant it shall conduct you through as many perplexities and contradictions to the very same state of skepticism that I myself am in at present.

Phil. I assure you, Hylas, I do not pretend to frame any hypothesis at all. I am of a vulgar cast, simple enough to believe my senses and leave things as I find them. To be plain, it is my opinion that the real things are those very things I see and feel, and perceive by my senses. These I know and, finding they answer all the necessities and purposes of life, have no reason to be solicitous about any other unknown beings. A piece of sensible bread, for instance, would stay my stomach better than ten thousand times as much of that insensible, unintelligible real bread you speak of. It is likewise my opinion that colors and other sensible qualities are on the objects. I cannot for my life help thinking that snow is white, and fire hot. You, indeed, who by "snow" and "fire" mean certain external, unperceived, unperceiving substances are in the right to deny whiteness or heat to be affections inherent in them. But I who understand by those words the things I see and feel am obliged to think like other folks. And as I am no skeptic with regard to the nature of things, so neither am I as to their existence. That a thing should be really perceived by my senses and at the same time not really exist is to me a plain contradiction, since I cannot prescind or abstract, even in thought, the existence of a sensible thing from its being perceived. Wood, stones, fire, water, flesh, iron, and the like things which I name and discourse of are things that I know. And I should not have known them but that I perceived them by my senses; and things perceived by the senses are immediately perceived; and things immediately perceived are ideas; and ideas cannot exist without the mind; their existence therefore consists in being perceived; when, therefore, they are actually perceived, there can be no doubt of their existence. Away then with all that skepticism, all those ridiculous philosophical doubts. What a jest is it for a philosopher to question the existence of sensible things till he has it proved to him from the veracity of God [7] or to pretend our knowledge in this point falls short of intuition or demonstration! [8] I might as well doubt of my own being as of the being of those things I actually see and feel.

[3.] *Hyl.* Not so fast, Philonous: You say you cannot conceive how sensible things should exist without the mind. Do you not?

Phil. I do.

Hyl. Supposing you were annihilated, cannot you conceive it possible that things perceivable by sense may still exist?

Phil. I can, but then it must be in another mind. When I deny sensible things an existence out of the mind, I do not mean my mind in particular, but all minds. Now it is plain they have an existence exterior to my mind, since I find them by experience to be independent of it. There is therefore some other mind wherein they exist during the intervals between the times of my perceiving them, as likewise they did before my birth, and would do after my supposed annihilation. And as the same is true with regard to all other finite created spirits, it necessarily follows there is an *omnipresent eternal Mind* which knows and comprehends all things, and exhibits them to our view in such a manner and according to such rules as He Himself has ordained and are by us termed the "laws of nature."

[4.] *Hyl.* Answer me, Philonous. Are all our ideas perfectly inert beings? Or have they any agency included in them?

Phil. They are altogether passive and inert.

Hyl. And is not God an agent, a being purely active?

Phil. I acknowledge it.

Hyl. No idea, therefore, can be like unto or represent the nature of God.

Phil. It cannot.

Hyl. Since, therefore, you have no idea of the mind of God,

---

[7] [I.e., Descartes, *Meditationes de prima philosophia* (Paris, 1641), Sixth Meditation, and elsewhere.]

[8] [I.e., Locke, *Essay*, Bk. IV, chap. 11, sec. 3.]

how can you conceive it possible that things should exist in His mind? Or, if you can conceive the mind of God without having an idea of it, why may not I be allowed to conceive the existence of matter, notwithstanding I have no idea of it?

Phil. As to your first question: I own I have properly no *idea* either of God or any other spirit; for these, being active, cannot be represented by things perfectly inert as our ideas are. I do nevertheless know that I, who am a spirit or thinking substance, exist as certainly as I know my ideas exist. Further, I know what I mean by the terms "I" and "myself"; and I know this immediately or intuitively, though I do not perceive it as I perceive a triangle, a color, or a sound. The mind, spirit, or soul is that indivisible unextended thing which thinks, acts, and perceives. I say "indivisible," because unextended; and "unextended," because extended, figured, movable things are ideas; and that which perceives ideas, which thinks and wills, is plainly itself no idea, nor like an idea. Ideas are things inactive and perceived. And spirits a sort of beings altogether different from them. I do not therefore say my soul is an idea, or like an idea. However, taking the word "idea" in a large sense, my soul may be said to furnish me with an idea, that is, an image or likeness of God, though indeed extremely inadequate. For all the notion I have of God is obtained by reflecting on my own soul, heightening its powers, and removing its imperfections. I have, therefore, though not an inactive idea, yet in *myself* some sort of an active thinking image of the Deity. And though I perceive Him not by sense, yet I have a notion of Him, or know Him by reflection and reasoning. My own mind and my own ideas I have an immediate knowledge of; and, by the help of these, do mediately apprehend the possibility of the existence of other spirits and ideas. Further, from my own being, and from the dependency I find in myself and my ideas, I do, by an act of reason, necessarily infer the existence of a God and of all created things in the mind of God. So much for your first question. For the second: I suppose by this time you can answer it yourself. For you neither perceive matter objectively, as you do an inactive being or idea, nor know it, as you do yourself by a reflex act; neither do you mediately apprehend it by similitude of the one or the other, nor yet collect it by reasoning from that which you know immediately. All which makes the case of *matter* widely different from that of the *Deity*.

[*Hyl*.[9] You say your own soul supplies you with some sort of an idea or image of God. But, at the same time, you acknowledge you have, properly speaking, no idea of your own soul. You even affirm that spirits are a sort of beings altogether different from ideas. Consequently, that no idea can be like a spirit. We have, therefore, no idea of any spirit. You admit nevertheless that there is spiritual substance, although you have no idea of it, while you deny there can be such a thing as material substance, because you have no notion or idea of it. Is this fair dealing? To act consistently, you must either admit matter or reject spirit. What say you to this?

Phil. I say, in the first place, that I do not deny the existence of material substance merely because I have no notion of it, but because the notion of it is inconsistent, or, in other words, because it is repugnant that there should be a notion of it. Many things, for aught I know, may exist whereof neither I nor any other man has or can have any idea or notion whatsoever. But then those things must be possible, that is, nothing inconsistent must be included in their definition. I say, secondly, that, although we believe things to exist which we do not perceive, yet we may not believe that any particular thing exists without some reason for such belief; but I have no reason for believing the existence of matter. I have no immediate intuition thereof, neither can I immediately from my sensations, ideas, notions, actions, or passions infer an unthinking, unperceiving, inactive substance, either by probable deduction or necessary consequence. Whereas the being of my self, that is, my own soul, mind, or thinking principle, I evidently know by reflection. You will forgive me if I repeat the

[9] [The four paragraphs following were added in the 1734 edition. See *Principles*, note 8, p. 35.]

same things in answer to the same objections. In the very notion or definition of "material substance" there is included a manifest repugnance and inconsistency. But this cannot be said of the notion of spirit. That ideas should exist in what does not perceive, or be produced by what does not act, is repugnant. But it is no repugnancy to say that a perceiving thing should be the subject of ideas, or an active thing the cause of them. It is granted we have neither an immediate evidence nor a demonstrative knowledge of the existence of other finite spirits, but it will not thence follow that such spirits are on a foot with material substances, if to suppose the one be inconsistent, and it be not inconsistent to suppose the other; if the one can be inferred by no argument, and there is a probability for the other; if we see signs and effects indicating distinct finite agents like ourselves, and see no sign or symptom whatever that leads to a rational belief of matter. I say, lastly, that I have a notion of spirit, though I have not, strictly speaking, an idea of it. I do not perceive it as an idea, or by means of an idea, but know it by reflection.

Hyl. Notwithstanding all you have said, to me it seems that, according to your own way of thinking, and in consequence of your own principles, it should follow that you are only a system of floating ideas without any substance to support them.[10] Words are not to be used without a meaning. And, as there is no more meaning in *spiritual* substance than in *material* substance, the one is to be exploded as well as the other.

Phil. How often must I repeat that I know or am conscious of my own being, and that *I myself* am not my ideas, but somewhat else, a thinking, active principle that perceives, knows, wills, and operates about ideas. I know that I, one and the same self, perceive both colors and sounds, that a color cannot perceive a sound, nor a sound a color, that I am there-

---

[10] [Cf. David Hume, *A Treatise of Human Nature* (London, 1739), Bk. I, Pt. IV, sec. 6: "The mind is a kind of theater, where several perceptions make their appearance. . . . There is properly no *simplicity* in it at one time, nor *identity* in different. . . . The comparison of the theater must not mislead us. They are the successive perceptions only that constitute the mind."]

fore one individual principle distinct from color and sound, and, for the same reason, from all other sensible things and inert ideas. But I am not in like manner conscious either of the existence or essence of matter. On the contrary, I know that nothing inconsistent can exist, and that the existence of matter implies an inconsistency. Further, I know what I mean when I affirm that there is a spiritual substance or support of ideas, that is, that a spirit knows and perceives ideas. But I do not know what is meant when it is said that an unperceiving substance has inherent in it and supports either ideas or the archetypes of ideas. There is, therefore, upon the whole no parity of case between spirit and matter.]

[5.] *Hyl.* I own myself satisfied in this point. But do you in earnest think the real existence of sensible things consists in their being actually perceived? If so, how comes it that all mankind distinguish between them? Ask the first man you meet, and he shall tell you, "to be perceived" is one thing, and "to exist" is another.

Phil. I am content, Hylas, to appeal to the common sense of the world for the truth of my notion. Ask the gardener why he thinks yonder cherry tree exists in the garden, and he shall tell you, because he sees and feels it; in a word, because he perceives it by his senses. Ask him why he thinks an orange tree not to be there, and he shall tell you, because he does not perceive it. What he perceives by sense, that he terms a real being and says it "is" or "exists"; but that which is not perceivable, the same, he says, has no being.

Hyl. Yes, Philonous, I grant the existence of a sensible thing consists in being perceivable, but not in being actually perceived.

Phil. And what is perceivable but an idea? And can an idea exist without being actually perceived? These are points long since agreed between us.

Hyl. But be your opinion never so true, yet surely you will not deny it is shocking and contrary to the common sense of men. Ask the fellow whether yonder tree has an existence out of his mind; what answer think you he would make?

Phil. The same that I should myself, to wit, that it does exist out of his mind. But then to a Christian it cannot surely be shocking to say, the real tree, existing without his mind, is truly known and comprehended by (that is, *exists in*) the infinite mind of God. Probably he may not at first glance be aware of the direct and immediate proof there is of this, inasmuch as the very being of a tree, or any other sensible thing, implies a mind wherein it is. But the point itself he cannot deny. The question between the materialists and me is not whether things have a *real* existence out of the mind of this or that person, but, whether they have an *absolute* existence, distinct from being perceived by God, and exterior to all minds. This, indeed, some heathens and philosophers have affirmed, but whoever entertains notions of the *Deity* suitable to the Holy Scriptures will be of another opinion.

[6.] *Hyl.* But, according to your notions, what difference is there between real things and chimeras formed by the imagination or the visions of a dream, since they are all equally in the mind?

Phil. The ideas formed by the imagination are faint and indistinct; they have, besides, an entire dependence on the will. But the ideas perceived by sense, that is, real things, are more vivid and clear, and, being imprinted on the mind by a spirit distinct from us, have not the like dependence on our will. There is, therefore, no danger of confounding these with the foregoing, and there is as little of confounding them with the visions of a dream, which are dim, irregular, and confused. And though they should happen to be never so lively and natural, yet, by their not being connected and of a piece with the preceding and subsequent transaction of our lives, they might easily be distinguished from realities. In short, by whatever method you distinguish *things* from *chimeras* on your own scheme, the same, it is evident, will hold also upon mine. For it must be, I presume, by some perceived difference, and I am not for depriving you of any one thing that you perceive.

Hyl. But still, Philonous, you hold there is nothing in the world but spirits and ideas. And this you must needs acknowledge sounds very oddly.

Phil. I own the word "idea," not being commonly used for "thing," sounds something out of the way. My reason for using it was because a necessary relation to the mind is understood to be implied by the term; and it is now commonly used by philosophers to denote the immediate objects of the understanding. But however oddly the proposition may sound in words, yet it includes nothing so very strange or shocking in its sense, which in effect amounts to no more than this, to wit, that there are only things perceiving and things perceived, or that every unthinking being is necessarily, and from the very nature of its existence, perceived by some mind, if not by any finite created mind, yet certainly by the infinite mind of God, in whom "we live, and move, and have our being." Is this as strange as to say the sensible qualities are not on the object or that we cannot be sure of the existence of things, or know anything of their real natures, though we both see and feel them and perceive them by all our senses?

[7.] *Hyl.* And, in consequence of this, must we not think there are no such things as physical or corporeal causes, but that a spirit is the immediate cause of all the *phenomena* in nature? Can there be anything more extravagant than this?

Phil. Yes, it is infinitely more extravagant to say a thing which is inert operates on the mind, and which is unperceiving is the cause of our perceptions. Besides, that which to you I know not for what reason seems so extravagant is no more than the Holy Scriptures assert in a hundred places. In them God is represented as the sole and immediate Author of all those effects which some heathens and philosophers are wont to ascribe to Nature, Matter, Fate, or the like unthinking principle. This is so much the constant language of Scripture that it were needless to confirm it by citations.

Hyl. You are not aware, Philonous, that, in making God the immediate Author of all the motions in nature, you make Him the Author of murder, sacrilege, adultery, and the like heinous sins.

Phil. In answer to that I observe, first, that the imputation of guilt is the same whether a person commits an action with or without an instrument. In case, therefore, you suppose God to act by the mediation of an instrument or occasion called "matter," you as truly make Him the Author of sin as I, who think Him the immediate agent in all those operations vulgarly ascribed to Nature. I further observe that sin or moral turpitude does not consist in the outward physical action or motion, but in the internal deviation of the will from the laws of reason and religion. This is plain, in that the killing an enemy in a battle or putting a criminal legally to death is not thought sinful, though the outward act be the very same with that in the case of murder. Since, therefore, sin does not consist in the physical action, the making God an immediate cause of all such actions is not making Him the Author of sin. Lastly, I have nowhere said that God is the only agent who produces all the motions in bodies. It is true I have denied there are any other agents besides spirits, but this is very consistent with allowing to thinking rational beings, in the production of motions, the use of limited powers, ultimately, indeed, derived from God but immediately under the direction of their own wills, which is sufficient to entitle them to all the guilt of their actions.

[8.] *Hyl.* But the denying matter, Philonous, or corporeal substance; there is the point. You can never persuade me that this is not repugnant to the universal sense of mankind. Were our dispute to be determined by most voices, I am confident you would give up the point without gathering the votes.

Phil. I wish both our opinions were fairly stated and submitted to the judgment of men who had plain common sense, without the prejudices of a learned education. Let me be represented as one who trusts his senses, who thinks he knows the things he sees and feels, and entertains no doubts of their existence; and you fairly set forth with all your doubts, your paradoxes, and your skepticism about you, and I shall willingly acquiesce in the determination of any indifferent person. That there is no substance wherein ideas can exist besides spirit is to me evident. And that the objects immediately perceived are ideas is on all hands agreed. And that sensible qualities are objects immediately perceived no one can deny. It is therefore evident there can be no *substratum* of those qualities but spirit, in which they exist, not by way of mode or property, but as a thing perceived in that which perceives it. I deny, therefore, that there is any unthinking *substratum* of the objects of sense, and in that acceptation that there is any material substance. But if by "material substance" is meant only sensible body, that which is seen and felt (and the unphilosophical part of the world, I dare say, mean no more), then I am more certain of matter's existence than you or any other philosopher pretend to be. If there be anything which makes the generality of mankind averse from the notions I espouse, it is a misapprehension that I deny the reality of sensible things; but as it is you who are guilty of that and not I, it follows that in truth their aversion is against your notions and not mine. I do therefore assert that I am as certain as of my own being that there are bodies or corporeal substances (meaning the things I perceive by my senses), and that, granting this, the bulk of mankind will take no thought about, nor think themselves at all concerned in the fate of, those unknown natures and philosophical quiddities which some men are so fond of.

[9.] *Hyl.* What say you to this? Since, according to you, men judge of the reality of things by their senses, how can a man be mistaken in thinking the moon a plain lucid surface, about a foot in diameter, or a square tower, seen at a distance, round, or an oar, with one end in the water, crooked?

Phil. He is not mistaken with regard to the ideas he actually perceives, but in the inferences he makes from his present perceptions. Thus, in the case of the oar, what he immediately perceives by sight is certainly crooked, and so far he is in the right. But if he thence conclude that upon taking the oar out of the water he shall perceive the same crookedness, or that it would affect his touch as crooked things are wont to do, in that he is mistaken. In like manner, if he shall conclude, from what he perceives in one station, that, in case he advances toward the moon or tower, he should still be affected with the like ideas, he is mistaken. But his mistake lies not in what he perceives immediately and at present (it being a manifest contradiction to suppose he should err in respect of that), but in the wrong judgment he makes concerning the ideas he apprehends to be connected with those immediately perceived, or, concerning the ideas, that from what he perceives at present he imagines would be perceived in other circumstances. The case is the same with regard to the Copernican system. We do not here perceive any motion of the earth, but it were erroneous thence to conclude that, in case we were placed at as great a distance from that as we are now from the other planets, we should not then perceive its motion.

[10.] *Hyl.* I understand you and must needs own you say things plausible enough, but give me leave to put you in mind of one thing. Pray, Philonous, were you not formerly as positive that matter existed as you are now that it does not?

Phil. I was. But here lies the difference. Before, my positiveness was founded, without examination, upon prejudice, but now, after inquiry, upon evidence.

Hyl. After all, it seems our dispute is rather about words than things. We agree in the thing, but differ in the name. That we are affected with ideas from without is evident; and it is no less evident that there must be (I will not say archetypes, but) powers without the mind corresponding to those ideas. And as these powers cannot subsist by themselves, there is some subject of them necessarily to be admitted, which I call "matter," and you call "spirit." This is all the difference.

Phil. Pray, Hylas, is that powerful being, or subject of powers, extended?

Hyl. It has not extension, but it has the power to raise in you the idea of extension.

Phil. It is therefore itself unextended?

Hyl. I grant it.

Phil. Is it not also active?

Hyl. Without doubt; otherwise, how could we attribute powers to it?

Phil. Now let me ask you two questions: *First,* whether it be agreeable to the usage either of philosophers or others to give the name "matter" to an unextended active being? And, *secondly,* whether it be not ridiculously absurd to misapply names contrary to the common use of language?

Hyl. Well then, let it not be called "matter," since you will have it so, but some "third nature," distinct from matter and spirit. For what reason is there why you should call it "spirit"? Does not the notion of spirit imply that it is thinking as well as active and unextended?

Phil. My reason is this: because I have a mind to have some notion or meaning in what I say, but I have no notion of any action distinct from volition, neither can I conceive volition to be anywhere but in a spirit; therefore, when I speak of an active being I am obliged to mean a spirit. Besides, what can be plainer than that a thing which has no ideas in itself cannot impart them to me; and, if it has ideas, surely it must be a spirit. To make you comprehend the point still more clearly, if it be possible: I assert as well as you that, since we are affected from without, we must allow powers to be without, in a being distinct from ourselves. So far we are agreed. But then we differ as to the kind of this powerful being. I will have it to be spirit, you matter or I know not what (I may add, too, you know not what) third nature. Thus I prove it to be spirit. From the effects I see produced I conclude there are actions; and because actions, volitions; and because there are volitions, there must be a will. Again, the things I perceive must have an existence, they or their archetypes, out of my mind; but, being ideas, neither they nor their archetypes can exist otherwise than in an understanding; there is therefore an understanding. But will and understanding constitute in the strictest sense a mind or spirit. The powerful cause, therefore, of my ideas is in strict propriety of speech a *spirit.*

[11.] *Hyl.* And now I warrant you think you have made the point very clear, little suspecting that what you advance leads directly to a contradiction. Is it not an absurdity to imagine any imperfection in God?
Phil. Without a doubt.
Hyl. To suffer pain is an imperfection?
Phil. It is.
Hyl. Are we not sometimes affected with pain and uneasiness by some other being?
Phil. We are.
Hyl. And have you not said that being is a spirit, and is not that spirit God?
Phil. I grant it.
Hyl. But you have asserted that whatever ideas we perceive from without are in the mind which affects us. The ideas, therefore, of pain and uneasiness are in God, or, in other words, God suffers pain; that is to say, there is an imperfection in the divine nature, which, you acknowledge, was absurd. So you are caught in a plain contradiction.
Phil. That God knows or understands all things, and that He knows, among other things, what pain is, even every sort of painful sensation, and what it is for His creatures to suffer pain, I make no question. But that God, though He knows and sometimes causes painful sensations in us, can Himself suffer pain I positively deny. We, who are limited and dependent spirits, are liable to impressions of sense, the effects of an external agent, which, being produced against our wills, are sometimes painful and uneasy. But God, whom no external being can affect, who perceives nothing by sense as we do, whose will is absolute and independent, causing all things, and liable to be thwarted or resisted by nothing, it is evident such a Being as this can suffer nothing, nor be affected with any painful sensation or, indeed, any sensation at all. We are chained to a body; that is to say, our perceptions are connected with corporeal motions. By the law of our nature we are affected upon every alteration in the nervous parts of our sensible body; which sensible body, rightly considered, is noth-

ing but a complexion of such qualities or ideas as have no existence distinct from being perceived by a mind; so that this connection of sensations with corporeal motions means no more than a correspondence in the order of nature between two sets of ideas, or things immediately perceivable. But God is a pure spirit, disengaged from all such sympathy or natural ties. No corporeal motions are attended with the sensations of pain or pleasure in His mind. To know everything knowable is certainly a perfection, but to endure or suffer or feel anything by sense is an imperfection. The former, I say, agrees to God, but not the latter. God knows or has ideas, but His ideas are not conveyed to Him by sense, as ours are. Your not distinguishing where there is so manifest a difference makes you fancy you see an absurdity where there is none.

[12.] *Hyl.* But all this while you have not considered that the quantity of matter has been demonstrated to be proportional to the gravity of bodies. And what can withstand demonstration?

Phil. Let me see how you demonstrate that point.

Hyl. I lay it down for a principle that the moments or quantities of motion in bodies are in a direct compounded reason of the velocities and quantities of matter contained in them. Hence, where the velocities are equal, it follows the moments are directly as the quantity of matter in each. But it is found by experience that all bodies (bating the small inequalities arising from the resistance of the air) descend with an equal velocity; the motion therefore of descending bodies, and consequently their gravity, which is the cause or principle of that motion, is proportional to the quantity of matter, which was to be demonstrated.

Phil. You lay it down as a self-evident principle that the quantity of motion in any body is proportional to the velocity and matter taken together; and this is made use of to prove a proposition from whence the existence of matter is inferred. Pray is not this arguing in a circle?

Hyl. In the premise I only mean that the motion is proportional to the velocity, jointly with the extension and solidity.

Phil. But allowing this to be true, yet it will not thence follow that gravity is proportional to matter in your philosophic sense of the word, except you take it for granted that unknown *substratum,* or whatever else you call it, is proportional to those sensible qualities which to suppose is plainly begging the question. That there is magnitude and solidity or resistance perceived by sense I readily grant, as likewise, that gravity may be proportional to those qualities I will not dispute. But that either these qualities as perceived by us, or the powers producing them, do exist in a *material substratum* —this is what I deny, and you, indeed, affirm but, notwithstanding your demonstration, have not yet proved.

[13.] *Hyl.* I shall insist no longer on that point. Do you think, however, you shall persuade me the natural philosophers have been dreaming all this while? Pray what becomes of all their hypotheses and explications of the phenomena which suppose the existence of matter?

Phil. What mean you, Hylas, by the "phenomena"?

Hyl. I mean the appearances which I perceive by my senses.

Phil. And the appearances perceived by sense, are they not ideas?

Hyl. I have told you so a hundred times.

Phil. Therefore, to explain the phenomena is to show how we come to be affected with ideas in that manner and order wherein they are imprinted on our senses. Is it not?

Hyl. It is.

Phil. Now, if you can prove that any philosopher has explained the production of any one idea in our minds by the help of *matter,* I shall forever acquiesce and look on all that has been said against it as nothing; but if you cannot, it is vain to urge the explication of phenomena. That a being endowed with knowledge and will should produce or exhibit ideas is easily understood. But that a being which is utterly destitute of these faculties should be able to produce ideas, or in any sort to affect an intelligence, this I can never understand. This I say, though we had some positive conception of matter, though we knew its qualities and could comprehend its existence, would yet be so far from explaining things that it is itself the most inexplicable thing in the world. And yet, for all this, it will not follow that philosophers have been doing nothing; for by observing and reasoning upon the connection of ideas, they discover the laws and methods of nature, which is a part of knowledge both useful and entertaining.

[14.] *Hyl.* After all, can it be supposed God would deceive all mankind? Do you imagine He would have induced the whole world to believe the being of matter if there was no such thing?

Phil. That every epidemical opinion arising from prejudice, or passion, or thoughtlessness may be imputed to God, as the Author of it, I believe you will not affirm. Whatsoever opinion we father on Him, it must be either because He has discovered it to us by supernatural revelation or because it is so evident to our natural faculties, which were framed and given us by God, that it is impossible we should withhold our assent from it. But where is the revelation? Or where is the evidence that extorts the belief of matter? Nay, how does it appear that matter, taken for something distinct from what we perceive by our senses, is thought to exist by all mankind, or, indeed, by any except a few philosophers who do not know what they would be at? Your question supposes these points are clear; and, when you have cleared them, I shall think myself obliged to give you another answer. In the meantime let it suffice that I tell you I do not suppose God has deceived mankind at all.

Hyl. But the novelty, Philonous, the novelty! There lies the danger. New notions should always be discountenanced; they unsettle men's minds, and nobody knows where they will end.

Phil. Why the rejecting a notion that has no foundation, either in sense or in reason or in Divine authority, should be thought to unsettle the belief of such opinions as are grounded on all or any of these, I cannot imagine. That innovations in government and religion are dangerous and ought to be discountenanced, I freely own. But is there the like reason why they should be discouraged in philosophy? The making anything known which was unknown before is an innovation in knowledge; and if all such innovations had been forbidden, men would [not] have made a notable progress in the arts and sciences. But it is none of my business to plead for novelties and paradoxes. That the qualities we perceive are not on the objects, that we must not believe our senses, that we know nothing of the real nature of things and can never be assured even of their existence, that real colors and sounds are nothing but certain unknown figures and motions, that motions are in themselves neither swift nor slow, that there are in bodies absolute extensions without any particular magnitude or figure, that a thing stupid, thoughtless, and inactive operates on a spirit, that the least particle of a body contains innumerable extended parts—these are the novelties, these are the strange notions which shock the genuine uncorrupted judgment of all mankind, and, being once admitted, embarrass the mind with endless doubts and difficulties. And it is against these and the like innovations I endeavor to vindicate Common Sense. It is true, in doing this I may, perhaps, be obliged to use some ambages and ways of speech not common. But if my notions are once thoroughly understood, that which is most singular in them will, in effect, be found to amount to no more than this—that it is absolutely impossible and a plain contradiction to suppose any unthinking being should exist without being perceived by a mind. And if this notion be singular, it is a shame it should be so at this time of day and in a Christian country.

[15.] *Hyl.* As for the difficulties other opinions may be liable to, those are out of the question. It is your business to defend your own opinion. Can anything be plainer than that you are for changing all things into ideas? You, I say, who are not ashamed to charge me with skepticism. This is so plain, there is no denying it.

Phil. You mistake me. I am not for changing things into ideas but rather ideas into things, since those immediate objects of perception, which, according to you, are only appearances of things, I take to be the real things themselves.

Hyl. Things! you may pretend what you please; but it is certain you leave us nothing but the empty forms of things, the outside only which strikes the senses.

Phil. What you call the empty forms and outside of things seem to me the very things themselves. Nor are they empty or incomplete otherwise than upon your supposition that matter is an essential part of all corporeal things. We both, therefore, agree in this, that we perceive only sensible forms; but herein we differ: you will have them to be empty appearances, I real beings. In short, you do not trust your senses, I do.

[16.] *Hyl.* You say you believe your senses, and seem to applaud yourself that in this you agree with the vulgar. According to you, therefore, the true nature of a thing is discovered by the senses. If so, whence comes that disagreement? Why, is not the same figure, and other sensible qualities, perceived all manner of ways? And why should we use a microscope the better to discover the true nature of a body, if it were discoverable to the naked eye?

Phil. Strictly speaking, Hylas, we do not see the same object that we feel; neither is the same object perceived by the microscope which was by the naked eye. But in case every variation was thought sufficient to constitute a new kind or individual, the endless number or confusion of names would render language impracticable. Therefore, to avoid this as well as other inconveniences which are obvious upon a little thought, men combine together several ideas, apprehended by divers senses, or by the same sense at different times or in different circumstances, but observed, however, to have some connection in nature, either with respect to coexistence or succession; all which they refer to one name and consider as one thing. Hence it follows that when I examine by my other senses a thing I have seen, it is not in order to understand better the same object which I had perceived by sight, the object of one sense not being perceived by the other senses. And when I look through a microscope, it is not that I may perceive more clearly what I perceived already with my bare eyes, the object perceived by the glass being quite different from the former. But in both cases my aim is only to know what ideas are connected together; and the more a man knows of the connection of ideas, the more he is said to know of the nature of things. What, therefore, if our ideas are variable, what if our senses are not in all circumstances affected with the same appearances? It will not thence follow they are not to be trusted or that they are inconsistent either with themselves or anything else, except it be with your preconceived notion of (I know not what) one single, unchanged, unperceivable, real nature, marked by each name; which prejudice seems to have taken its rise from not rightly understanding the common language of men speaking of several distinct ideas as united into one thing by the mind. And, indeed, there is cause to suspect several erroneous conceits of the philosophers are owing to the same original: while they began to build their schemes not so much on notions as words which were framed by the vulgar merely for convenience and dispatch in the common actions of life, without any regard to speculation.

Hyl. Methinks I apprehend your meaning.

[17.] *Phil.* It is your opinion the ideas we perceive by our senses are not real things, but images or copies of them. Our knowledge, therefore, is no further real than as our ideas are the true representations of those originals. But as these supposed originals are in themselves unknown, it is impossible to know how far our ideas resemble them, or whether they resemble them at all. We cannot, therefore, be sure we have any real knowledge. Further, as our ideas are perpetually varied, without any change in the supposed real things, it necessarily follows they cannot all be true copies of them, or, if some are and others are not, it is impossible to distinguish the former from the latter. And this plunges us yet deeper in uncertainty. Again, when we consider the point, we cannot conceive how any idea, or anything like an idea, should have an absolute existence out of a mind, nor consequently, according to you, how there should be any real thing in nature. The result of all which is that we are thrown into the most hopeless and abandoned skepticism. Now give me leave to ask you, *first,* whether your referring ideas to certain absolutely existing unperceived substances, as their originals, be not the source of all this skepticism? *Secondly,* whether you are informed, either by sense or reason, of the existence of those unknown originals? And in case you are not, whether it be not absurd to suppose them? *Thirdly,* whether, upon inquiry, you find there is anything distinctly conceived or meant by the "absolute or external existence of unperceiving substances"? *Lastly,* whether, the premises considered, it be not the wisest way to follow nature, trust your senses, and, laying aside all anxious thought about unknown natures or substances, admit with the vulgar those for real things which are perceived by the senses?

[18.] *Hyl.* For the present I have no inclination to the answering part. I would much rather see how you can get over what follows. Pray, are not the objects perceived by the senses of one likewise perceivable to others present? If there were a hundred more here, they would all see the garden, the trees and flowers, as I see them. But they are not in the same manner affected with the ideas I frame in my imagination. Does not this make a difference between the former sort of objects and the latter?

Phil. I grant it does. Nor have I ever denied a difference between the objects of sense and those of imagination. But what would you infer from thence? You cannot say that sensible objects exist unperceived because they are perceived by many.

Hyl. I own I can make nothing of that objection, but it has led me into another. Is it not your opinion that by our senses we perceive only the ideas existing in our minds?

Phil. It is.

Hyl. But the same idea which is in my mind cannot be in yours or in any other mind. Does it not, therefore, follow from your principles that no two can see the same thing? And is not this highly absurd?

Phil. If the term "same" be taken in the vulgar acceptation, it is certain (and not at all repugnant to the principles I maintain) that different persons may perceive the same thing, or the same thing or idea exist in different minds. Words are of arbitrary imposition; and since men are used to apply the word "same" where no distinction or variety is perceived, and I do not pretend to alter their perceptions, it follows that, as men have said before, *several saw the same thing,* so they may, upon like occasions, still continue to use the same phrase without any deviation either from propriety of language or the truth of things. But if the term "same" be used in the acceptation of philosophers who pretend to an abstracted notion of identity, then, according to their sundry definitions of this notion (for it is not yet agreed wherein that philosophic identity consists), it may or may not be possible for divers persons to perceive the same thing. But whether philosophers shall think fit to call a thing the "same" or no is, I conceive, of small importance. Let us suppose several men together, all endued with the same faculties, and consequently affected in like sort by their senses, and who had yet never known the use of language; they would without question agree in their perceptions. Though perhaps, when they came to the use of speech, some regarding the uniformness of what was perceived might call it the "same" thing; others, especially regarding the diversity of persons who perceived, might choose the denomination of "different" things. But who sees not that all the dispute is about a word, to wit, whether what is perceived by different persons may yet have the term "same" applied to it? Or suppose a house whose walls or outward shell remaining unaltered, the chambers are all pulled down, and new ones built in their place, and that you should call this the "same," and I should say it was not the "same" house—would we not, for all this, perfectly agree in our thoughts of the house considered in itself? And would not all the difference consist in a sound? If you should say we differed in our notions, for that you superadded to your idea of the house the simple abstracted idea of identity, whereas I did not, I would tell you I know not what you mean by that "abstracted idea of identity," and should desire you to look into your own thoughts and be sure you understood yourself.— Why so silent, Hylas? Are you not yet satisfied men may dispute about identity and diversity without any real difference in their thoughts and opinions abstracted from names? Take this further reflection with you— that, whether matter be allowed to exist or no, the case is exactly the same as to the point in hand. For the materialists themselves acknowledge what we immediately perceive by our senses to be our own ideas. Your difficulty, therefore, that no two see the same thing makes equally against the materialists and me.

Hyl. But they suppose an external archetype to which referring their several ideas they may truly be said to perceive the same thing.

Phil. And (not to mention your having discarded those archetypes) so may you suppose an external archetype on my principles; *external,* I mean, to your own mind, though, indeed, it must be supposed to exist in that mind which comprehends all things; but then, this serves all the ends of *identity,* as well as if it existed out of a mind. And I am sure you yourself will not say it is less intelligible.

Hyl. You have indeed clearly satisfied me either that there is no difficulty at bottom in this point or, if there be, that it makes equally against both opinions.

Phil. But that which makes equally against two contradictory opinions can be a proof against neither.

[19.] *Hyl.* I acknowledge it. But, after all, Philonous, when I consider the substance of what you advance against skepticism, it amounts to no more than this: we are sure that we really see, hear, feel, in a word, that we are affected with sensible impressions.

Phil. And how are we concerned any further? I see this cherry, I feel it, I taste it, and I am sure *nothing* cannot be seen or felt or tasted; it is therefore *real*. Take away the sensations of softness, moisture, redness, tartness, and you take away the cherry. Since it is not a being distinct from sensations, a cherry, I say, is nothing but a congeries of sensible impressions, or ideas perceived by various senses, which ideas are united into one thing (or have one name given them) by the mind because they are observed to attend each other. Thus, when the palate is affected with such a particular taste, the sight is affected with a red color, the touch with roundness, softness, etc. Hence, when I see and feel and taste in sundry certain manners, I am sure the cherry exists or is real, its reality being in my opinion nothing abstracted from those sensations. But if by the word "cherry" you mean an unknown nature distinct from all those sensible qualities, and by its "existence" something distinct from its being perceived, then, indeed, I own neither you nor I, nor anyone else, can be sure it exists.

[20.] *Hyl.* But what would you say, Philonous, if I should bring the very same reasons against the existence of sensible things in a mind which you have offered against their existing in a material *substratum?*

Phil. When I see your reasons, you shall hear what I have to say to them.

Hyl. Is the mind extended or unextended?

Phil. Unextended, without doubt.

Hyl. Do you say the things you perceive are in your mind?

Phil. They are.

Hyl. Again, have I not heard you speak of sensible impressions?

Phil. I believe you may.

Hyl. Explain to me now, O Philonous! how is it possible there should be room for all those trees and houses to exist in your mind. Can extended things be contained in that which is unextended? Or are we to imagine impressions made on a thing void of all solidity? You cannot say objects are in your mind, as books in your study, or that things are imprinted on it, as the figure of a seal upon wax. In what sense, therefore, are we to understand those expressions? Explain me this if you can, and I shall then be able to answer all those queries you formerly put to me about my *substratum.*

Phil. Look you, Hylas, when I speak of objects as existing in the mind or imprinted on the senses, I would not be understood in the gross literal sense—as when bodies are said to exist in a place or a seal to make an impression upon wax. My meaning is only that the mind comprehends or perceives them, and that it is affected from without or by some being distinct from itself. This is my explication of your difficulty; and how it can serve to make your tenet of an unperceiving material *substratum* intelligible, I would fain know.

Hyl. Nay, if that be all, I confess I do not see what use can be made of it. But are you not guilty of some abuse of language in this?

Phil. None at all. It is no more than common custom, which you know is the rule of language, has authorized, nothing being more usual than for philosophers to speak of the immediate objects of the understanding as things existing in the mind. Nor is there anything in this but what is conformable to the general analogy of language; most part of the mental operations being signified by words borrowed from sensible things, as is plain in the terms "comprehend," "reflect," "discourse," etc., which, being applied to the mind, must not be taken in their gross original sense.

[21.] *Hyl.* You have, I own, satisfied me in this point. But there still remains one great difficulty which I know not how you will get over. And, indeed, it is of such importance that if you could solve all others without being able to find a solution for this, you must never expect to make me a proselyte to your principles.

Phil. Let me know this mighty difficulty.

Hyl. The Scripture account of the creation is what appears to me utterly irreconcilable with your notions. Moses tells us of a creation—a creation of what? of ideas? No, certainly, but of things, of real things, solid corporeal substances. Bring your principles to agree with this and I shall perhaps agree with you.

Phil. Moses mentions the sun, moon, and stars, earth and sea, plants and animals. That all these do really exist and were in the beginning created by God, I make no question.

If by "ideas" you mean fictions and fancies of the mind, then these are no ideas. If by "ideas" you mean immediate objects of the understanding, or sensible things which cannot exist unperceived, or out of a mind, then these things are ideas. But whether you do or do not call them "ideas," it matters little. The difference is only about a name. And whether that name be retained or rejected, the sense, the truth, and reality of things continues the same. In common talk, the objects of our senses are not termed "ideas" but "things." Call them so still, provided you do not attribute to them any absolute external existence, and I shall never quarrel with you for a word. The creation, therefore, I allow to have been a creation of things, of *real* things. Neither is this in the least inconsistent with my principles, as is evident from what I have now said; and would have been evident to you without this if you had not forgotten what had been so often said before. But as for solid corporeal substances, I desire you to show where Moses makes any mention of them; and if they should be mentioned by him or any other inspired writer, it would still be incumbent on you to show those words were not taken in the vulgar acceptation for things falling under our senses, but in the philosophic acceptation for matter or an unknown quiddity with an absolute existence. When you have proved these points, then (and not till then) may you bring the authority of Moses into our dispute.

Hyl. It is in vain to dispute about a point so clear. I am content to refer it to your own conscience. Are you not satisfied there is some peculiar repugnancy between the Mosaic account of the creation and your notions?

Phil. If all possible sense which can be put on the first chapter of Genesis may be conceived as consistently with my principles as any other, then it has no peculiar repugnancy with them. But there is no sense you may not as well conceive, believing as I do. Since, besides spirits, all you conceive are ideas, and the existence of these I do not deny. Neither do you pretend they exist without the mind.

Hyl. Pray let me see any sense you can understand it in.

Phil. Why, I imagine that if I had been present at the creation, I should have seen things produced into being—that is become perceptible—in the order prescribed by the sacred historian. I ever before believed the Mosaic account of the creation, and now find no alteration in my manner of believing it. When things are said to begin or end their existence, we do not mean this with regard to God, but His creatures. All objects are eternally known by God, or, which is the same thing, have an eternal existence in His mind; but when things, before imperceptible to creatures, are, by a decree of God, made perceptible to them, then are they said to begin a relative existence with respect to created minds. Upon reading therefore the Mosaic account of the creation, I understand that the several parts of the world became gradually perceivable to finite spirits endowed with proper faculties, so that, whoever such were present, they were in truth perceived by them. This is the literal obvious sense suggested to me by the words of the Holy Scripture, in which is included no mention or thought either of *substratum,* instrument, occasion, or absolute existence. And, upon inquiry, I doubt not it will be found that most plain honest men who believe the creation never think of those things any more than I. What metaphysical sense you may understand it in, you only can tell.

Hyl. But, Philonous, you do not seem to be aware that you allow created things in the beginning only a relative and consequently hypothetical being; that is to say, upon supposition there were men to perceive them, without which they have no actuality of absolute existence wherein creation might terminate. Is it not, therefore, according to you, plainly impossible the creation of any inanimate creatures should precede that of man? And is not this directly contrary to the Mosaic account?

Phil. In answer to that, I say, *first,* created beings might begin to exist in the mind of other created intelligences besides men. You will not, therefore, be able to prove any contradiction beween Moses and my notions unless you first show there was no other order of finite created spirits in being before man. I say further, in case we conceive the creation as we should at this time a parcel of plants or vegetables of all sorts produced by an invisible power in a desert where nobody was present—that this way of explaining or conceiving it is consistent with my principles, since they deprive you of nothing, either sensible or imaginable; that it exactly suits with the common, natural, and undebauched notions of mankind; that it manifests the dependence of all things on God, and consequently has all the good effect or influence, which it is possible that important article of our faith should have in making men humble, thankful, and resigned to their Creator. I say, moreover, that, in this naked conception of things, divested of words, there will not be found any notion of what you call the "actuality of absolute existence." You may indeed raise a dust with those terms and so lengthen our dispute to no purpose. But I entreat you calmly to look into your own thoughts and then tell me if they are not a useless and unintelligible jargon.

Hyl. I own I have no very clear notion annexed to them. But what say you to this? Do you not make the existence of sensible things consist in their being in a mind? And were not all things eternally in the mind of God? Did they not therefore exist from all eternity, according to you? And how could that which was eternal be created in time? Can anything be clearer or better connected than this?

Phil. And are not you too of opinion that God knew all things from eternity?

Hyl. I am.

Phil. Consequently, they always had a being in the Divine intellect.

Hyl. This I acknowledge.

Phil. By your own confession, therefore, nothing is new, or begins to be, in respect of the mind of God. So we are agreed in that point.

Hyl. What shall we make then of the creation?

Phil. May we not understand it to have been entirely in respect of finite spirits, so that things, with regard to us, may properly be said to begin their existence, or be created, when God decreed they should become perceptible to intelligent creatures in that order and manner which He then established and we now call the laws of nature? You may call this a "relative," or "hypothetical existence," if you please. But so long as it supplies us with the most natural, obvious, and literal sense of the Mosaic history of the creation, so long as it answers all the religious ends of that great article, in a word, so long as you can assign no other sense or meaning in its stead, why should we reject this? Is it to comply with a ridiculous skeptical humor of making everything nonsense and unintelligible? I am sure you cannot say it is for the glory of God. For allowing it to be a thing possible and conceivable that the corporeal world should have an absolute subsistence extrinsical to the mind of God, as well as to the minds of all created spirits, yet how could this set forth either the immensity or omniscience of the Deity or the necessary and immediate dependence of all things on Him? Nay, would it not rather seem to derogate from those attributes?

Hyl. Well, but as to this decree of God's for making things perceptible, what say you, Philonous, is it not plain God did either execute that decree from all eternity or at some certain time began to will what He had not actually willed before, but only designed to will? If the former, then there could be no creation or beginning of existence in finite things. If the latter, then we must acknowledge something new to befall the Deity, which implies a sort of change; and all change argues imperfection.

Phil. Pray consider what you are doing. Is it not evident this objection concludes equally against a creation in any sense, nay, against every other act of the Deity discoverable by the light of nature? None of which can we conceive otherwise than as performed in time and having a beginning. God is a Being of transcendent and unlimited perfections; His Nature, therefore, is incomprehensible to finite spirits. It is not, therefore, to be expected that any man, whether *materialist* or *immaterialist,* should have exactly just notions of the Deity,

His attributes, and ways of operation. If then you would infer anything against me, your difficulty must not be drawn from the inadequateness of our conceptions of the Divine nature, which is unavoidable on any scheme, but from the denial of matter, of which there is not one word, directly or indirectly, in what you have now objected.

Hyl. I must acknowledge the difficulties you are concerned to clear are such only as arise from the nonexistence of matter and are peculiar to that notion. So far you are in the right. But I cannot by any means bring myself to think there is no such peculiar repugnancy between the creation and your opinion, though, indeed, where to fix it I do not distinctly know.

Phil. What would you have? Do I not acknowledge a twofold state of things, the one ectypal or natural, the other archetypal and eternal? The former was created in time, the latter existed from everlasting in the mind of God. Is not this agreeable to the common notions of divines? Or is any more than this necessary in order to conceive the creation? But you suspect some peculiar repugnancy, though you know not where it lies. To take away all possibility of scruple in the case, do but consider this one point: either you are not able to conceive the creation on any hypothesis whatsoever, and if so, there is no ground for dislike or complaint against my particular opinion on that score; or you are able to conceive it, and if so, why not on my principles, since thereby nothing conceivable is taken away? You have all along been allowed the full scope of sense, imagination, and reason. Whatever, therefore, you could before apprehend, either immediately or mediately by your senses, or by ratiocination from your senses, whatever you could perceive, imagine, or understand, remains still with you. If, therefore, the notion you have of the creation by other principles be intelligible, you have it still upon mine; if it be not intelligible, I conceive it to be no notion at all, and so there is no loss of it. And, indeed, it seems to me very plain that the supposition of matter, that is, a thing perfectly unknown and inconceivable, cannot serve to make us conceive anything. And I hope it need not be proved to you that if the existence of matter does not make the creation conceivable, the creation's being without it inconceivable can be no objection against its nonexistence.

Hyl. I confess, Philonous, you have almost satisfied me in this point of the creation.

Phil. I would fain know why you are not quite satisfied. You tell me indeed of a repugnancy between the Mosaic history and immaterialism, but you know not where it lies. Is this reasonable, Hylas? Can you expect I should solve a difficulty without knowing what it is? But, to pass by all that, would not a man think you were assured there is no repugnancy between the received notions of materialists and the inspired writings?

Hyl. And so I am.

Phil. Ought the historical part of Scripture to be understood in a plain obvious sense or in a sense which is metaphysical and out of the way?

Hyl. In the plain sense, doubtless.

Phil. When Moses speaks of herbs, earth, water, etc., as having been created by God, think you not the sensible things commonly signified by those words are suggested to every unphilosophical reader?

Hyl. I cannot help thinking so.

Phil. And are not all ideas, or things perceived by sense, to be denied a real existence by the doctrine of the materialists?

Hyl. This I have already acknowledged.

Phil. The creation, therefore, according to them, was not the creation of things sensible, which have only a relative being, but of certain unknown natures which have an absolute being wherein creation might terminate?

Hyl. True.

Phil. Is it not, therefore, evident the assertors of matter destroy the plain obvious sense of Moses, with which their notions are utterly inconsistent, and instead of it obtrude on us I know not what, something equally unintelligible to themselves and me?

Hyl. I cannot contradict you.

Phil. Moses tells us of a creation. A creation of what? of unknown quiddities, of occasions, or *substratums?* No, certainly, but of things obvious to the senses. You must first reconcile this with your notions if you expect I should be reconciled to them.

Hyl. I see you can assault me with my own weapons.

Phil. Then as to *absolute existence,* was there ever known a more jejune notion than that? Something it is so abstracted and unintelligible that you have frankly owned you could not conceive it, much less explain anything by it. But allowing matter to exist and the notion of absolute existence to be as clear as light, yet, was this ever known to make the creation more credible? Nay, has it not furnished the atheists and infidels of all ages with the most plausible arguments against a creation? That a corporeal substance which has an absolute existence without the minds of spirits should be produced out of nothing, by the mere will of a spirit, has been looked upon as a thing so contrary to all reason, so impossible and absurd, that not only the most celebrated among the ancients, but even divers modern and Christian philosophers have thought matter coeternal with the Deity. Lay these things together and then judge you whether materialism disposes men to believe the creation of things.

[22.] *Hyl.* I own, Philonous, I think it does not. This of the creation is the last objection I can think of; and I must needs own it has been sufficiently answered as well as the rest. Nothing now remains to be overcome but a sort of unaccountable backwardness that I find in myself toward your notions.

Phil. When a man is swayed, he knows not why, to one side of a question, can this, think you, be anything else but the effect of prejudice, which never fails to attend old and rooted notions? And, indeed, in this respect I cannot deny the belief of matter to have very much the advantage over the contrary opinion with men of a learned education.

Hyl. I confess it seems to be as you say.

Phil. As a balance, therefore, to this weight of prejudice, let us throw into the scale the great advantages that arise from the belief of immaterialism, both in regard to religion and human learning. The being of a God and incorruptibility of the soul, those great articles of religion, are they not proved with the clearest and most immediate evidence? When I say the being of a *God*, I do not mean an obscure general cause of things whereof we have no conception, but *God* in the strict and proper sense of the word, a Being whose spirituality, omnipresence, providence, omniscience, infinite power, and goodness are as conspicuous as the existence of sensible things, of which (notwithstanding the fallacious pretenses and affected scruples of skeptics) there is no more reason to doubt than of our own being. Then, with relation to human sciences: in Natural Philosophy, what intricacies, what obscurities, what contradictions has the belief of matter led men into! To say nothing of the numberless disputes about its extent, continuity, homogeneity, gravity, divisibility, etc.—do they not pretend to explain all things by bodies operating on bodies, according to the laws of motion? And yet, are they able to comprehend how any one body should move another? Nay, admitting there was no difficulty in reconciling the notion of an inert being with a cause, or in conceiving how an accident might pass from one body to another, yet, by all their strained thoughts and extravagant suppositions, have they been able to reach the mechanical production of any one animal or vegetable body? Can they account, by the laws of motion, for sounds, tastes, smells, or colors, or for the regular course of things? Have they accounted, by physical principles, for the aptitude and contrivance even of the most inconsiderable parts of the universe? But laying aside matter and corporeal causes and admitting only the efficiency of an all-perfect Mind, are not all the effects of nature easy and intelligible? If the *phenomena* are nothing else but *ideas*, God is a *spirit*, but matter an unintelligent, unperceiving being. If they demonstrate an unlimited power in their cause, God is active and omnipotent, but matter an inert mass. If the order, regularity, and usefulness of them can never be sufficiently admired, God is infinitely wise and provident, but matter destitute of all contrivance and design. These surely are great advantages in physics. Not to mention that the apprehension of a distant Deity naturally disposes men to a negligence of their moral actions, which they would be more cautious of, in case they thought him immediately present and acting on their minds without the interposition of matter or unthinking second causes. Then in metaphysics: what difficulties concerning entity in abstract, substantial forms, hylarchic principles, plastic natures, substance and accident, principle of individuation, possibility of matter's thinking, origin of ideas, the manner how two independent substances so widely different as *spirit* and *matter* should mutually operate on each other? What difficulties, I say, and endless disquisitions concerning these and innumerable other the like points do we escape by supposing only spirits and ideas? Even the mathematics themselves, if we take away the absolute existence of extended things, become much more clear and easy, the most shocking paradoxes and intricate speculations in those sciences depending on the infinite divisibility of finite extension, which depends on that supposition. But what need is there to insist on the particular sciences? Is not that opposition to all science whatsoever, that frenzy of the ancient and modern skeptics, built on the same foundation? Or can you produce so much as one argument against the reality of corporeal things or in behalf of that avowed utter ignorance of their natures which does not suppose their reality to consist in an external absolute existence? Upon this supposition, indeed, the objections from the change of colors in a pigeon's neck, or the appearance of the broken oar in the water, must be allowed to have weight. But these and the like objections vanish if we do not maintain the being of absolute external originals, but place the reality of things in ideas, fleeting, indeed, and changeable; however, not changed at random, but according to the fixed order of nature. For herein consists that constancy and truth of things which secures all the concerns of life, and distinguishes that which is real from the irregular visions of the fancy.

Hyl. I agree to all you have now said and must own that nothing can incline me to embrace your opinion more than the advantages I see it is attended with. I am by nature lazy, and this would be a mighty abridgment in knowledge. What doubts, what hypotheses, what labyrinths of amusement, what fields of disputation, what an ocean of false learning may be avoided by that single notion of *immaterialism!*

Phil. After all, is there anything further remaining to be done? You may remember you promised to embrace that opinion which upon examination should appear most agreeable to common sense and remote from skepticism. This, by your own confession, is that which denies matter or the absolute existence of corporeal things. Nor is this all; the same notion has been proved several ways, viewed in different lights, pursued in its consequences, and all objections against it cleared. Can there be a greater evidence of its truth? Or is it possible it should have all the marks of a true opinion and yet be false?

[23.] *Hyl.* I own myself entirely satisfied for the present in all respects. But what security can I have that I shall still continue the same full assent to your opinion and that no unthought-of objection or difficulty will occur hereafter?

Phil. Pray, Hylas, do you in other cases, when a point is once evidently proved, withhold your assent on account of objections or difficulties it may be liable to? Are the difficulties that attend the doctrine of incommensurable quantities, of the angle of contact, of the asymptotes to curves, or the like, sufficient to make you hold out against mathematical demonstration? Or will you disbelieve the Providence of God because there may be some particular things which you know not how to reconcile with it? If there are difficulties attending immaterialism, there are at the same time direct and evident proofs of it. But for the existence of matter there is not one proof, and far more numerous and insurmountable objections lie against it. But where are those mighty difficulties you insist on? Alas! you know not where or what they are; something which may possibly occur hereafter. If this be a sufficient pretense for withholding your full assent, you should never yield it to any proposition, how free soever from exceptions, how clearly and solidly soever demonstrated.

Hyl. You have satisfied me, Philonous.

Phil. But to arm you against all future objections, do but consider that which bears equally hard on two contradictory opinions can be proof against neither. Whenever, therefore, any difficulty occurs, try if you can find a solution for it on the hypothesis of the materialists. Be not deceived by words, but sound your own thoughts. And in case you cannot conceive it easier by the help of materialism, it is plain it can be no objection against immaterialism. Had you proceeded all along by this rule, you would probably have spared yourself abundance of trouble in objecting, since of all your difficulties I challenge you to show one that is explained by matter, nay, which is not more unintelligible with than without that supposition, and consequently makes rather *against* than *for* it. You should consider, in each particular, whether the difficulty arises from the *nonexistence of matter*. If it does not, you might as well argue from the infinite divisibility of extension against the Divine prescience as from such a difficulty against immaterialism. And yet, upon recollection, I believe you will find this to have been often if not always the case. You should likewise take heed not to argue on a *petitio principii*. One is apt to say the unknown substances ought to be esteemed real things rather than the ideas in our minds; and who can tell but the unthinking external substance may concur as a cause or instrument in the production of our ideas? But is not this proceeding on a supposition that there are such external substances? And to suppose this, is it not begging the question? But above all things, you should beware of imposing on yourself by that vulgar sophism which is called *ignoratio elenchi*. You talked often as if you thought I maintained the nonexistence of sensible things, whereas in truth no one can be more thoroughly assured of their existence than I am; and it is you who doubt, I should have said, positively deny it. Everything that is seen, felt, heard, or any way perceived by the senses is, on the principles I embrace, a real being, but not on yours. Remember, the matter you contend for is an unknown somewhat (if indeed it may be termed "somewhat"), which is quite stripped of all sensible qualities, and can neither be perceived by sense, nor apprehended by the mind. Remember, I say that it is not any object which is hard or soft, hot or cold, blue or white, round or square, etc.—for all these things I affirm do exist. Though, indeed, I deny they have an existence distinct from being perceived, or that they exist out of all minds whatsoever. Think on these points; let them be attentively considered and still kept in view. Otherwise you will not comprehend the state of the question, without which your objections will always be wide of the mark and, instead of mine, may possibly be directed (as more than once they have been) against your own notions.

Hyl. I must needs own, Philonous, nothing seems to have kept me from agreeing with you more than this same *mistaking the question*. In denying matter, at first glimpse I am tempted to imagine you deny the things we see and feel, but, upon reflection, find there is no ground for it. What think you, therefore, of retaining the name "matter" and applying it to *sensible things?* This may be done without any change in your sentiments; and, believe me, it would be a means of reconciling them to some persons who may be more shocked at an innovation in words than in opinion.

Phil. With all my heart; retain the word "matter" and apply it to the objects of sense, if you please, provided you do not attribute to them any subsistence distinct from their being perceived. I shall never quarrel with you for an expression. "Matter" or "material substance" are terms introduced by philosophers , and, as used by them, imply a sort of independence, or a subsistence distinct from being perceived by a mind; but are never used by common people, or, if ever, it is to signify the immediate objects of sense. One would think, therefore, so long as the names of all particular things with the terms "sensible," "substance," "body," "stuff," and the like, are retained, the word "matter" should be never missed in common talk. And in philosophical discourses it seems the best way to leave it quite out, since there is not, perhaps, any one thing that has more favored and strengthened the depraved bent of the mind toward atheism than the use of that general confused term.

Hyl. Well, but, Philonous, since I am content to give up the notion of an unthinking substance exterior to the mind, I think you ought not to deny me the privilege of using the word "matter" as I please, and annexing it to a collection of sensible qualities subsisting only in the mind. I freely own there is no other substance, in a strict sense, than spirit. But I have been so long accustomed to the term "matter" that I know not how to part with it. To say there is no matter in the world is still shocking to me. Whereas to say there is no matter if by that term be meant an unthinking substance existing without the mind, but if by matter is meant some sensible thing whose existence consists in being perceived, then there is matter—this distinction gives it quite another turn; and men will come into your notions with small difficulty when they are proposed in that manner. For, after all, the controversy about matter in the strict acceptation of it lies altogether between you and the philosophers, whose principles, I acknowledge, are not near so natural or so agreeable to the common sense of mankind and Holy Scripture as yours. There is nothing we either desire or shun but as it makes, or is apprehended to make, some part of our happiness or misery. But what has happiness or misery, joy or grief, pleasure or pain to do with absolute existence or with unknown entities abstracted from all relation to us? It is evident things regard us only as they are pleasing or displeasing; and they can please or displease only so far forth as they are perceived. Further, therefore, we are not concerned; and thus far you leave things as you found them. Yet still there is something new in this doctrine. It is plain, I do not now think with the philosophers, nor yet altogether with the vulgar. I would know how the case stands in that respect, precisely what you have added to or altered in my former notions.

[24.] *Phil.* I do not pretend to be a setter-up of new notions.

My endeavors tend only to unite and place in a clearer light that truth which was before shared between the vulgar and the philosophers, the former being of opinion that *those things they immediately perceive are the real things,* and the latter, that *the things immediately perceived are ideas which exist only in the mind.* Which two notions put together do, in effect, constitute the substance of what I advance.

Hyl. I have been a long time distrusting my senses; methought I saw things by a dim light and through false glasses.[11] Now the glasses are removed and a new light breaks in upon my understanding. I am clearly convinced that I see things in their native forms and am no longer in pain about their *unknown natures* or *absolute existence.* This is the state I find myself in at present, though, indeed, the course that brought me to it I do not yet thoroughly comprehend. You set out upon the same principles that Academics,[12] Cartesians, and the like sects usually do, and for a long time it looked as if you were advancing their philosophical skepticism; but, in the end, your conclusions are directly opposite to theirs.

Phil. You see, Hylas, the water of yonder fountain, how it is forced upwards, in a round column, to a certain height, at which it breaks and falls back into the basin from whence it rose, its ascent as well as descent proceeding from the same uniform law or principle of gravitation. Just so, the same principles which, at first view, lead to skepticism, pursued to a certain point, bring men back to common sense.

---

[11] [Cf. I Corinthians 13:12: "For now we see through a glass darkly, but then face to face. . . ."]

[12] [The Academics referred to were probably the members of the second or middle Academy founded by Arcesilaus (315–241 B.C.), or those of the third or new Academy founded by Carneades (214–129 B.C.). Both advanced skepticism. "Arcesilaus . . . seems to me to have very much in common with the Pyrrhonean teachings, so that his school and ours are almost one." Sextus Empiricus (*fl.* third century), *Outlines of Pyrrhonism,* trans. Mary Mills Patrick (Chicago, Ill.: Henry Regnery Company, 1949), p. 63. The skepticism of Carneades was less extreme than Pyrrhonism. The former avoided extreme skepticism by making probability the guide of life. On the Cartesians, see *Principles,* note 13, p. 55.]

PHILOSOPHICAL CORRESPONDENCE
BETWEEN
BERKELEY AND SAMUEL JOHNSON

1729–1730

I. JOHNSON TO BERKELEY

A letter to the Rev'd Dr. Berkeley, Dean of London Derry, upon reading his books of the Principles of Human Knowledge and Dialogues

Stratford, Sept. 10, 1729

Rev'd Sir:

The kind invitation you gave me to lay before you any difficulties that should occur to me in reading those excellent books which you was pleased to order into my hands, is all the apology I shall offer for the trouble I now presume to give you. But nothing could encourage me to expose to your view my low and mean way of thinking and writing, but my hopes of an interest in that candor and tenderness which are so conspicuous both in your writings and conversation.

These books (for which I stand humbly obliged to you) contain speculations the most surprisingly ingenious I have ever met with; and I must confess that the reading of them has almost convinced me that matter as it has been commonly defined for an unknown Quiddity is but a mere non-entity. That it is a strong presumption against the existence of it, that there never could be conceived any manner of connection between it and our ideas. That the *esse* of things is only their *percipi;* and that the rescuing us from the absurdities of abstract ideas and the gross notion of matter that have so much obtained, deserves well of the learned world, in that it clears away very many difficulties and perplexities in the sciences.

And I am of opinion that this way of thinking can't fail of prevailing in the world, because it is likely to prevail very much among us in these parts, several ingenious men having entirely come in to it. But there are many others on the other hand that cannot be reconciled to it; tho' of these there are some who have a very good opinion of it and plainly see many happy consequences attending it, on account of which they are well inclined to embrace it, but think they find some difficulties in their way which they can't get over, and some objections not sufficiently answered to their satisfaction. And since you have condescended to give me leave to do so, I will make bold to lay before you sundry things, which yet remain in the dark either to myself or to others, and which I can't account for either to my own, or at least to their satisfaction.

1. The greatest prejudice that lies against it with some is its repugnancy to and subversion of Sir I. Newton's philosophy in sundry points; to which they have been so much attached that they can't suffer themselves in the least to call it in question in any instance, but indeed it does not appear to me so inconsistent therewith as at first blush it did, for the laws of nature which he so happily explains are the same whether matter be supposed or not. However, let Sir Isaac Newton, or any other man, be heard only so far as his opinion is supported by reason:—but after all I confess I have so great a regard for the philosophy of that great man, that I would gladly see as much of it as may be, to obtain in this ideal scheme.

2. The objection, that it takes away all subordinate natural causes, and accounts for all appearances merely by the immediate will of the supreme spirit, does not seem to many to be answered to their satisfaction. It is readily granted that our ideas are inert, and can't cause one another, and are truly only signs one of another. For instance my idea of fire is not the cause of my idea of burning and of ashes. But inasmuch as these ideas are so connected as that they seem necessarily to point out to us the relations of cause and effect, we can't help thinking that our ideas are pictures of things without our minds at least, tho' not without the Great Mind, and which are their archetypes, between which these relations do obtain. I kindle a fire and leave it, no created mind beholds it; I return again and find a great alteration in the fuel; has there not been in my absence all the while that gradual al-

teration making in the archetype of my idea of wood which I should have had the idea of if I had been present? And is there not some archetype of my idea of the fire, which under the agency of the Divine Will has gradually caused this alteration? And so in all other instances, our ideas are so connected, that they seem necessarily to refer our minds to some originals which are properly (tho' subordinate) causes and effects one of another; insomuch that unless they be so, we can't help thinking ourselves under a perpetual delusion.

3. That all the phenomena of nature, must ultimately be referred to the will of the Infinite Spirit, is what must be allowed; but to suppose his immediate energy in the production of every effect, does not seem to impress so lively and great a sense of his power and wisdom upon our minds, as to suppose a subordination of causes and effects among the archetypes of our ideas, as he that should make a watch or clock of ever so beautiful an appearance and that should measure the time ever so exactly yet if he should be obliged to stand by it and influence and direct all its motions, he would seem but very deficient in both his ability and skill in comparison with him who should be able to make one that would regularly keep on its motion and measure the time for a considerable while without the intervention of any immediate force of its author or any one else impressed upon it.

4. And as this tenet seems thus to abate our sense of the wisdom and power of God, so there are some that cannot be persuaded that it is sufficiently cleared from bearing hard on his holiness; those who suppose that the corrupt affections of our souls and evil practices consequent to them, are occasioned by certain irregular mechanical motions of our bodies, and that these motions come to have an habitual irregular bias and tendency by means of our own voluntary indulgence to them, which we might have governed to better purpose, do in this way of thinking, sufficiently bring the guilt of those ill habits and actions upon ourselves; but if in an habitual sinner, every object and motion be but an idea, and every wicked appetite the effect of such a set of ideas, and these

ideas, the immediate effect of the Almighty upon his mind; it seems to follow, that the immediate cause of such ideas must be the cause of those immoral appetites and actions; because he is borne down before them seemingly, even in spite of himself. At first indeed they were only occasions, which might be withstood, and so, proper means of trial, but now they become causes of his immoralities. When therefore a person is under the power of a vicious habit, and it can't but be foreseen that the suggestion of such and such ideas will unavoidably produce those immoralities, how can it consist with the holiness of God to suggest them?

5. It is, after all that has been said on that head, still something shocking to many to think that there should be nothing but a mere show in all the art and contrivance appearing in the structure (for instance) of a human body, particularly of the organs of sense. The curious structure of the eye, what can it be more than merely a fine show, if there be no connection more than you admit of, between that and vision? It seems from the make of it to be designed for an instrument or means of conveying the images of external things to the perceptive faculty within; and if it be not so, if it be really of no use in conveying visible objects to our minds, and if our visible ideas are immediately created in them by the will of the Almighty, why should it be made to seem to be an instrument or medium as much as if indeed it really were so? It is evident, from the conveying of images into a dark room thro' a lens, that the eye is a lens, and that the images of things are painted on the bottom of it. But to what purpose is all this, if there be no connection between this fine apparatus and the act of vision; can it be thought a sufficient argument that there is no connection between them because we can't discover it, or conceive how it should be?

6. There are some who say, that if our sensations don't depend on any bodily organs—they don't see how death can be supposed to make any alteration in the manner of our perception, or indeed how there should be (properly speaking) any separate state of the soul at all. For if our bodies are

nothing but ideas, and if our having ideas in this present state does not depend upon what are thought to be the organs of sense, and lastly, if we are supposed (as doubtless we must) to have ideas in that state; it should seem that immediately upon our remove from our present situation, we should still be attended with the same ideas of bodies as we have now, and consequently with the same bodies or at least with bodies however different, and if so, what room is there left for any resurrection, properly so-called? So that while this tenet delivers us from the embarrassments that attend the doctrine of a material resurrection, it seems to have no place for any resurrection at all, at least in the sense that word seems to bear in St. John 5:28, 29.

7. Some of us are at a loss to understand your meaning when you speak of archetypes. You say the beings of things consists in their being perceived. And that things are nothing but ideas, that our ideas have no unperceived archetypes, but yet you allow archetypes to our ideas when things are not perceived by our minds; they exist in, i.e., are perceived by, some other mind. Now I understand you, that there is a twofold existence of things or ideas, one in the divine mind, and the other in created minds; the one archetypal, and the other ectypal; that, therefore, the real original and permanent existence of things is archetypal, being ideas in *mente Divinâ*, and that our ideas are copies of them, and so far forth real things as they are correspondent to their archetypes and exhibited to us, or begotten in us by the will of the Almighty, in such measure and degrees and by such stated laws and rules as He is pleased to observe; that, therefore, there is no unperceived substance intervening between the divine ideas and ours as a medium, occasion or instrument by which He begets our ideas in us, but that which was thought to be the material existence of things is in truth only ideal in the divine mind. Do I understand you right? Is it not therefore your meaning, that the existence of our ideas (i.e., the ectypal things) depends upon our perceiving them, yet there are external to any created mind, in the all-comprehending Spirit, real and perma-

nent archetypes (as stable and permanent as ever matter was thought to be), to which these ideas of ours are correspondent, and so that (tho' our visible and tangible ideas are *toto coelo* different and distinct things, yet) there may be said to be external to my mind, in the divine mind, an archetype (for instance of the candle that is before me) in which the originals of both my visible and tangible ideas, light, heat, whiteness, softness, etc., under such a particular cylindrical figure, are united, so that it may be properly said to be the same thing that I both see and feel?

8. If this, or something like it might be understood to be your meaning, it would seem less shocking to say that we don't see and feel the same thing, because we can't dispossess our minds of the notion of an external world, and would be allowed to conceive that, tho' there were no intelligent creature before Adam to be a spectator of it, yet the world was really six days in *archetypo,* gradually proceeding from an informal chaotic state into that beautiful show wherein it first appeared to his mind, and that the comet that appeared in 1680 (for instance) has now, tho' no created mind beholds it, a real existence in the all-comprehending spirit, and is making its prodigious tour through the vast fields of ether, and lastly that the whole vast congeries of heaven and earth, the mighty systems of worlds with all their furniture, have a real being in the eternal mind antecedent to and independent on the perception of created spirit, and that when we see and feel, etc., that that almighty mind, by his immediate *fiat*, begets in our minds (*pro nostro modulo*) ideas correspondent to them, and which may be imagined in some degree resemblances of them.

9. But if there be archetypes to our ideas, will it not follow that there is external space, extension, figure and motion, as being archetypes of our ideas, to which we give these names. And indeed for my part I cannot disengage my mind from the persuasion that there is external space; when I have been trying ever so much to conceive of space as being nothing but an idea in my mind, it will return upon me even in spite of my

utmost efforts, certainly there must be, there can't but be, external space. The length, breadth, and thickness of any idea, it's true, are but ideas; the distance between two trees in my mind is but an idea, but if there are archetypes to the ideas of the trees, there must be an archetype to the idea of the distance between them. Nor can I see how it follows that there is no external absolute height, bigness, or distance of things, because they appear greater or less to us according as we are nearer or remote from them, or see them with our naked eyes, or with glasses; any more than it follows that a man, for instance, is not really absolutely six foot high measured by a two foot rule applied to his body, because divers pictures of him may be drawn some six, some four, some two foot long according to the same measure. Nobody ever imagined that the idea of distance is without the mind, but does it therefore follow that there is no external distance to which the idea is correspondent, for instance, between Rhode Island and Stratford? Truly I wish it were not so great, that I might be so happy as to have a more easy access to you, and more nearly enjoy the advantages of your instructions.

10. You allow spirits to have a real existence external to one another. Methinks, if so, there must be distance between them, and space wherein they exist, or else they must all exist in one individual spot or point, and as it were coincide one with another. I can't see how external space and duration are any more abstract ideas than spirits. As we have (properly speaking) no ideas of spirits, so, indeed, neither have we of external space and duration. But it seems to me that the existence of these must unavoidably follow from the existence of those, insomuch that I can no more conceive of their not being, than I can conceive of the non-existence of the infinite and eternal mind. They seem as necessarily existent independent of any created mind as the Deity Himself. Or must we say there is nothing in Dr. Clarke's [1] argument *a priori*, in his demonstration of the being and attributes of God, or in

---

[1] [Samuel Clarke (1675–1729), author of *On the Being and Attributes of God* (1704–1705).]

what Sir Isaac Newton says about the infinity and eternity of God in his *Scholium Generale* to his *Principia*? I should be glad to know your sense of what those two authors say upon this subject.

11. You will forgive the confusedness of my thoughts and not wonder at my writing like a man something bewildered, since I am, as it were, got into a new world amazed at everything about me. These ideas of ours, what are they? Is the substance of the mind the *substratum* to its ideas? Is it proper to call them modifications of our minds? Or impressions upon them? Or what? Truly I can't tell what to make of them, any more than of matter itself. What is the *esse* of spirits?—you seem to think it impossible to abstract their existence from their thinking. *Princ.* p. 143. sec. 98. Is then the *esse* of minds nothing else but *percipere,* as the *esse* of ideas is *percipi?* Certainly, methinks there must be an unknown somewhat that thinks and acts, as difficult to be conceived of as matter, and the creation of which, as much beyond us as the creation of matter. Can actions be the *esse* of any thing? Can they exist or be exerted without some being who is the agent? And may not that being be easily imagined to exist without acting, e.g., without thinking? And consequently (for you are there speaking of duration) may he not be said *durare, etsi non cogitet,* to persist in being, tho' thinking were intermitted for a while? And is not this sometimes fact? The duration of the eternal mind, must certainly imply some thing besides an eternal succession of ideas. May I not then conceive that, tho' I get my idea of duration by observing the succession of ideas in my mind, yet there is a *perseverare in existendo,* a duration of my being, and of the being of other spirits distinct from, and independent of, this succession of ideas.

But, Sir, I doubt I have more than tired your patience with so many (and I fear you will think them impertinent) questions; for tho' they are difficulties with me, or at least with some in my neighborhood, for whose sake, in part, I write, yet I don't imagine they can appear such to you, who have so perfectly digested your thoughts upon this subject. And perhaps they may vanish before me upon a more mature consideration of it. However, I should be very thankful for your assistance, if it were not a pity you should waste your time (which would be employed to much better purposes) in writing to a person so obscure and so unworthy of such a favor as I am. But I shall live with some impatience till I see the second part of your design accomplished, wherein I hope to see these (if they can be thought such) or any other objections, that may have occurred to you since your writing the first part, obviated; and the usefulness of this doctrine more particularly displayed in the further application of it to the arts and sciences. May we not hope to see logic, mathematics, and natural philosophy, pneumatology, theology and morality, all in their order, appearing with a new lustre under the advantages they may receive from it? You have at least given us to hope for a geometry cleared of many perplexities that render that sort of study troublesome, which I shall be very glad of, who have found that science more irksome to me than any other, tho', indeed, I am but very little versed in any of them. But I will not trespass any further upon your patience. My very humble service to Mr. James and Mr. Dalton, and I am with the greatest veneration,

Rev'd Sir,
your most obliged
and most obedient
humble servant
Samuel Johnson

II. BERKELEY TO JOHNSON

Nov. 25, 1729

Rev. Sir:

The ingenious letter you favored me with found me very much indisposed with a gathering or imposthumation in my head, which confined me several weeks, and is now, I thank God, relieved. The objections of a candid thinking man to what I have written will always be welcome, and I shall not fail to give all the satisfaction I am able, not without hopes either of convincing or being convinced. It is a common fault for men to hate opposition, and be too much wedded to their own opinions. I am so sensible of this in others that I could not pardon it to myself, if I considered mine any further than they seem to me to be true, which I shall the better be able to judge of when they have passed the scrutiny of persons so well qualified to examine them as you and your friends appear to be, to whom my illness must be an apology for not sending this answer sooner.

1. The true use and end of natural philosophy is to explain the phenomena of nature, which is done by discovering the laws of nature, and reducing particular appearances to them. This is Sir Isaac Newton's method; and such method or design is not in the least inconsistent with the principles I lay down. This mechanical philosophy doth not assign or suppose any one natural efficient cause in the strict and proper sense; nor is it, as to its use, concerned about *matter;* nor is matter connected therewith; nor doth it infer the being of matter. It must be owned, indeed, that the mechanical philosophers do suppose (though unnecessarily) the being of matter. They do even pretend to demonstrate that matter is proportional to gravity, which, if they could, this indeed would furnish an

unanswerable objection. But let us examine their demonstration—it is laid down in the first place, that the momentum of any body is the product of its quantity by its velocity, *moles in celeritatem ducta*. If, therefore, the velocity is given, the momentum will be as its quantity. But it is observed that bodies of all kinds descend *in vacuo* with the same velocity; therefore, the momentum of descending bodies is as the quantity of moles, i.e., gravity is as matter. But this argument concludes nothing, and is a mere circle. For, I ask, when it is premised that the momentum is equal to the *moles in celeritatem ducta,* how the moles or quantity of matter is estimated. If you say, by extent, the proposition is not true; if by weight, then you suppose that the quantity of matter is proportional to matter: i.e., the conclusion is taken for granted in one of the premises. As for absolute space and motion, which are also supposed without any necessity or use, I refer you to what I have already published; particularly in a Latin treatise, *De Motu*,[2] which I shall take care to send you.

2. Cause is taken in different senses. A proper active efficient cause I can conceive none but spirit; nor any action, strictly speaking, but where there is will. But this doth not hinder the allowing occasional causes (which are in truth but signs), and more is not requisite in the best physics, i.e., the mechanical philosophy. Neither doth it hinder the admitting other causes besides God; such as spirits of different orders, which may be termed active causes, as acting indeed, though by limited and derivative powers. But as for an unthinking agent, no point of physics is explained by it, nor is it conceivable.

3. Those who have all along contended for a material world, have yet acknowledged that *natura naturans* (to use the language of the Schoolmen) is God; and that the divine conservation of things is equipollent to, and in fact, the same thing with a continued repeated creation; in a word, that conservation and creation differ only in the *terminus a quo*. These are the common opinions of the Schoolmen; and

[2] [Published in London, 1721.]

Durandus,[3] who held the world to be a machine like a clock, made and put in motion by God, but afterwards continuing to go of itself, was therein particular and had few followers. The very poets teach a doctrine not unlike the schools,—*Mens agitat molem.* (Virg. *Aeneid* VI.) The Stoics and Platonists are everywhere full of the same notion. I am not therefore singular in this point itself, so much as in my way of proving it. Further, it seems to me that the power and wisdom of God are as worthily set forth by supposing Him to act immediately as an omnipresent, infinitely active spirit, as by supposing Him to act by the mediation of subordinate causes, in preserving and governing the natural world. A clock may indeed go independent of its maker or artificer, inasmuch as the gravitation of its pendulum proceeds from another cause, and that the artificer is not the adequate cause of the clock; so that the analogy would not be just to suppose a clock is in respect of its artist what the world is in respect of its creator. For aught I can see, it is no disparagement to the perfection of God to say that all things necessarily depend on Him as their conservator as well as creator, and that all nature would shrink to nothing, if not upheld and preserved in being by the same force that first created it. This, I am sure, is agreeable to Holy Scripture, as well as to the writings of the most esteemed philosophers; and if it is to be considered that men make use of tools and machines to supply defect of power in themselves, we shall think it no honor to the divinity to attribute such things to him.

4. As to guilt, it is the same thing whether I kill a man with my hands or an instrument; whether I do it myself or make use of a ruffian. The imputation therefore upon the sanctity of God is equal, whether we suppose our sensations to be produced immediately by God, or by the mediation of instruments and subordinate causes, all which are his creatures, and moved by his laws. This theological consideration, there-

---

[3] [Probably Durandus of St. Pourcain, i.e., Guillaume Durand (d. 1332), author of *De statu animarum sanctarum* and *In Sententias Petri Lombardi* (Paris, 1508).]

fore, may be waived, as leading besides the question; for such I hold are points to be which bear equally hard on both sides of it. Difficulties about the principle of moral actions will cease, if we consider that all guilt is in the will, and that our ideas, from whatever cause they are produced, are alike inert.

5. As to the art and contrivance in the parts of animals, etc., I have considered that matter in the *Principles of Human Knowledge,* and, if I mistake not, sufficiently shown the wisdom and use thereof, considered as signs and means of information. I do not indeed wonder that on first reading what I have written, men are not thoroughly convinced. On the contrary, I should very much wonder if prejudices, which have been many years taking root, should be extirpated in a few hours' reading. I had no inclination to trouble the world with large volumes. What I have done was rather with a view of giving hints to thinking men, who have leisure and curiosity to go to the bottom of things, and pursue them in their own minds. Two or three times reading these small tracts, and making what is read the occasion of thinking, would, I believe, render the whole familiar and easy to the mind, and take off that shocking appearance which hath often been observed to attend speculative truths.

6. I see no difficulty in conceiving a change of state, such as is vulgarly called death, as well without as with material substance. It is sufficient for that purpose that we allow sensible bodies, i.e., such as are immediately perceived by sight and touch; the existence of which I am so far from questioning (as philosophers are used to do) that I establish it, I think, upon evident principles. Now, it seems very easy to conceive the soul to exist in a separate state (i.e., divested from those limits and laws of motion and perception with which she is embarrassed here), and to exercise herself on new ideas, without the intervention of these tangible things we call bodies. It is even very possible to apprehend how the soul may have ideas of color without an eye, or of sounds without an ear. . . .

And now, Sir, I submit these hints (which I have hastily thrown together as soon as my illness gave me leave) to your own maturer thoughts, which after all you will find the best instructors. What you have seen of mine was published when I was very young, and without doubt hath many defects. For though the notions should be true (as I verily think they are), yet it is difficult to express them clearly and consistently, language being framed to common use and received prejudices. I do not therefore pretend that my books can teach truth. All I hope for is that they may be an occasion to inquisitive men of discovering truth by consulting their own minds and looking into their own thoughts. As to the second part of my treatise concerning the principles of human knowledge, the fact is that I had made a considerable progress in it, but the manuscript was lost about fourteen years ago during my travels in Italy; and I never had leisure since to do so disagreeable a thing as writing twice on the same subject.

Objections passing through your hands have their full force and clearness. I like them the better. This intercourse with a man of parts and a philosophic genius is very agreeable. I sincerely wish we were nearer neighbors. In the meantime whenever either you or your friends favor me with your thoughts, you may be sure of a punctual correspondence on my part. Before I have done I will venture to recommend three points: (1) To consider well the answers I have already given in my books to several objections. (2) To consider whether any new objection that shall occur doth not suppose the doctrine of abstract general ideas. (3) Whether the difficulties proposed in objection to my scheme can be solved by the contrary, for if they cannot, it is plain they can be no objection to mine.

I know not whether you have got my treatise concerning the principles of human knowledge. I intend to send it with my tract *De Motu*. If you know of a safe hand favor me with a line, and I will make use of that opportunity to send them. My humble service to your friends, to whom I understand myself indebted for some part of your letter.

I am, your very faithful, humble servant,

Geor. Berkeley

III. JOHNSON TO BERKELEY

A SECOND LETTER TO THE REV'D DR. BERKELEY IN ANSWER TO HIS REPLY TO THE FOREGOING LETTER

Feb. 5, 1730

REV'D SIR:

Yours of November 25th, I received not till January 17th, and this being the first convenient opportunity I now return you my humblest thanks for it.

I am very sorry to understand that you have labored under the illness you mention; but am exceeding glad and thankful for your recovery; I pray God preserve your life and health, that you may have opportunity to perfect these great and good designs for the advancement of learning and religion wherewith your mind labors.

I am very much obliged to you for the favorable opinion you are pleased to express at what I made bold to write to you and that you have so kindly vouchsafed so large and particular an answer to it. But you have done me too great an honor in putting any value on my judgment; for it is impossible my thoughts on this subject should be of any consequence, who have been bred up under the greatest disadvantages, and have had so little ability and opportunity to be instructed in things of this nature. And therefore I should be very vain to pretend any thing else but to be a learner; 'tis merely with this view that I give you this trouble.

I am sensible that the greatest part of what I wrote was owing to not sufficiently attending to those three important considerations you suggest at the end of your letter: And I hope a little more time and a more careful attention to and application of them, will clear up what difficulties yet lie in the way of our entirely coming into your sentiments. Indeed I had not had opportunity sufficiently to digest your books;

for no sooner had I just read them over, but they were greedily demanded by my friends, who live much scattered up and down, and who expected I would bring them home with me, because I had told them before that if these books were to be had in Boston, I intended to purchase a set of them; and indeed they have not yet quite finished their tour. The *Theory of Vision* is still at New York and the *Dialogues* just gone to Long Island. But I am the better content to want them because I know they are doing good.

For my part I am content to give up the cause of matter, glad to get rid of the absurdities thereon depending if it be defensible, I am sure, at least, it is not in my power to defend it. And being spoiled of that sandy foundation, I only want now to be more thoroughly taught how and where to set down my foot again and make out a clear and consistent scheme without it. And of all the particulars I troubled you with before, there remain only these that I have any difficulty about, viz., archetypes, space and duration, and the *esse* of spirits. And indeed these were the chief of my difficulties before. Most of the rest were such objections as I found by conversation among my acquaintance, did not appear to them sufficiently answered. But I believe upon a more mature consideration of the matter, and especially of this kind reply, they will see reason to be better satisfied. They that have seen it (especially my friend Mr. Wetmore) join with me in thankfully acknowledging your kindness, and return their very humble service to you.

1. As to those difficulties that yet remain with me, I believe all my hesitation about the first of them (and very likely the rest) is owing to my dullness and want of attention so as not rightly to apprehend your meaning. I believe I expressed myself uncouthly about archetypes in my 7th and 8th articles, but upon looking back upon your *Dialogues,* and comparing again three or four passages, I can't think I meant any thing different from what you intend.

You allow, *Dial.* p. 74,[4] "That things have an existence dis-

[4] [See above, II, sec. 3.]

tinct from being perceived by us" (i.e., any created spirits), "and that they exist in, i.e., are perceived by, the infinite and omnipresent mind who contains and supports this sensible world as being perceived by him." And p. 109,[5] "That things have an existence exterior to our minds, and that during the intervals of their being perceived by us, they exist in another (i.e., the infinite) mind"; from whence you justly and excellently infer the certainty of his existence, "who knows and comprehends all things and exhibits them to our view in such manner and according to such rules as he himself has ordained." And p. 113,[6] "That, e.g., a tree, when we don't perceive it, exists without our minds in the infinite mind of God." And this exterior existence of things (if I understand you right) is what you call the archetypal state of things, p. 150.[7]

From these and the like expressions, I gathered what I said about the archetypes of our ideas, and thence inferred that there is exterior to us, in the divine mind, a system of universal nature, whereof the ideas we have are in such a degree resemblances as the Almighty is pleased to communicate to us. And I cannot yet see but my inference was just; because according to you, the idea we see is not in the divine mind, but in our own. When, therefore, you say sensible things exist in, as being perceived by, the infinite mind I humbly conceive you must be understood that the originals or archetypes of our sensible things or ideas exist independent of us in the infinite mind, or that sensible things exist *in archetypo* in the divine mind. The divine idea, therefore, of a tree I suppose (or a tree in the divine mind), must be the original or archetype of ours, and ours a copy or image of His (our ideas images of His, in the same sense as our souls are images of Him) of which there may be several, in several created minds, like so many several pictures of the same original to which they are all to be referred.

---

[5] [See above, III, sec. 3.]
[6] [See above, III, sec. 5.]
[7] [See above, III, sec. 21.]

When therefore, several people are said to see the same tree or star, etc., whether at the same or at so many several distances from it, it is (if I understand you) *unum et idem in Archetypo,* tho' *multiplex et diversum in Ectypo,* for it is as evident that your idea is not mine nor mine yours when we say we both look on the same tree, as that you are not I nor I you. But in having each our idea we being dependent upon and impressed upon by the same almighty mind, wherein you say this tree exists, while we shut our eyes (and doubtless you mean the same also, while they are open), our several trees must, I think be so many pictures (if I may so call them) of the one original, the tree in the infinite mind, and so of all other things. Thus I understand you not indeed that our ideas are in any measure adequate resemblances of the system in the divine mind, but however that they are just and true resemblances or copies of it, so far as He is pleased to communicate His mind to us.

2. As to space and duration, I do not pretend to have any other notion of their exterior existence than what is necessarily implied in the notion we have of God; I do not suppose they are any thing distinct from, or exterior to, the infinite and eternal mind; for I conclude with you that there is nothing exterior to my mind but God and other spirits with the attributes or properties belonging to them and ideas contained in them.

External space and duration therefore I take to be those properties or attributes in God, to which our ideas, which we signify by those names, are correspondent, and of which they are the faint shadows. This I take to be Sir Isaac Newton's meaning when he says, *Schol. General. Deus—durat semper et adest ubique et existendo semper et ubique, durationem et spacium, eternitatem et infinitatem constituit.*[8] And in his

---

[8] ["He endures forever, and is everywhere present; and by existing always and everywhere, he constitutes duration and space." *Sir Isaac Newton's Mathematical Principles of Natural Philosophy,* trans. Andrew Motte, ed. Florian Cajori (2nd. edn.; Berkeley: University of California Press, 1946), p. 545.]

Optics calls space *as it were God's boundless sensorium*,[9] nor can I think you have a different notion of these attributes from that great philosopher, tho' you may differ in your ways of expressing or explaining yourselves. However it be, when you call the Deity infinite and eternal, and in that most beautiful and charming description, *Dial.* p. 71,[10] etc., when you speak of the *abyss of space and boundless extent beyond thought* and imagination, I don't know how to understand you any otherwise than I understood Sir Isaac, when he uses the like expressions. The truth is we have no proper ideas of God or His attributes, and conceive of them only by analogy from what we find in ourselves; and so, I think we conceive His immensity and eternity to be what in Him are correspondent to our space and duration.

As for the *punctum stans* of the Schools, and the *to nun* of the Platonists, they are notions too fine for my gross thoughts; I can't tell what to make of those words, they don't seem to convey any ideas or notions to my mind, and whatever the matter is, the longer I think of them, the more they disappear, and seem to dwindle away into nothing. Indeed they seem to me very much like abstract ideas, but I doubt the reason is because I never rightly understood them. I don't see why the term *punctum stans* may not as well, at least, be applied to the immortality as the eternity of God; for the word *punctum* is more commonly used in relation to extension or space than duration; and to say that a being is immense, and yet that it is but a point, and that its duration is perpetual without beginning or end, and yet that it is but a *to nun,* looks to me like a contradiction.

I can't therefore understand the term *to nun* unless it be designed to adumbrate the divine omnisciency or the perfec-

---

[9] [*Opticks* (London, 1730; first published 1704), Question 28: ". . . does it not appear from phenomena that there is a being incorporeal, living, intelligent, omnipresent, who in infinite space, as it were in his sensory, sees the things themselves intimately . . . ?"]

[10] [See above, II, sec. 2.]

tion of the divine knowledge, by the more perfect notion we have of things present than of things past; and in this sense it would imply that all things past, present and to come are always at every point of duration equally perfectly known or present to God's mind (tho' in a manner infinitely more perfect), as the things that are known to us are present to our minds at any point of our duration which we call *now*. So that with respect to His equally perfect knowledge of things past, present or to come, it is in effect always now with Him. To this purpose it seems well applied and intelligible enough, but His duration I take to be a different thing from this, as that point of our duration which we call *now*, is a different thing from our actual knowledge of things, as distinguished from our remembrance. And it may as well be said that God's immensity consists in His knowing at once what is, and is transacted in all places (e.g., China, Jupiter, Saturn, all the systems of fixed stars, etc.) everywhere, however so remote from us (tho' in a manner infinitely more perfect), as we know what is, and is transacted in us and about us just at hand; as that His eternity consists in this *to nun* as above explained, i.e., in His knowing things present, past and to come, however so remote, all at once or equally perfectly as we know the things that are present to us *now*.

In short our ideas expressed by the terms immensity and eternity are only space and duration considered as boundless or with the negation of any limits, and I can't help thinking there is something analogous to them without us, being in and belonging to, or attributes of, that glorious mind, whom for that reason we call immense and eternal, in whom we and all other spirits, *live, move and have their being*, not all in a point, but in so many different points, places, or *alicubis*, and variously situated with respect one to another, or else as I said before, it seems as if we should all coincide one with another.

I conclude, if I am wrong in my notion of external space, and duration, it is owing to the riveted prejudices of abstract ideas; but really when I have thought it over and over again in my feeble way of thinking, I can't see any connection between them (as I understand them) and that doctrine. They don't seem to be any more abstract ideas than spirits, for, as I said, I take them to be attributes of the necessarily existing spirit; and consequently the same reasons that convince me of his existence, bring with them the existence of these attributes. So that of the ways of coming to the knowledge of things that you mention, it is that of inference or deduction by which I seem to know that there is external infinite space and duration because there is without me a mind infinite and eternal.

3. As to the *esse* of spirits,[11] I know Descartes held the soul always thinks, but I thought Mr. Locke had sufficiently confuted this notion, which he seems to have entertained only to serve an hypothesis. The Schoolmen, it is true, call the soul *Actus* and God *Actus purus;* but I confess I never could well understand their meaning perhaps because I never had opportunity to be much versed in their writings. I should have thought the Schoolmen to be of all sorts of writers the most unlikely to have had recourse to for the understanding of your sentiments, because they of all others, deal the most in abstract ideas; tho' to place the very being of spirits in the mere act of thinking, seems to me very much like making abstract ideas of them.

There is certainly something passive in our souls, we are purely passive in the reception of our ideas; and reasoning and willing are actions of something that reasons and wills, and therefore must be only modalities of that something. Nor does it seem to me that when I say [something] I mean an abstract idea. It is true I have no idea of it, but I feel it; I feel that it is, because I feel or am conscious of the exertions of it; but the exertions of it are not the thing but the modalities of it

---

11 [See *Principles*, sec. 98; Descartes, *Discourse on Method*, Part IV; Locke, *Essay*, Bk. II, chap. 1, sec. 13: "Thus, methinks, every drowsy nod shakes their doctrine who teach that the soul is always thinking."]

distinguished from it as actions from an agent, which seem to me distinguishable without having recourse to abstract ideas.

And, therefore, when I suppose the existence of a spirit while it does not actually think, it does not appear to me that I do it by supposing an abstract idea of existence, and another of absolute time. The existence of John asleep by me, without so much as a dream is not an abstract idea. Nor is the time passing the while an abstract idea, they are only partial considerations of him. *Perseverare in existendo* in general, without reflecting on any particular thing existing, I take to be what is called an abstract idea of time or duration; but the *perseverare in existendo* of John is, if I mistake not, a partial consideration of him. And I think it is as easy to conceive of him as continuing to exist without thinking as without seeing.

Has a child no soul till it actually perceives? And is there not such a thing as sleeping without dreaming, or being in a *deliquium* without a thought? If there be, and yet at the same time the *esse* of a spirit be nothing else but its actual thinking, the soul must be dead during those intervals; and if ceasing or intermitting to think be the ceasing to be, or death of the soul, it is many times and easily put to death. According to this tenet, it seems to me the soul may sleep on to the resurrection, or rather may wake up in the resurrection state, the next moment after death. Nay I don't see upon what we can build any natural argument for the soul's immortality. I think I once heard you allow a principle of perception and spontaneous motion in beasts. Now if their *esse* as well as ours consists in perceiving, upon what is the natural immortality of our souls founded that will not equally conclude in favor of them? I mention this last consideration because I am at a loss to understand how you state the argument for the soul's natural immortality; for the argument from thinking to immaterial and from thence to indiscerpible, and from thence to immortal don't seem to obtain in your way of thinking.

If *esse* be only *percipere*, upon what is our consciousness founded? I perceived yesterday, and I perceive now, but last night between my yesterday's and today's perception there has been an intermission when I perceived nothing. It seems to me there must be some principle common to these perceptions, whose *esse* don't depend on them, but in which they are, as it were, connected, and on which they depend, whereby I am and continue conscious of them.

Lastly, Mr. Locke's argument (Bk. II, chap. 19, sec. 4) from the intention and remission of thought, appears to me very considerable; according to which, upon this supposition the soul must exist more or have a greater degree of being at one time than at another, according as it thinks more intensely or more remissly.

I own I said very wrong when I said I did not know what to make of ideas more than of matter. My meaning was, in effect, the same as I expressed afterwards about the substance of the soul's being a somewhat as unknown as matter. And what I intended by those questions was whether our ideas are not the substance of the soul itself, under so many various modifications, according to that saying (if I understand it right) *Intellectus intelligendo fit omnia?* [12] It is true, those expressions (modifications, impressions, etc.) are metaphorical, and it seems to me to be no less so, to say that ideas exist in the mind, and I am under some doubt whether this last way of speaking don't carry us further from the thing, than to say ideas are the mind variously modified; but as you observe, it is scarce possible to speak of the mind without a metaphor.

Thus Sir, your goodness has tempted me to presume again to trouble you once more; and I submit the whole to your correction; but I can't conclude without saying that I am so much persuaded that your *books teach truth*, indeed the most excellent truths, and that in the most excellent manner, that I can't but express myself again very solicitously desirous that

---

[12] [Cf. Aristotle, *De Anima* III. 5: "Mind . . . is what it is by virtue of becoming all things." *The Works of Aristotle*, ed. W. D. Ross and J. A. Smith (12 vols.; Oxford: Oxford University Press, 1928–1952), Vol. III (trans. Smith, 1931).]

the noble design you have begun may be yet further pursued in the second part. And everybody that has seen the first is earnestly with me in this request. In hopes of which I will not desire you to waste your time in writing to me (tho' otherwise I should esteem it the greatest favor), at least till I have endeavored further to gain satisfaction by another perusal of the books I have, with the other pieces you are so kind as to offer, which I will thankfully accept, for I had not *The Principles* of my own, it was a borrowed one I used.

The bearer hereof, Capt. Gorham, is a coaster bound now to Boston, which trade he constantly uses (except that it has been now long interrupted by the winter). But he always touches at Newport, and will wait on the Rev'd Mr. Honyman both going and returning, by whom you will have opportunity to send those books.

I am, Rev'd Sir,
>with the greatest gratitude,
>your most devoted humble servant,

S. Johnson

Stratford, *Feb. 5, 1730*

IV. BERKELEY TO JOHNSON

March 24, 1730

REV. SIR:

Yours of Feb. 5th came not to my hands before yesterday; and this afternoon being informed that a sloop is ready to sail towards your town, I would not let slip the opportunity of returning you an answer, though wrote in a hurry.

1. I have no objection against calling the ideas in the mind of God, archetypes of ours. But I object against those archetypes by philosophers supposed to be real things, and to have an absolute rational existence distinct from their being perceived by any mind whatsoever, it being the opinion of all materialists that an ideal existence in the divine mind is one thing, and the real existence of material things another.

2. As to space, I have no notion of any but that which is relative. I know some late philosophers have attributed extension to God, particularly mathematicians; one [13] of whom, in a treatise *de Spatio Reali,* pretends to find out fifteen of the incommunicable attributes of God in space. But it seems to me, that they being all negative, he might as well have found them in nothing; and that it would have been as justly inferred from space being impassive, uncreated, indivisible, etc., that it was nothing, as that it was God.

Sir Isaac Newton supposeth an absolute space different from relative, and consequent thereto, absolute motion different from relative motion; and with all other mathematicians, he supposeth the infinite divisibility of the finite parts of this absolute space; he also supposeth material bodies to drift therein. Now, though I do acknowledge Sir Isaac to have been

---

[13] [Joseph Raphson, F.R.S. (d. 1715 or 1716), in *De Spatio Reali seu Ente Infinito* (1697).]

an extraordinary man and most profound mathematician, yet I cannot agree with him in these particulars. I make no scruple to use the word space, as well as other words in common use, but I do not mean thereby a distinct absolute being. For my meaning I refer you to what I have published.

By the *to nun* I suppose to be implied that all things past and to come are actually present to the mind of God, and that there is in Him no change, variation, or succession—a succession of ideas I take to constitute time and not to be only the sensible measure thereof, as Mr. Locke [14] and others think. But in these matters every man is to think for himself, and speak as he finds. One of my earliest inquiries was about time, which led me into several paradoxes that I did not think fit or necessary to publish, particularly into the notion that the resurrection follows the next moment to death. We are confounded and perplexed about time. (1) Supposing a succession in God. (2) Conceiving that we have an abstract idea of time. (3) Supposing that the time in one mind is to be measured by the succession of ideas in another. (4) Not considering the true use and end of words, which as often terminate in the will as in the understanding, being employed rather to excite influence, and direct action than to produce clear and distinct ideas.

3. That the soul of man is passive as well as active I make no doubt. Abstract general ideas was a notion that Mr. Locke [15] held in common with the Schoolmen, and I think all other philosophers; it runs through his whole book *Of Human Understanding*. He holds an abstract idea of existence exclusive of perceiving and being perceived. I cannot find I have any such idea, and this is my reason against it. Descartes proceeds upon other principles. One square foot of snow is as white as one thousand yards; one single perception is as truly a perception as one hundred. Now any degree of perception being sufficient to existence, it will not follow that we should

[14] [*Essay*, Bk. II, chap. 14.]
[15] [See *Principles*, Introduction, sec. 11.]

say one existed more at one time than another, any more than we should say one thousand yards of snow are whiter than one yard. But after all, this comes to a verbal dispute. I think it might prevent a good deal of obscurity and dispute to examine well what I have said about abstraction, and about the true sense and significancy of words, in several parts of these things that I have published, though much remains to be said on that subject.

You say you agree with me that there is nothing within your mind but God and other spirits, with the attributes or properties belonging to them, and the ideas contained in them. This is a principle or main point from which, and from what I had laid down about abstract ideas, much may be deduced. But if in every inference we should not agree, so long as the main points are settled and well understood, I should be less solicitous about particular conjectures. I could wish that all the things I have published on these philosophical subjects were read in the order wherein I published them, once to take in the design and connection of them, and a second time with a critical eye, adding your own thought and observation upon every part as you went along. I send you herewith ten bound books and one unbound. You will take yourself what you have not already. You will give the *Principles,* the *Theory,* the *Dialogues,* one of each, with my service to the gentleman who is Fellow of New Haven College, whose compliments you brought me. What remains you will give as you please.

If at any time your affairs should draw you into these parts, you shall be very welcome to pass as many days as you can spend at my house. Four or five days' conversation would set several things in a fuller and clearer light than writing could do in as many months. In the meantime I shall be glad to hear from you or your friends when ever you please to favor,

Rev. Sir,
Your very humble servant,
Geor. Berkeley

Pray let me know whether they would admit the writings of

Hooker and Chillingworth into the library of the College in New Haven.[16]

Rhode Island, *March 24, 1730*

---

[16] [Later Yale University. Richard Hooker (1553–1600), author of *Laws of Ecclesicastical Polity* (1594), and William Chillingworth (1602–1644), author of *The Religion of Protestants a Safe Way to Salvation* (1637), were Anglican theologians and possibly unacceptable at Yale. Berkeley gave nearly a thousand books to Yale. See Andrew Keogh, "Bishop Berkeley's Gifts of Books to Yale in 1733," *Yale University Library Gazette*, VIII (1933), 1–41.]

INDEX*

Absolute existence. *See* Relativity
Abstract ideas, ix ff., 28, 240–241; criticism of, *Introduction*, **10–17**; distinct from being perceived, *Principles*, **5–6**; of extension and motion, *Principles*, **10, 11**, 99, 125, *Dialogues*, **I, 8**; of goodness, happiness, justice, and virtue, *Principles*, **100**; nature of doctrine, *Introduction*, **6–9**; of number, *Principles*, **12, 119–122**; of object from sensation, 134–135; source of, in language, *Introduction*, **18–20**; of space, *Principles*, **116**; of a spirit's existence from thinking, 235–236, *Principles*, **98**; of time, 240, *Principles*, **97, 98**; of unity, *Principles*, **13, 120**
Academics, 211
Action of the mind: in perception, *Dialogues*, **I, 9**; in volition, 159, 185, 235
Albigenses, 99n.
America, Berkeley in, xviii ff.
"America, or the Muses Refuge," xix
Arcesilaus, 211n.
Archetypes, 26, 42, 64, 70, 145, 156, 185, 195, 202, 217, 219, 230–231, 239; and ectypes, 202, 219–220, 232; and external space, 220

Aristotle, 18, 27, 237n.
Atheism, *Principles*, **92–96**, *Dialogues*, **III, 22**
Attraction, *Principles*, **103–106**
Augustine, Saint, 99n.
Author of Nature, 35, 36, 52, 54, 75, 95, 152, 157

Bacon, Francis, 46n.
Baxter, Andrew, ix, xi, xxvii, xxxiii
Bayle, Pierre, xxix
Beattie, James, ix, xi, xxix–xxx
Bergson, Henri, xxxii
Berkeley, Anne xiv, xx
Bermuda, xix–xxi
Bracken, Harry M., xxv–xxvi

Carneades, 211n.
Cartesians, 211
Causality, *Principles*, **25–33**, 65, 66
Causes: efficient and final, 225, *Principles*, **107**; second, physical, or occasional, *Principles*, **32, 51–53, 60–66**, *Dialogues*, **II, 5, 7**, *Correspondence*, **I, 2–5, II, 2–5**; as signs, 225–226. *See also* Signs and things signified
Chambers, Ephraim, xxv–xxvi
Chillingworth, William, 242
Clarke, Samuel, 55n., 221
"Clockwork of nature," 50, 226

* In the Index, references to whole sections of the *Principles*, *Dialogues*, and *Correspondence* are given in boldface numbers. *Introduction* refers to Berkeley's Introduction to the *Principles*.

Collections of ideas. *See* Combinations of qualities
Colors, *Dialogues*, I, 5; apparent and real, 123 ff.
Combinations of qualities, ix, 6, 9, 22, 23, 27, 38, 39, 53, 66, 70–71, 112, 140, 191, 195–196
Condillac, Étienne de, vii, xxiii
Congreve, William, xii
Context theory of meaning, x–xi
Copernican system, 46, 49, 184
Creation: continued, Correspondence, II, 3; explanation of, 199–204; Mosaic account of, 197–198

Davie, George E., xxvi
Death. *See* Resurrection
Descartes, René, 175n., 235
Diderot, Denis, vii, xxiii
"Distance or outness," 41, 142
"Distances of time," 41
Durand, Guillaume (Durandus), 226

Einstein, Albert, vii
Epicureans, 68
Esse is *percipi*, vii, xxxi, 23
"Existence," 23, 61, 65, 113, 153, 168, 175, 179–180, 185, 195–196, 201
Explanation, nature of physical, 45, 51–52, 72 ff., 224
Extension, *Principles*, 11, 99, 123–132, *Dialogues*, I, 6

Figure, *Dialogues*, I, 6

Geulincx, Arnold, 55n.
God. *See* Mind, Mind, divine
Gravitation. *See* Attraction
Guilt, and instruments, 226–227

Heat and cold, 112 ff.

Helmholtz, Hermann von, vii
Hendel, Charles W., xxviii
Hobbes, Thomas, 154
Hobbists, 68
Hooker, Richard, 242
Hume, David, viii–ix, xxvi, xxviii, xxx–xxxi; on Berkeley's rejection of abstract ideas, ix, xxviii; on Berkeley's skepticism, xxviii–xxix, 178n.

Ideas, *Principles*, **86–134**; changed into things, 190, 211; defense of use of word, 39, 181; distinct from minds, 23, 65, 178–179; exist independently of human minds, 175, 180; exist only in minds, 23, 66; explanation of production of, 149 ff.; fleeting and variable, 147; immediately perceived, 174, 179–180, 211; none of mind, 34, 176 ff.; as objects of knowledge, 22, 66; passive, 33–34, 175; the same perceived by many, 193–194; of sense and imagination, 35–36. *See also* "Existence," Mind, Sensible things
Illusions, 37, 38, 49, 180, 183–184
Immaterialism, 201, 207; advantages of, *Dialogues*, III, **22**
"In the mind," the metaphor, 196–197
Infinite divisibility, *Principles*, 48, **123–132**
Infinitesimals, vii, 87 ff.

Jessop, T. E., xv n., xxxiii n.
Johnson, Samuel (English), ix, x
Johnson, Samuel (President of King's College, New York), vii–viii, xxi–xxii, 215 ff.

INDEX

Kant, Immanuel, ix; relation to Berkeley, xxx ff.

Language: of Author of Nature, *Principles*, **65, 66,** 108–110; errors of the source of doctrine of abstract ideas, *Introduction*, **18–20;** framed for "convenience and dispatch," 192; meditating without words, *Introduction*, **21–25;** and proper use of words, 158, 241, *Principles*, 83; purposes of, xiv, 17–18; "think with the learned and speak with the vulgar," *Principles*, **51, 52;** use of metaphors for describing mind, 197; visible ideas form a, *Principles*, **43, 44**

Laws of nature. See Rules

Leibniz, G. W. von, x

Locke, John, xii, xvii, xxi–xxii, 175n., 235, 237, 240; on abstract ideas, 9–10, 12; on pure substance in general, 29n.

Luce, A. A., xiv n., xv n.

Mach, Ernst, vii, xxxi–xxxii

Maclaurin, Colin, xxiii, xxvi

Malebranche, N., xii, 55n., 96n.

Manichaean heresy, 99

Matter, xvii, 26, 109; as Aristotle's *materia prima*, 27; and atheism, *Principles*, **92–96;** as "bare possibility," 146, *Principles*, **22–23;** Berkeley's use of the word, 209–210; cause of belief in, *Principles*, **56, 57;** and common sense, *Principles*, **54, 55,** *Dialogues*, III, **14;** as explanatory principle, *Principles*, **19, 50,** *Dialogues*, II, **5, 10,** IV, **13;** how known, 146, 163, *Principles*, **18, 20;** impossibility of, *Dialogues*, II, **11;** as instrument, 218, *Principles*, **60–66,** *Dialogues*, II, **6;** as material *substratum*, *Principles*, **7–10, 16–17,** *Dialogues*, I, **10;** not necessary in physics, *Principles*, 50; as occasion, *Principles*, **67–79,** *Dialogues*, II, **7;** proportional to gravity, 224–225, *Dialogues*, III, **12;** and skepticism, *Principles*, **85–91,** *Dialogues*, III, **1;** as unknown somewhat, *Principles*, **80, 81,** *Dialogues*, II, **9**

Microscopes, 123–124, 191–192

Mind, *Principles*, **135–149;** and abstraction, 70, 221, *Principles*, **143;** as cause or will, *Principles*, **26–33,** *Dialogues*, II, **4;** distinct from ideas, *Principles*, **2, 139, 142;** and instruments, 161; knowledge of other minds, 178, *Principles*, **145–149;** knowledge or notion of. 34–35, 65–66, 93, 176 ff.; no idea of, *Principles*, **27, 135–142,** *Dialogues*, III, **4;** as only substance or support of ideas, 179, *Principles*, **7, 49, 73, 135;** as perceiving being or understanding, *Principles*, **27;** skepticism about nature of, 178, *Principles*, **137;** as "system of floating ideas," 178

Mind, divine: and blemishes and defects of nature, *Principles*, **151–154;** as cause or will, 185, *Principles*, **26–33, 102, 105, 146,** *Dialogues*, II, **4;** our knowledge of, *Principles*, **146–149,** *Dialogues*, II, **3, 4,** III, **4, 5;** and pain, *Dialogues*, III, **11;** and sin, 181–182

Minimum sensibile, 89. See also Infinitesimals

Miracles, *Principles*, 84
Molyneux, William, xii
Mossner, E. C., xxvi
Motion, *Principles*, 11, 99, *Dialogues*, I, 7; absolute and relative, i, *Principles*, 110–115

"Nature," meaning of, 97
Newton, Sir Isaac, xii–xiii, xvii, xxi–xxii, 76n., 216, 222, 224, 232–233, 239–240; on absolute and relative space and motion, *Principles*, 110–117; on absolute time, *Principles*, 97, 98
Niphus, Augustine, 46n.
Norris, John, 55n.
Notions, 34–35, 65–66, 93, 177–178
Number, *Principles*, 12, 119–122

Objections, rules for answering, *Dialogues*, III, 23
Objects: of arithmetic, *Principles*, 119, 122; of geometry, *Principles*, 123; of human knowledge, *Principles*, 1, 86, 89, 135; immediately and mediately perceived, *Principles*, 43, 44, *Dialogues*, I, 2, 12, 13, III, 9
Occasionalism, *Principles*, 67–79, *Dialogues*, II, 4, 7
Occult qualities, 72

Pain or uneasiness, 99, 113 ff., 186–187
Paradoxes, ix ff.
Particulars, how become general, *Introduction*, 12. *See also* Universality
Passivity of the mind, 235–236, 240; in perception, 235, *Dialogues*, I, 9
Perception, action and passivity of mind in, 134 ff.; immediate and mediate, *Dialogues*, I, 2, 12, 13, III, 9. *See also* Representative or Copy Theory
Percival, Sir John, xvi–xvii, xix, xxv, 55n.
Personal identity, 237
Plato, xiii, xviii–xix
Platonists, 233
Pope, Alexander, xii
Popkin, Richard H., xxxi n.
Primary and secondary qualities, *Principles*, 9–15, *Dialogues*, I, 3–8, 11
Prior, Thomas, 55n.
Pyrrhonism, 211n.

de Quincey, Thomas, 56n.

Rankenian Club, vii, xxvi ff., xxxiii
Raphson, Joseph, 239
Reality, 152, 167–168, 183, 211; how distinguished from illusion, *Principles*, 34–40, 41, *Dialogues*, III, 6
Reid, Thomas, ix, xxvii, xxix
Relativity: of extension, *Principles*, 123–132; of number, *Principles*, 12; of physical objects to perception, 153, 201, *Principles*, 3–6, 22–24, 133, *Dialogues*, I, 11; of primary and secondary qualities, *Dialogues*, I, 3–8, 11; of primary qualities to perception, *Principles*, 14–15; of space and motion, 239–240, *Principles*, 110–117; of time, 240, *Principles*, 97, 98
Representative or Copy Theory, *Principles*, 8–10, *Dialogues*, I, 13, III, 17
Resurrection, 218–219, 227, 240
Rules, as laws of nature, *Princi-*

ples, 30–33, 62–65, 105–10, *Dialogues,* II, 2, III, 3
Russell, Bertrand, xxxii

"Same thing," meaning of, *Dialogues,* III, **16, 18**
Schopenhauer, Arthur, xxxi–xxxii
Sensible things, defined, *Dialogues,* II, **2**. See also Combinations of qualities, Ideas
Sextus Empiricus, 211n.
Signs and things signified, *Principles,* 43, 44, **65, 66,** 108, 121, 122, 145
Skepticism, viii ff., xxv ff., xxx–xxxi, 105–106, 109 ff., 115, 148, 152–153, 173–174, 192–193, 207, 211; Berkeley's and Kant's use of, xxxi; the fault of false principles, *Introduction,* **1–5**; follows from supposing difference between things and ideas, 173, *Principles,* **86–88**; about the nature of mind, *Principles,* **137**; refutation of, *Principles,* **88, 89,** *Dialogues,* III, **19**
Smells, 119
Smibert, John, xxvi
Socinians, 68
Solidity, *Dialogues,* I, **7**
Soul. See Mind
Sounds, 119 ff.
South Sea Bubble, xv, xix
Sozini, Lelio Francesco Maria, 68n.
Sozzini, Fausto Paolo, 68n.
Space, 232 ff., *Principles,* 43, 44; absolute and relative, 239–240, *Principles,* **110–117**; only relative, Correspondence, IV, **2**
Spinoza, Baruch, 154
Spirit. See Mind
Stevenson, John, xxvi
Stock, Joseph, xiii, xxiii, 55n.
Substance: material, *see* Matter; mental, *see* Mind
Substance-attribute, *Principles,* **49**
Swift, Jonathan, xii

Tar-water, Berkeley's promotion of, xxiv
Tastes, 118–119
Time, 202, 232 ff., 240, *Principles,* **97, 98, 110, 111**; and eternity, *Dialogues,* III, **21**
Turnbull, George, xxvi

Unity, *Principles,* **13, 120**
Universality, nature of, *Introduction,* **12, 15–16, 18,** *Principles,* **126–128**

Vanini, Lucilio, 154
Vision, *Principles,* **42–44,** *Dialogues,* I, **12**
Voltaire (Francois Marie Arouet de), vii, xxiii

Walpole, Sir Robert, xx
Ware, Robert, xxxiii n.
Whitehead, Alfred North, xxv, xxxiii

Zeno the Eleatic, vii